S0-DQZ-433

Retraining - not redundancy
Innovative approaches to industrial
restructuring in Germany and France

Retraining - not redundancy

Innovative approaches to industrial restructuring in Germany and France

Gerhard Bosch

International Institute for Labour Studies Geneva

Original title: *Qualifizieren statt entlassen - Beschäftigungspläne in der Praxis*

© Westdeutscher Verlag GmbH, Opladen, 1990

© English edition, International Labour Organisation (International Institute for Labour Studies) 1992

Short excerpts from this publication may be reproduced without authorisation, on condition that the source is indicated. For rights of reproduction or translation, application should be made to the Editor, International Institute for Labour Studies, P.O. Box 6, CH-1211 Geneva 22 (Switzerland).

ISBN 92-9014-473-4

The responsibility for opinions expressed in signed articles, studies and other contributions rests solely with their authors, and publication does not constitute an endorsement by the International Institute for Labour Studies of the opinions expressed in them.

Copies can be ordered from: ILO Publications, International Labour Office, CH-1211 Geneva 22.

Foreword to the English edition

In the course of the 1970s and 1980s, we witnessed a major wave of industrial restructuring in virtually all the advanced industrial countries. In many sectors, this structural change led to workforce reduction and employment dislocation on a large scale. The term "de-industrialisation" was coined to describe the scrapping of major industrial activities, and the corresponding huge employment losses of whole regions and countries.

This book, which was originally published in German under the title *Qualifizieren statt entlassen - Beschäftigungspläne in der Praxis* tells us, first of all, how the retrenchment of employment was accomplished in the Federal Republic of Germany and France. Although there are many important differences, we do find a number of similarities in this regard in the two countries, such as the increasing recourse in the 1970s to redundancy payments and early retirement to resolve the problem of excess labour. Early retirement may be seen as a "soft", but also largely "passive" and reactive measure of labour market policy. It cuts back labour supply, but does nothing to generate new job opportunities. In the 1980s, this measure reached its limits: there were hardly any older employees left in the shrinking sectors who could be released, and the public funds that helped to finance the measure were depleted.

Yet, the threat of massive redundancy continued in the 1980s. This led to substantial conflict, especially in core industries with strong trade unions. In France and the Federal Republic of Germany, instead of resorting again solely to redundancy payment contracts, initiatives were taken to cope with restructuring needs by using more active measures of labour market policy. Employment planning in the Federal Republic of Germany and reconversion plans in France may be seen as two important innovations which introduce elements of such active policy. Employees threatened by dismissal were offered the opportunity for retraining, and ways were found to finance this by regrouping private and public aid. The plans were specifically aimed at preventing redundancies by creating new, more competitive employment at the place where the redundancy occurred. This approach, which amounts to nothing less than a departure from the "classic" process of structural change, demands much greater commitment to worker retraining. In France and the Federal Republic of Germany, this commitment was apparently facilitated through the combination of company funds and funding from public labour market and structural policy.

Employment and reconversion plans succeeded in stemming part of the threat of mass dismissal, notably among the ranks of unskilled and semi-skilled workers with long service in the firm. They were the most likely candidates for redundancy and subsequent long-term unemployment. The study provides evidence that their chances of re-employment were significantly enhanced thanks to employment planning practised in the two countries.

The reason why employment and reconversion planning occurred in France and the Federal Republic of Germany can be found in the peculiar institutional setting in those countries. No doubt push forces for such policies emanated from legal and contractual employment protection, which had the effect of a legal restriction on dismissal and/or the effect of making redundancy more expensive to the firm. This, then, provided incentives to look for alternative solutions. In addition, the existing social standards in the two countries provided room for trade unions, works councils and government to negotiate a new combination of existing private and public means of worker compensation, such as redundancy payments and unemployment benefits, to be able to finance active restructuring measures. That is to say that the prevailing standards were not made subject to so-called "deregulation", but were instead revised. The author makes it quite clear that following the deregulation approach would have hollowed out the employer obligation to share in the financing of employment plans, and would thus have made more difficult a high road approach to restructuring.

Alongside push forces, there were also pull forces at work in the two countries. Most important among these was the provision of public financial support for retraining. The pooling of public and private resources, including financial support, staff, counselling, and expertise, permitted the attainment of a much higher effectiveness of the labour market measures taken. Experts from the industrial plants took part in designing the training measures; works councils (in the German case) advised and motivated employees to take up training in a way not available from public agencies. Support was especially targeted to the disadvantaged groups of workers, such as older and less skilled workers. Hence, attention was paid to the redistribution of employment opportunities in such a way as to avert labour market segmentation. Again, to make this possible, existing labour standards were of key importance. In the German case, for example, had the right of works councils to negotiate with management over the selection of workers for dismissal, and the use of social selection criteria, not existed, the workforce reduction would most likely have proceeded in the normal fashion: that is the companies would have retained the most efficient employees and laid off the least efficient.

The author, who himself was involved in the creation of the first German employment plan concluded at Grundig, identifies further positive long-term effects of employment and reconversion agreements, while maintaining all along a reserved optimism on the success of employment plans in general. He rightly points to the increasing importance of the "qualitative" dimension of structural change, which demands ever higher levels of worker qualification. Unless workers possess versatility through polyvalent skills, they will not be able to cope with the demands of an accelerated pace of change. In the cases investigated, the level of qualification of the labour force in the region was raised, and there was a new impetus to regional and labour market policy stemming from the co-operation of representatives of the companies, the public employment agencies, and government in designing and implementing the plans. Such co-operative networks were perpetuated even when the mass redundancy problem by which they were prompted had disappeared. In some cases, new agencies for vocational training were set up. In France particularly, large companies that were involved in reconversion planning created their own economic development agencies with the objective of promoting small and medium-sized enterprises. Finally, firms came to take a more long-term view of human resource management and were thus able to enhance their personnel and training policies.

Co-operative regional networks are, furthermore, a prerequisite for extending employment and reconversion planning to the sector of small and medium-sized enterprises. As ample experience attests, small enterprises on their own are hardly capable of designing and implementing training. They need either to enlist the support of large companies or, alternatively, form local communities of small firms, such as industrial districts, which enable them to jointly set up training institutions [cf. Pyke et al., 1990: *Industrial districts and inter-firm co-operation in Italy*, Geneva, International Institute for Labour Studies].

Employment and reconversion plans may be seen as an important instrument to "internal" industrial restructuring, i.e. one in which the readjustment of resources is carried out within organisational units such as plants, enterprises, or regions, rather than through resource mobility between them. Such internal restructuring normally consists of two components: the switch to new products and processes within the unit, and the concomitant reallocation of the labour force, with the retraining measures required to allow the employees to adapt to the new job demands. In other words, worker readjustment takes place through the internal labour market of the company, and this market may be extended to include workers outside the firm's present employed workforce for which it takes responsibility. This happened under German employment planning when workers were reinstated to the company after passing through a period of external vocational training. Similarly, in France, companies involved in the reconversion policies were obliged to make commitments to the future of workers who had been dismissed. The former employers were released from their obligations only after the worker found a new job. Taking responsibility for the fate of redundant workers may help not only to prevent the external labour market from being flooded with workers with obsolete skills, but may serve proactively as an inducement to the firm to find imaginative and creative solutions for the redeployment of workers.

In the meantime, the important social groups in the Federal Republic of Germany, including the employers' and workers' organisations, government, and the state agency *Treuhandanstalt* entrusted with the privatisation and restructuring of the East German economy after unification, have joined forces and agreed on establishing in the Eastern part of the country so-called "employment promotion and training companies" modelled after the earlier training-related employment plans in West Germany. In the face of quickly rising unemployment, it was generally felt that an instrument of this kind is indispensable for accomplishing the transition to a market-type economy in a "socially acceptable" fashion. Firms are not unduly burdened financially as part of the training cost is covered from public funds. The measures will foster the availability of a better trained labour force. Finally, the workers affected in East Germany would not be exposed immediately, but only gradually, to full competition in the labour market, a situation to which they had in no way been accustomed in the past.

Could employment and reconversion plans serve as a "model" instrument in helping to restructure industry in the countries of Central and Eastern Europe? To the extent that these countries will be exposed to international competition, they will presumably be confronted with an outdated industrial structure that will have to be reshaped by scrapping old industries and expanding the modern ones. Thus, there will be a vast agenda of restructuring. How could this be accomplished without generating too much social damage? It seems that it makes little sense to scrap the existing enterprises and let whole industries collapse in order to rebuild them laboriously from scratch. Such an approach would, among other things, overlook the fact that the existing workforces, where they are still intact, constitute one of the most important assets of an economy. To take them apart would clearly destroy productive strength. All this would speak in favour of internal restructuring, at least to some extent.

But while the potential utility of employment and reconversion planning in Central and Eastern Europe is obvious, there is the question of whether it is feasible. There are doubts. For example, there may be a shortage of an infrastructure of retraining institutions which were of vital importance in the Federal Republic of Germany and France to promote the requalification of redundant workers. Such institutions would have to be built on a regional base, together with active personnel policies in the enterprises geared to the pursuit of reconversion and diversification, and also the creation of a viable sector of small and medium-sized enterprises that would permit the diversification of the local industrial spectrum of activities. While such a programme of building local and regional infrastructures appears immense, it would nevertheless seem indispensable if the object is to move gradually to an effective market economy.

By presenting an English version of the study, we intend to make the pioneering innovation of employment plans accessible to a broader audience. This book fits well into the objective of the Labour Institutions and New Industrial Organisation Programme of the International Institute for Labour Studies to identify, debate and publicise forms of industrial organisation which seek to harmonise employees' interests in employment security and continuity with the employer interests in flexible responses to a new economic environment.

Werner Sengenberger
Head, Labour Institutions and
New Industrial Organisation Programme (NIO)

Acknowledgements

The original edition of this book, which appeared in German under the title *Qualifizieren statt entlassen - Beschäftigungspläne in der Praxis* (Opladen, Westdeutscher Verlag GmbH, 1990), was supported by the Minister of Labour, Health and Social Affairs of the *Land* of North Rhine-Westphalia as part of its programme entitled "Man and technology - Socially acceptable design of technology".

The English translation of the book was financially supported by the Hans-Böckler-Foundation of the German Trade Union Federation DGB. The International Institute for Labour Studies gratefully acknowledges this support.

In addition, thanks are due to Andrew Wilson for the translation of the book from German into English, to Hazel Cecconi for editorial assistance, text design, graphic work, formatting and proof-reading, to Ximena Subercaseaux for the cover design, and to the Publications Unit of the Institute for their assistance.

Acknowledgements

List of acronyms

AuB	*Ausbildungs- und Beschäftigungsgesellschaft* (Thomson Training and Employment Company)
CAD	Computer-aided design
CFDT	*Confédération française démocratique du travail*
CGT	*Confédération générale du travail*
CNC	Computer numerically controlled
DGB	Deutscher Gewerkschaftsbund (German TUC)
DM	Deutschmarks
EC	European Community
EWD	Electronic-Werke Deutschland
FDP	Free Democrat Party (in the Hamburg Senate)
FF	French francs
FLO	Federal Labour Office
HDW	Howaldt Deutsche Werft
ITM	*Industrie- und technologiepark Management-Gesellschaft* (Villingen Industry and Technology Park Management Company)
KHD	Klöckner-Humboldt-Deutz
NATO	North Atlantic Treaty Organisation
OECD	Organisation for Economic Co-operation and Development
TCL	Training and conversion leave

Table of contents

Chapter 4 - Employment plans in practice (contd.)

Chapter 1

The subject under investigation:
employment plans

I.   The issue outlined

In many countries, large firms announcing mass redundancies or plant closures have now accepted joint responsibility for creating new jobs or helping displaced workers find alternative employment. A fairly recent international survey of the very different experiences in a number of countries revealed, in the cases of the Federal Republic of Germany[1] and Japan, that firms were still adopting a defensive attitude towards an active employment policy in times of crisis. The situation in both countries was characterised, strikingly, in the following terms: "In Japan and the Federal Republic, large companies assume that, in order to create jobs, they must above all be competitive and profitable. The problems of structural change cannot be overcome by large companies themselves, but remain the responsibility of government or of other institutions" [Sagét, 1986, pp. 26-27].

In the second half of the 1980s, however, primarily as a result of pressure exerted by trade unions and works councils, so-called *employment plans* have been concluded in between 30 and 40 West German establishments. In contrast to the prevailing trend towards making dismissals easier again, or avoiding the need for them altogether, as reflected in the easing of regulations governing fixed-term employment contracts [cf. Bosch and Seifert, 1984; Dragendorf et al., 1988], these employment plans make provision for employees to undergo a period of training before, or even instead of, any final decision on redundancy.

The concept of employment plans arose at the end of the 1970s. It combines proposals for product diversification developed in trade union working parties on alternative production with recommendations for the establishment of a labour pool, in which employees can be trained in times of crisis and substitute tasks can be carried out. The concept of the labour pool was formulated as part

---

[1] The research for this study was undertaken prior to the unification of Germany and is therefore focused on the Federal Republic of Germany (former West Germany).

of a project carried out in 1981 by the public body Humanisation of Working Life (*Humanisierung des Arbeitslebens*) organisation for Howald Deutsche Werft, a Hamburg shipyard, but was not subsequently adopted by the company. However, without these various conceptual precursors, the first employment plan would not have been implemented in 1985 by Grundig.

The philosophy of the employment plan can be summarised as follows:

(1) The financial resources devoted by companies to personnel policies should be supplemented by a combination of the company funds devoted to "social plans"[2] and additional public money from the Federal Labour Office or from the regional development funds. In this way, companies and even whole regions win time to implement a policy of diversification through which unemployment can be avoided and employment found soon after the end of the retraining period.

(2) Employees remain tied to the firm while being retrained. Even unskilled and semi-skilled workers, as well as skilled workers whose training is out of date, can take part in the company's restructuring processes after an appropriate period of retraining. In this way, they can avoid becoming the victims of their company's structural change, as is so frequently the case with less well qualified employees, who are dismissed and replaced with better qualified workers as part of the company's rotation strategy.

(3) In the case of groups already at a disadvantage in the labour market, it is easier to offer further training in the familiar setting of their firm than in the anonymity of unemployment, which is so destructive of personality. The possibility, however vague, of finding a new job, the support of workmates who find themselves in the same position and the continuing protection provided by their contract of employment and the collective representation of their interests, may all serve to increase motivation. Employment plans can even help to reach groups of workers who have hardly benefited from the "training offensive" of recent years.

It is estimated that, in 1987 and 1988, only 2,000 to 3,000 people received training under such employment plans; this is a meagre figure, compared to the almost 550,000 individuals who took part in further training programmes offered by the Federal Labour Office in 1987 alone.

In periods of rapid change, however, topics for research cannot be chosen solely on the basis of high percentages. New developments necessarily make their presence felt initially as phenomena of only peripheral importance. The ability of researchers accurately to predict future trends depends on their sensitivity to new developments. The trends outlined below suggest that at least several elements of employment plans may become increasingly important in the future:

---

[2] For a definition and context of social plans, see pp. 30-37.

- *Rapid structural change, both technological and economic,* associated particularly in key industrial sectors with increased skill requirements and more systematic selection of personnel [cf., among others, Kern and Schumann, 1985; Jürgens et al., 1989], means that firms require increasingly broadly-based skills in order that changes in products and processes can be mastered without excessive difficulty (long learning periods, large numbers of rejects, etc.).

- It is likely that *additional sectors* of manufacturing industry in the Federal Republic of Germany will in the near future be threatened with *employment losses* (e.g. the motor industry). Unskilled and semi-skilled workers will be the ones most at risk of losing their jobs, so that the government of the Federal Republic will also be subject to increased political pressure to introduce measures to cope with the social aspects of structural change.

- In reaction to and in anticipation of these developments, the *trade unions* are increasingly trying to influence the course of structural change in the economy. They are demanding that the opportunities in the labour market for workers whose jobs are at risk should be improved by the acquisition of skills that look to the future and the timely development of new products at threatened sites.

- *Companies* know that in the 1990s financial problems in the pension system and the expiry of the regulations governing early retirement will make it more difficult to shed labour through early retirement schemes. In consequence, they will have to look for new, socially acceptable ways of reducing their workforce and of coping with periods of under-utilisation. Since further training within firms is being expanded at the same time - in part through union-inspired collective agreements - it is likely that retraining will play a role in this area.

- The *government* may well wish to ensure that companies do not pass on the entire cost of structural change to the external labour market, since this will be a long-term burden on public funds (e.g. the Federal Labour Force will have to spend a larger proportion of its budget on benefits for the long-term unemployed) and will hinder regional structural change. The government may therefore urge employers to use more of the resources they devote to social plans for labour market purposes, for example for further training for employees threatened by dismissal.

- On the *European level*, there is a consensus that, in the event of industrial restructuring, funds from the European Structural Fund should not be granted solely for traditional social plans and the establishment of new firms or industries, but should be used increasingly to encourage the retraining of workers affected by restructuring. Retraining is thus being seen as the "bridge" between past and future employment that has hitherto been missing.

- *Workers themselves*, both within firms and in the labour market, are
  increasingly realising the importance of formal qualifications [Gottsleben,
  1987], since access to jobs with good prospects will depend increasingly on
  the possession of such qualifications. This will make workers in sectors
  undergoing rapid structural change more interested not only in initial
  training but also in further training and retraining.

It is not our intention here to be falsely optimistic about the clarity and
unambiguousness of emerging trends. It is not difficult to discern counter trends:
older and less well-qualified workers, who do not see much advantage in
retraining, are more likely to be dismissed. In order to implement new
production strategies and achieve higher standards of performance, companies
do seek to shed those parts of their workforce that are less well qualified and
less productive. From the companies' point of view, it is either unrealistic, too
costly or simply a poor investment to retrain such workers. They prefer to shed
labour quickly, in order subsequently to be able to restructure their workforce.
By so doing, they avoid responsibility for making structural change socially
acceptable, and externalise its consequences. Budget reductions at the Federal
Labour Office have given rise to fears that the requirement to make retraining
programmes part of employment plans was only a temporary phase. The
conservative government is seeking to force the pace of structural change and,
by eliminating employment programmes and cutting the resources available for
labour market policy, to shift labour market pressure on to the individual in
order to force those facing unemployment to accept lower wages and less
favourable working conditions.

These contradictory trends show there is scope for political developments
in either direction. It is also conceivable, as a result of increasing segmentation
in the labour market, that individual regions, sectors or companies, will develop
in different ways. In areas with well-qualified workforces and strong trade
unions, employment plans may be one strategy for promoting internal structural
change, while in sectors with weak unions, a poorly qualified workforce and
rapidly increasing skill requirements, a hire-and-fire policy is more likely to
predominate. So long as employment plans continue to be concluded at plant or
company level and are not made a general legal requirement, it is more likely
that different trends will emerge in different sectors rather than one unambiguous
trend dominating in most areas. In contrast to the first 25 years of the existence
of the Federal Republic of Germany, it can no longer be assumed - as was the
case with social plans - that arrangements initially negotiated by unions and
management at company level will subsequently become generalised through
legislation; this model for the development of the social state, in which gains
made by trade unions in large firms spread gradually into economically weaker
companies and sectors, seems today to be under threat. The legislature is now

under increasing pressure to introduce laws that will reduce the standards achieved in company agreements and collective negotiations.[3]

II. Internal or external structural change

Employment plans represent an intervention in the mechanisms of economic structural change. They are an attempt to shift the burdens from external change, mediated by the market, to internal change, carried out at plant, firm or group level. Thus *the differences between external and internal structural change* prove to be central to an analysis of the origins and the practical consequences of employment plans. In order to be able to clarify the issues to be investigated here, these differences should be examined in greater depth.

Structural change can involve jobs as well as workers.[4] The term internal change is used when productive resources, like capital and labour, are reallocated *within* organisational units, such as firms or establishments. External change means reshuffling of resources *across* units [Sengenberger, 1990, pp. 144-146]. Such internal change in the labour market takes place when quantitative and qualitative changes[5] are dealt with primarily at plant or company level, with existing employees being given preferential treatment over outsiders [Sengenberger, 1987, p. 150]. An internal adjustment of labour to quantitative fluctuations in production means, for example, the use of overtime or short-time working instead of hiring or firing. Reductions in working hours, particularly in periods of downturn, may also contribute to internal adjustments (see Table 1). If new products, new production processes or different forms of work organisation necessitate a qualitative change in the demands on workers, a company adopting an internal solution will provide further training for its workers or transfer them; an external solution, on the other hand, would involve the replacement of part of the workforce with better or differently qualified workers.

---

[3] An example of such a reduction in the standards reached in collective agreements is the addition of paragraph 112a to the Law on Labour Relations at the Workplace (*Betriebsverfassungsgesetz*), which relates redundancy payments more closely to individual labour market opportunities, and also increases the threshold level of redundancies at which social plans become obligatory. It is quite obvious that further attacks on the provisions contained in social plans are planned. The deregulation commission appointed by the Federal Government, for example, is considering adapting social plans solely to meet the demands of individuals, making them dependent on the resumption of reasonable employment and differentiating the provisions in accordance with the employment situation in the various regions.

[4] Sagét makes a distinction between social structural change (affecting workers) and economic structural change (affecting jobs). However, since the social dimension also includes economic aspects and vice versa, the distinction is not a happy one [Sagét, 1986, p. 15].

[5] In the literature, the somewhat more abstract but synonymous pair of concepts "numerical or functional flexibility" is used [Atkinson, 1986].

Table 1:   External and internal structural change

Form of structural change	Consequences of structural change on Labour		Consequences of structural change on Jobs	
	Quantitative	Qualitative	Quantitative	Qualitative
Internal (establishment, company, group, combine)	(1) Variations in working hours (overtime, short time, reduction in working hours)	(2) Retraining/transfer of production in the firm	(5) Extension/restructuration of production	(6) Diversification
External	(3) Recruitment and dismissal	(4) Rotation: Dismissals and immediate recruitment of workers with different skills	(7) Growth in production in other firms/new start-ups in the same sector	(8) Diversification of other firms/new start-ups in other sectors
No structural change	(9) Unemployment		(10) Reduction in the number of jobs	

Similar processes are possible with respect to capital and jobs. A company can make quantitative and qualitative changes by increasing and/or diversifying its production. Changes can also be mediated through the market, with some firms contracting or disappearing while others expand or start up.

Obviously there are close correlations between the kind of *structural change in the labour market and that in the product market*. An internal change in the labour market can be sustained in the long term only if internal change dominates on the product side. This is the explanation for the formation of internal labour markets in the Federal Republic of Germany in the 1950s and 1960s, in which existing employees were given preferential treatment in adjustment processes, particularly when high growth rates made it possible to expand and stabilise the workforce (strategies 1 and 5 in Table 1) [Lutz and Sengenberger, 1974]. Because of the relative lack of technological change and the long-term stability of the system of work organisation, the permanent workforces built up in this way were limited in their flexibility and were tied for the most part to particular departments and hierarchies.[6]

The demands made on permanent workforces today have changed significantly. The qualitative changes in jobs are greater than before, not only because of more rapid product diversification, but more particularly because of technological changes in production processes and new forms of work organisation [see, for example, Roth and Kohl, 1988]. Structural change today increasingly has a qualitative as well as a quantitative component. Workers must have reserves of skills in order to be able to participate in the technological and organisational changes which their jobs are undergoing; moreover, they have to be able to substitute for other employees, which is now a general requirement because of reductions in staffing levels. In the medium term, many employees have to reckon with job changes and the need for further training if they want to remain with their company (strategies 2 and 6 in Table 1).

There are increasing indications that *firms are seeking partially to decouple structural change in the labour market from that in the product market*. Firms that are expanding or diversifying are trying to sever their ties with the less well-qualified sections of their permanent workforce and restructuring their workforce through an increase in voluntary and involuntary mobility between plants (strategies 4 and 6 in Table 1). In extreme cases of rapid increases in the skills required, this may be the only way of ensuring the firm's survival [Ardenti and Vrain, 1988, p. 91]. Recourse to the external labour market appears particularly attractive when more highly qualified staff can be found there than are available within firms, as a result of government funded training programmes for the unemployed; as a consequence, firms can save themselves the cost of providing further training programmes.

---

[6] This is typified by the following finding from a case study in the steel industry: about 80 per cent of the workforce in a tube-rolling mill that was shut down in 1972 were working at the time of closure in the department in which they had started their employment, mostly in the 1950s [Bosch, 1978a, p.53].

Thus an internal structural change in jobs is consistent with an external adjustment of the workforce, and can be accomplished entirely at the cost of part of the workforce. In contrast, an internal adjustment of the workforce can be sustained as a long-term company strategy only when internal change predominates on the product side as well. Of course this last statement applies only to the labour market as a whole, and certainly not to individual workers or the workforces of individual firms. Since there is significant mobility of labour unconnected with changes in product markets (entry of younger and exit of older workers, fluctuation between economic activity and inactivity, changes of job for personal reasons), internal labour strategies are also conceivable in plants that are contracting and not diversifying. The economically necessary reduction in staffing levels - particularly if it is stretched over a long period of time - may be exceeded as a result of these fluctuations, so that there is a chance not only that employment may stabilise but that there may even be scope for recruitment.

The differences between the two types of structural change for the workforce arise out of the difference in social protection inside and outside the firm. Within the firm, workers have individual rights based on the employment contract (e.g. classification in a particular grade, protection against unfair dismissal, retention of salary when transferred to a different job) as well as collective employment rights (representation by the works council).[7] They lose these rights when they leave the firm. It is true - at least in most Western European countries - that they are not then wholly without social protection (unemployment benefit, early retirement in the event of unemployment and employment policy measures such as further training programmes and job creation schemes). However, in the competition for jobs in the external labour market, the cards are always being reshuffled. Without the protection of the employment contract and labour relations legislation, many people have to accept a worse hand; in some circumstances, they may face wage cuts and increased job requirements, and further training is no longer the firm's problem, but one for the individual or the state. External structural change offers firms an opportunity for rapid redistribution, to the disadvantage of its employees. Plants may be wholly or partially shut down and new products introduced elsewhere, or orders may be transferred to subcontractors. Such strategies mean that existing company agreements and trade union structures can be by-passed; they also make it easier to shed less productive employees and to hire replacements from the growing pool of people who have received training at outside institutions.

The purpose of employment plans is precisely to halt this redistribution of employment opportunities at the expense of a part of the workforce by *mobilising the individual and collective rights that have been won in order to shape the process of structural change*. The aim is to use these rights as a basis

---

[7] A number of rights can be implemented only through a works council (e.g. protest against dismissals, co-determination with respect to further training programmes, negotiation of a social plan) and cannot be sued for by individuals.

for establishing a "corridor of protection" for those affected, within which the *necessary internal or external mobility* can take place.

This objective can be achieved by means of various strategies (see Table 1), which can be divided into four basic types:

(1) *Retraining and diversification*: continued employment within the firm is encouraged by a combination of training for the workforce and a simultaneous widening of the product range (strategies 2 and 6 in Table 1).

(2) *Training only*: continued employment within the firm is ensured solely through training (strategy 2 only). This training "wins time" and makes it possible for employees to be reintegrated into a job made available through normal turnover.

(3) *Placement in external jobs and assistance in creating jobs*: the company does not itself diversify, but supports the establishment of new companies or the placement of workers in other firms. The "corridor of protection" is thus extended to the external labour market and stretches from the firm of origin to the receiving company (strategies 3 and 8). This strategy could also be described as a partial extension of the internal labour market.[8]

(4) *Placement in external firms only*: the above approach can be pursued solely in relation to the workforce. The responsibility of the original firm extends only to the placement of workers in another job, which is not, however, newly created.

The aim of the last two basic types is restricted to external change in the workforce. Some of the "trauma" of changing to a new job is reduced by certain guarantees made by both the discharging and the receiving firm.

All these strategies can be employed by *individual firms* wishing to shed labour, but at the same time they can also be *implemented on a regional level*. Measures which apply to one company, and thus to a situation of mass redundancy, are presumably - depending on the circumstances - only temporary and restricted to the reintegration of a given number of workers.

However, if the state is to intervene in structural change, in order to ensure that such change is not left solely to the external labour market, a broader and more long-term perspective must be adopted. The difference between in-firm and public employment plans can be summarised as follows:

---

[8] The term "extended internal labour market" has hitherto been used in labour market theory to describe the situation in which firms subcontract production or forge exclusive links with subcontractors, without taking any responsibility for the employment aspects of the product and labour markets which they thus control. The logic for capital in these extended internal labour markets is precisely that workers' rights can thereby be diminished. Employment plans, in contrast, extend firms' responsibility for workers outside the company (on the concept of extended internal labour markets see Sengenberger [1987, p. 273]).

(1) *In-firm versus public training programmes*: structural change within a company can be accomplished by training a certain number of workers and subsequently placing them in jobs. At the regional level, however, the integration and training of the next generation, or of workers who fall victim to other redundancies, remains a problem.

(2) *In-firm versus regional job creation and/or diversification*: a company can consider the internal or external diversification made necessary by manpower reductions as completed if, for example, it simply creates short-term jobs for a part of its workforce that will last until the workers reach retirement age. A regional programme, on the other hand, will have to be concerned with the development of permanent jobs and/or company expansion.

Thus public employment policy must be broader in scope, extend over a longer period of time, cover a wider area and apply to more workers than in-firm employment policies, if it is to take up the initiatives already contained in in-firm employment plans. In the first instance, the creation of new in-firm instruments of structural change gives rise to an *area of tension between firm-based and state activities and interests*, in which the main issue is essentially the extent to which new instruments of structural change should be generalised, and the degree to which they should be tolerated or restricted. When public funds are involved, a necessary precondition for the functioning of employment plans, the government will question the use of such resources for the benefit of just one group of workers. There are basically three possible reciprocal relationships that, in individual cases, can be passed through in successive phases or "political cycles":

(1) In-firm arrangements for training and diversification become the *forerunners* of corresponding government activities and, by being generalised in this way, improve the chances of most workers of participating in structural change without personally paying any penalty. In order to gain political acceptance for such new standards, it is essential for the positive effects of employment plans in the accomplishment of socially acceptable structural change to be articulated and disseminated. This was the case, for example, in the 1950s and 1960s with many in-firm and collectively negotiated arrangements that provided the basis for subsequent legislation (social plans, protection against unfair dismissal).

(2) Firms and state act independently of each other. Structural change takes place with *differing social standards* for different groups of workers. There is a privileged group of workers in firms with employment plans and an area of "normal" external structural change, which proceeds in accordance with market principles. Since in-firm measures come to a halt after a certain time, coexistence is limited. The political domination of market solutions remains intact. Government will stress the special nature of each individual

case and the short-term nature of any assistance provided, while playing down the fundamental importance of employment plans.

(3) Finally, the state may try *to reduce the "corridors of protection" in the privileged area and cut the provisions of firms' employment plans down to a "normal level"*. In this case, public debate will concentrate not on the special assistance given to disadvantaged groups, but on the unjustified privileges employment plans supposedly give to individual groups of employees, which cannot be tolerated for reasons of equality.

The *political dynamic of employment plans can be seen from the nature of their relationship to state employment policy*. In the first place, of course, a one-dimensional perspective, focusing only on the financial provisions of the plans, would be inadequate. It is entirely conceivable, or even probable, that state employment policy will take on board proposals in certain areas (e.g. calls for more systematic planning of further training on a regional basis), while in other areas pressure will be exerted on firms to make downward adjustments (e.g in the level of redundancy payments or subsistence allowances). Secondly, all these policy variables can, under certain circumstances, be implemented several times over; depending on the government's scope for financial manoeuvring, the prevailing views on economic and social policy and the reactions of the parties involved (unions, employers, various public bodies), the state can force through a policy of employment plans for all, but then withdraw again from active involvement in employment policy, so that a standardised employment policy, in effect for only a short while, can be very rapidly superseded.

III.　The problems under investigation

The subject of our investigations was the origin and implementation of 13 employment plans in the Federal Republic of Germany and the so-called "reconversion policy" implemented in France between 1984 and 1988. Our observations on external and internal structural change make it possible to define more precisely this area of investigation and the six questions raised below by the research (see pp. 12-13).

In addition to elements traditionally included in social plans, the German employment plans contain provisions on training and diversification. The objective of most of the employment plans is internal structural change (the exceptions are Klöckner-Humboldt-Deutz, Thomson and HDW Ross) or the postponement of any decision on whether employees should remain with the firm or leave until the end of a training period; however, they are all in competition with instruments of external structural change (particularly redundancy payments). Almost all the agreements under investigation were concluded in 1987-88: at the time this research project came to an end (mid-1989), most of them were still being implemented; some of the retraining and diversification measures that had been agreed upon were not even fully under way. Consequently, the present investigation can offer only an *interim assessment*, and at best provide cautious evaluations of the interaction between employment plans and government policy. However, such evaluations would seem to be necessary, in order to illuminate the public debate on regional and sectoral policy, in which employment plans play a role, with empirical results based on current practice.

In France in the early 1980s, the customary social plans in the iron and steel industry, the shipyards and in other sectors affected by the recession were augmented by a number of additional instruments intended to help workers leaving these declining industries (help in entering self-employment, retraining, placement in other jobs, founding of new firms). From 1985 onwards, new legislation extended this reconversion policy to other sectors, although at a lower level than in the industries in which it had been pioneered. In contrast to the German employment plans, the sole aim of French reconversion policy was mobility of labour between firms. This policy has now become a generally accepted and much-used instrument of personnel policy. Moreover, the extensive experience of its use in France is well documented in numerous case studies and comparative analyses. This literature and our own discussions with experts on the French iron and steel industry will form the basis of our outline of the main features of reconversion policy in France, and of the differences and similarities between that policy and German employment plans. Since the French experience predates the West German one, and has already developed in several very different directions, this approach will both provide information on the political dynamics of the development over time of the philosophy and practice of restructuring, and enable us to draw some conclusions on possible scenarios for development in the Federal Republic of Germany. Furthermore, international comparisons help to increase our understanding of the institutional and structural characteristics of our own country, which can all too easily be seen as innate constants.

The aim of this research project was to discover the extent to which employment plans and reconversion policy have modified the mechanisms of structural change and its consequences for employees, and whether the use of such instruments of company and state employment policy can make external and internal job changes more socially acceptable than before. To this end, an in-depth investigation was made of the following questions:

(1) What were the objectives of the various employment plans? Were they intended to bring about changes in the workforce or in jobs, to enable workers to remain within the firm or to facilitate their transfer to another firm?

(2) To what extent were these objectives realised, and to what extent were they not achieved or altered? In particular, we wanted to determine how the various interests of the firms, the workers' representative bodies (works councils and trade unions), the workers affected and the state institutions involved influenced the outcome.

(3) What is the relationship of employment plans to social plans? Our initial position was that they should be seen as a development of social plans, but

not as an alternative to them. All the employment plans drawn up hitherto have followed in the tradition of the social plans: in addition to the retraining components, they all contain the usual repertoire of early retirement schemes and redundancy payments. These traditional measures were always present as alternatives to retraining measures, both in the decisions of individuals as well as in management policies for cutting back on staffing levels, and in some instances they continue to prevail.

(4) What role is played by the Federal Labour Office in the development of retraining measures? Despite the significantly wider-ranging structural and regional policy objectives, it soon became clear that the Federal Labour Office was virtually the only source of public funds. Employment plans and the Employment Promotion Law (see Chapter 3) had to be harmonised. There were so many problems that this has become an area for research in its own right. In particular, we wanted to examine under what conditions the Federal Labour Office supports *preventive further training*[9] programmes for workers threatened with unemployment.

(5) Do employment plans contain structural or regional policy components that extend beyond individual firms and which might possibly contribute to the spread of employment plans to other firms? The aim here is to investigate the extent to which employment plans have been integrated into structural or regional programmes, or have stimulated the further development of such programmes.

(6) What are the differences between the German retraining plans and the French reconversion programmes? What role do different economic and institutional situations play in this respect, in particular different trade union and labour market structures and policies?

IV. Methodology and structure of the study

In order to answer these questions, the following programme of research was carried out in 1988 and 1989:

- The employment plans of 13 firms were evaluated.

- Case studies were carried out in 12 of these firms. They were based on interviews with works councils, personnel managers, training managers and, in a few cases, with individual trainees (see Table 2).

- Other internal documents (training plans, the minutes of company committees, etc.) were evaluated.

---

[9] Further training geared to prevent workers from becoming unemployed because of the lack of appropriate skills.

- Representatives of the Federal Labour Office at federal, *Land*[10] and local level were interviewed about their department's opportunities for promoting employment plans and its practice in that respect, as well as its involvement in the employment plans in question.

- Expert discussions were held with other institutions involved (education and training establishments, government officials, trade unions).

Table 2: Overview of the expert interviews in the Federal Republic of Germany and France

	Federal Republic of Germany		France
	Interviews	Supplementary telephone surveys	Interviews
Employment office (local, regional, Federal Labour Office)	5	1	-
Works councils	12 [1]	12	1
Management/training managers	7 [1]	3	1
Officials (Department of Economics etc.)	5	1	-
External training agencies	2	-	-
Researchers	1	1	1
Trade unions	8	4	2
Total	39	22	5

Note: [1] In 3 firms, the interviews were carried out jointly with works councils and management. The table also includes the expert interviews on part-time training programmes in the mining industry.

Finally, the research report also includes practical experiences acquired in the development of the first employment plan in Germany, concluded at Grundig in 1985. The author contributed to the conceptual development of the Grundig plan and took part in the negotiations on retraining measures that took place at the time between the works council, IG Metall, the Grundig management, the Federal Labour Office in Nuremberg and the North Bavarian Employment Office. These negotiations, though occasionally tedious, were an ideal opportunity to gain an understanding of the difficulties involved in implementing these new ideas and in adequately assessing them.

The part-time training programmes for young workers in the Ruhr coal mining industry were also investigated. It was here that most comprehensive use was made of the support provided by the 1985 Employment Promotion Law for part-time training courses for young workers, thus enabling them to find full-time employment. However, these part-time training programmes were not introduced as part of employment plans; in accordance with the tradition of *IG Bergbau und Energie*, the mining and energy workers' union in Germany, whose

---

[10] *Land* refers to a region with legislative and executive powers of its own. Prior to unification in 1990, the Federal Republic of Germany consisted of 11 *Länder*. Through unification, 5 *Länder* in East Germany were added.

primary aim is to develop a strategy of co-operation with management (a policy which can be implemented successfully because of the union's organisational strength), their introduction was not accompanied by public debate on new concepts in employment policy. In practice, however, they amounted to the same thing, since their aim was to prevent the dismissal of workers through publicly funded retraining programmes. Discussions on these part-time training measures were held with the mining and energy workers' union, works councils and personnel managers in a colliery and managers at the head office of Ruhrkohle AG.

The example of the iron and steel industry in Lorraine was used to investigate French reconversion policy. Discussions were held with a personnel manager, works councils, representatives of two unions, the CGT (*Confédération générale du travail*) and the CFDT (*Confédération française démocratique du travail*), as well as with another group of researchers.[11] Experiences in other sectors of French industry have been gathered from the extensive literature in this area, and from discussions with other researchers.

---

[11] The author would like to thank Marie Claire Villeval and Philippe Méhaut for their co-operation.

Chapter 2

The origins of employment plans

I. Employees and individual or collective approaches to the labour market

The consequences of mass redundancies can be anticipated and dealt with both individually and collectively. If the reaction is purely individual, the dismissals are accepted more or less passively. There may be objective reasons for this: the situation in the labour market may be relatively favourable, or the workforce may be highly qualified. However, there may also be subjective reasons: the workforce may have little experience of fighting for their jobs, or there may be an inadequate level of trade union organisation, with the result that there is no alternative to individual action. Employment plans and French reconversion policy, on the other hand, are consequences of massive collective protests against dismissals and the inadequate redundancy payments offered to individuals by the traditional social plans. The aim of collective action, therefore, is to increase the options open to individuals in the labour market.

Once employment plans are agreed, each employee will have to weigh up his own individual interests and those of the workforce as a whole and decide between the new instruments contained in the employment plans and the provisions of the old social plans (particularly redundancy payments). This time, the decision is to be taken in the context of a concrete labour market situation, which may perhaps have already manifested itself in the form of job offers for individual workers. This choice is also influenced by subjective and objective arguments. The subjective arguments include the climate of debate within the firm about the new agreements, as well as the contribution made by works councils, trade unions, training agencies, employment offices and company managements to their development. The objective reasons are a function of the differing labour market opportunities open to individual members of the workforce. It is probable that there are lines of demarcation both between and within workforces. One section may be dependent on the employment plan, another will use redundancy payments as a cushion in order to conduct their own job searches. Collective and individual orientations may interact and strengthen the trend towards acceptance of the employment plan or towards an individual solution to the search for new jobs. They come into conflict, however, when individual members of the workforce withdraw from a collective decision and go their own way. *Thus tension between individual and collective labour market strategies may arise both in the conception and in the development of employment plans.*

Section II of this chapter summarises the results of empirical investigations of the consequences of mass redundancies. The results show the differing labour market opportunities of different groups of workers, which at least indicate the objective background to this area of conflict. The various subjective premises for action are clarified as far as possible in the case studies.

Traditional social plans are increasingly being seen as inadequate in the light of changed conditions in the labour market. Employment plans have emerged as a supplement or, in some cases, an alternative to social plans; nevertheless, they continue the tradition of the social plan. They are concluded on a legal basis (Law on Labour Relations at the Workplace para. 111 and 112 - see box below), and the new elements (training and diversification) have had to prove themselves in practice in competition with traditional instruments. In order to reconstruct the connection between social and employment plans, an overview of the provisions of typical social plans and the past history of employment plans will be given in section III.

Social Plans in Germany

The Law on Labour Relations at the Workplace of 1972, which is in force today, directs the employer with an establishment of more than 20 employees that he must inform the works council of "planned changes in the establishment" which could result in "specific disadvantages for the workforce". The disadvantages may not necessarily be dismissals, but could refer to loss of income or loss of qualification. The phrase "changes in the establishment" refers, above all, to works closures, removal of works or departments, amalgamations with other works, alterations in the organisation of an establishment and new methods of work or manufacture (para. 111: Law on Labour Relations at the Workplace, *Betriebsverfassungsgesetz*). With regard to such alterations the works council can demand that a "social plan" be drawn up, in order to minimise the disadvantages for the workforce. The Act does not contain any details of what the social plan has to regulate. Its detailed contents are a matter for negotiations between works councils and senior management. Should there be no agreement, the social plan is drawn up by the Arbitration Commission. The Arbitration Commission is a bipartite body, made up of an equal number of representatives of the works council and management, with a "neutral" chairperson whose appointment must be approved by both sides (para. 76: Law on Labour Relations at the Workplace). The arbitrators have "to take account of the social interest of the employees involved as well as ensuring that their decision, as far as the employer is concerned, can be defended on economic grounds" (para. 112: Law on Labour Relations at the Workplace).

II.   The social consequences
of mass redundancies

In the post-war period, the consequences of mass redundancies in the Federal Republic of Germany, England, Sweden, France and the United States of America have been investigated in more than 100 case studies, most of them using plant closures as examples. The results of these investigations differ very considerably. For example, the unemployment rate in the year after closure ranges from 0 per cent in a Swedish shipyard to 87 per cent in an English shipyard [Gerdes et al., 1990, p. 193]. Similar differences can be observed in other indicators of the social consequences of dismissals, such as the evolution of earnings or changes in working conditions. The *peak unemployment rate* in a country or region is too superficial an explanation for these differences. It is true that the unemployment rate has a greater influence on the consequences of dismissals than any other measure. Nevertheless, the unemployment rate alone is not an adequate basis for a full understanding of the social problems, which can also be observed in situations of full employment, the distribution of problems among the various groups of workers or the effects of the respective institutional context and the specific economic and technological dynamic of development (e.g. trend towards more advanced skills, structural change no longer taking place mainly within manufacturing industry, but involving a simultaneous shift towards the service sector).

The consequences of closures can be understood only as the result of a number of overlapping factors, the most important of which (in addition to the unemployment rate) are outlined below in the context of the recent debate on labour market theory. They explain at least a large part of the different results obtained in the case studies and at the same time make it possible to more accurately assess the potential risk for individual workforces or groups of employees.

(1) *The structure of skills in the labour market*: Labour markets are today generally divided into three basic types, each of which has a decisive influence on the consequences of redundancies. In so-called *unstructured* labour markets, workers have only minimal qualifications and skills; they are employed in simple auxiliary functions and are easily substituted, and firms and workers do not develop any mutual ties. These workers are the first to be dismissed in crisis situations. Because of their lowly position, a move to another firm cannot represent a downturn in their employment history. However, problems may arise because of the wage differential between different firms and sectors and the pressure to relocate.

The consequences for workers in *internal labour markets* are completely different. In labour markets of this kind, a firm's employees are given preferential treatment over outsiders [Sengenberger, 1987, p. 150]. Adjustment processes, such as retraining or promotion within the firm, are usually managed through the use of existing employees and not by recourse to the external labour market. Employees have either already been promoted within the firm or have promotion prospects; as a result, they develop strong ties with the firm. In labour markets of this kind, the costs of an enforced change of job are very high, even in a situation of full employment [cf. Bosch, 1978a;1978b]. It is true in this situation that workers dismissed or made redundant hardly ever remain unemployed. Nevertheless, an enforced move to another firm is particularly serious for semi-skilled workers trained in-house who have worked their way up within the firm, sometimes into positions that are comparable with those occupied by skilled workers (e.g. 1st. smelter in the steelworks) (cf. Figure 1). If such workers lose their jobs, they are in the situation - as Weltz graphically described it - "of a gambler who has thrown the dice for a score of 35 and has to start again at 1" [cf. *Der Spiegel*, Vol. 18/1976, p. 189]. Their skill is not ratified by a recognised formal qualification, so that in firms in other sectors they have to start all over again at the bottom as unskilled workers, or as semi-skilled workers in a lower grade. It is true that they might be able to fill comparable posts in the same sector, but these jobs are usually reserved for established workers in each firm, so that it is necessary first to gain the required seniority. The entry-level jobs open to these recipients of in-firm training are significantly less well paid, and new recruits also have to take the least pleasant jobs. It is only after a gradual process of integration, often lasting several years, that they succeed in obtaining a job comparable to their previous one, provided they are not then too old.

The consequences of an enforced change of firm are less serious in *occupational labour markets*. Here, workers' skills have been ratified by recognised, and transferable, formal qualifications. Job grades within the firm correspond to generally recognised occupations, and entry to particular jobs is not dependent on a lengthy period of employment in the firm but on the possession of the required vocational qualification. A move to another firm is made easier by a job structure with fewer hierarchical levels. However, managerial posts (e.g. foremen) are usually filled by internal promotions, so that even occupational labour markets contain some of the elements of internal labour markets which are an obstacle to mobility (see Figure 1).

In comparison with the other types, therefore, occupational labour markets would appear to offer the best protection against loss of status in the case of dismissal or redundancy. However, occupational labour markets require a minimum density in any given region. If there are not enough jobs in a particular occupation in the region (because of the restricted size of the local labour market, its industrial structure or the specificity of the occupation), the chances of obtaining a similar job in a different firm are reduced. In order to avoid loss of status, the occupational labour market has to be expanded, either through physical mobility on the part of employees (as is already customary, for example, in many graduate professions) or by

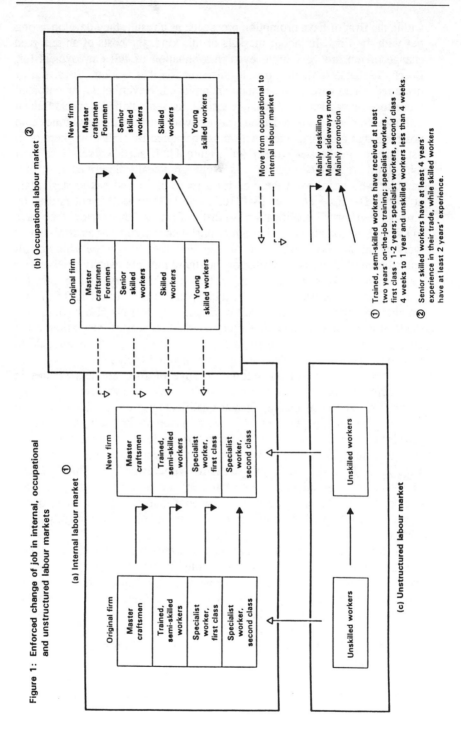

Figure 1: Enforced change of job in internal, occupational and unstructured labour markets

(a) Internal labour market ①

(b) Occupational labour market ②

(c) Unstructured labour market

- - - - - ▷   Move from occupational to internal labour market

——————▷   Mainly deskilling
Mainly sideways move
Mainly promotion

① Trained, semi-skilled workers have received at least two years' on-the-job training; specialist workers, first class - 1-2 years; specialist workers, second class - 4 weeks to 1 year and unskilled workers less than 4 weeks.

② Senior skilled workers have at least 4 years' experience in their trade, while skilled workers have at least 2 years' experience.

extending the scope of occupations in order to facilitate entry into different sectors or spheres of activity.[12]

If the occupations are too narrowly defined and perhaps specific to a particular sector, there is a risk, particularly at times of crisis in the sector, that previously functioning occupational labour markets might dry up (e.g. in occupations specific to the mining or steel industries). Those affected then have to transfer to internal labour markets, a move generally associated with loss of status (see Figure 1).

(2) *Age and health restrictions*: All the available studies come to the same conclusion, namely that the risk of occupational demotion increases as workers age and their health declines [cf., for example, Walker et al., 1984; Herron, 1975; Hillen, 1971; Bosch, 1978a]. The physical and psychological efficiency of older workers is either genuinely impaired relative to their competitors, or is generally reckoned to be weakened. In many cases, no individual assessment of performance is undertaken; instead, decisions in individual cases are made on the basis of general trends and conjectures (statistical discrimination). This is reflected in usually informal age limits, which have a decisive influence on firms' recruitment strategies. The age limit from which redundant workers experience reintegration problems ranges from 35 to 55 and varies in each individual case. This can be explained partly by different levels of unemployment. If unemployment is high, firms have greater choice in their recruitment strategies and can therefore reduce the age limit and increase the health requirements. However, the age limits and health requirements also depend on the qualifications required and on working conditions. The risk that these might become the only criteria for selection is greatest in an unstructured labour market. When unemployment is generally high, job opportunities for older, unskilled workers and for those with health problems are drastically reduced.[13] Workers with in-firm training may be thrown back into unstructured labour markets, with comparable social consequences; above a certain age, and with reduced efficiency, they no longer have any chance of climbing up again. In occupational labour markets, on the other hand, the age limit for successful inter-firm mobility is higher than in the other two

---

[12] The restructuring of occupations is intended to adapt occupational profiles to technological developments and at the same time extend their sphere of application. Between 1950 and 1987, the number of recognised occupations was reduced from 901 to 383 (Vocational Training Report 1988, p. 72). For example, 42 metalworking occupations were reduced to six basic occupations, with 16 areas of specialisation. The new metalworking occupations share a common basic training. Specialisation occurs relatively late, so that in the event of a change of activity, workers can be quickly trained to meet the requirements of their new job.

[13] Forty-nine per cent of all registered unemployed in September 1988 had no vocational qualification, while 56 per cent of the long-term unemployed had no vocational qualification [*Arbeitsmarktanalyse 1988 anhand ausgewählter Bestands- und Bewegungsdaten* (Labour Market Analysis 1988, based on selected stocks and flows)].

types of labour market. Professional skills and the corresponding job status mean that workers can be quickly integrated into new firms. In many highly-skilled occupations, lengthy experience is even an additional aid to integration;[14] here also, certain health problems are less likely to be a barrier to employment. Used as an instrument of labour market policy, therefore, vocational training is a means of raising the age limit above which employment opportunities deteriorate.

(3) *Discrimination by sex, nationality and race*: At right angles to the occupational structure and the restrictions on older and less efficient workers run the lines of discrimination or segregation which divide the labour market by sex, race or nationality. In Western industrial countries, white, male nationals receive preferential treatment in the competition for attractive jobs. Other workers are systematically disadvantaged in the competition for such jobs. This greatly influences the consequences of redundancies, as most studies show. The American studies all prove that blacks experience greater difficulties than whites in finding alternative employment, irrespective of their age or qualifications [cf., for example, Aiken et al., 1968]. In most countries - including the Federal Republic of Germany - foreign workers come across obstacles to employment. Daimler-Benz in Bremen, for example, is not currently recruiting any foreign nationals at all, so that after the closure of AG Weser many of the foreign workers made redundant were left with a choice between returning home, unemployment or unstable, temporary employment. In August 1985, 47.2 per cent of foreign workers remaining in the Federal Republic of Germany were on temporary or fixed-term employment contracts, compared with 11.4 per cent of German workers [Gerdes et al., 1987]. For women, the risk of remaining unemployed or ending up in unstable employment after redundancy is significantly higher than for men [Nowack and Snyder, 1983; Gonäs, 1989]. These lines of discrimination mean that strategies for integration into employment based solely on vocational training are limited in their effectiveness.

(4) *The local labour market*: The situation in the local labour markets is most certainly a decisive influence on the consequences of mass redundancies. There are two distinct types of situations. If the redundancies occur in a geographically isolated, small labour market dominated by a single industry or firm - such as the closure of the main employer in a rural area [e.g. Rhyope, 1970] - virtually all categories of employees are threatened by unemployment, or they must consider relocating in order to avoid unemployment. With increasing age, a conflict arises between burgeoning

---

[14] This applies not only to graduate occupations and management functions, but also to industrial occupations. Our case study in the mining industry (pp. 92-101) shows that an extreme reduction in the age of the workforce, who are not sufficiently aware of the risks of working underground, leads to irreplaceable losses of skills.

ties with the environment outside the workplace (starting a family, house ownership, social activities) and the need to be mobile. Particularly if employment opportunities are not good in other regions either (especially for older people in periods of high unemployment), the financial losses after redundancy may be increased still further by the costs of moving (enforced house sale, higher rents in the new location), without the additional expense being rewarded by a new job. There have been many investigations of redundancies in such isolated labour markets, particularly in the United Kingdom and the United States of America. This partly explains why, in these two countries, mass redundancies led in nearly all cases to an above-average level of unemployment and to its persistence.

In larger, geographically denser labour markets, in which the firm issuing the redundancy notices is just one of several large firms, the redundant workers do not remain as a homogeneous "mass of long-term unemployed". As time passes, career paths are differentiated in accordance with the structures outlined above. Firms help themselves from the pool of skilled and reliable redundant workers, substituting them for workers who are "less attractive" to them. In the case of mass redundancies, particularly closures, the workers made redundant are considered "innocent", and thus firms are more willing to employ them, which might not be the case with those dismissed individually. In some circumstances, public debate about the closures has even given rise to assistance by local firms and led to preferential treatment for the workers made redundant. In this way, the effects of mass redundancies are quickly mediated by the labour market and, through processes of displacement, affect less skilled workers, foreign workers, women and older employees in other firms.[15]

(5) *Closure or continued trading*: The consequences of redundancies differ according to whether or not the company continues to trade. Closures affect all employees without distinction. In this case, the consequences are the result of the selection procedures adopted by firms recruiting from the pool of redundant workers, as outlined above. However, if the firm continues trading, a selection process precedes any dismissals. In contrast to the process of recruitment, which is usually a matter for negotiation between a firm and individual workers, with the worker unable to call on institutional assistance in order to redress the unequal power relationship in the labour market, redundancies are subject to a multiplicity of institutional regulations. In the Federal Republic of Germany, for example, redundancies must be socially justified: works councils have a right of veto against dismissals (see box on p. 25), social plans are compulsory in firms with more than 20

---

[15] Direct displacement is, of course, the exception. For example, at the Vulkan shipyard in Bremen, foreign workers were "advised" to return home, and the jobs they vacated were offered to workers from AG Weser. In most other cases, former Weser employees were recruited some time after the dismissal of other workers, so that the displacement processes could not be perceived as important secondary effects of redundancies.

employees and many wage agreements contain special provisions protecting against dismissal, totally prohibiting, for example, the dismissal of employees aged over 50 or 55 [cf. Bosch, 1985a]. Thus, through the use of selection procedures which concentrate the risk of redundancy on specific groups of employees, the consequences of closures are determined to a certain extent by social considerations. In very broad terms, it can be said that protection from dismissal as a result of conditions prevailing in a firm increases with seniority and age.[16] As a result of the protection afforded to older workers and those with greater seniority within firms, there is no doubt that a certain preventive element with respect to the negative consequences of dismissals has been included in the law on dismissals. One of the basic findings of the labour market research presented here is that there is a greater degree of selectivity in recruitment than in dismissals.[17] On the other hand, if dismissals are subject to virtually no institutional regulations and restrictions, as in non-union American firms, the selection process is used both in recruitment and dismissals, thus aggravating the consequences for those categories of employees described above as being at risk.

(6) *The type of structural change*:   Recent French research[18] [e.g. Villeval, 1989; Ardenti and Vrain, 1988] has highlighted the influence of different types of structural change on the consequences of redundancies. In the 1950s and 1960s, industrial workers who had lost their jobs usually found

---

[16] Thus, in 1978, only 27 in 1,000 workers aged over 54 were dismissed, compared with 100 in the 25-34 age range [Falke, 1983, p. 15].

[17] In reaction to the extension of protection against dismissal, firms adopted new strategies for dealing with dismissals. On the whole, the proportion of dismissals caused by circumstances prevailing within firms has decreased. This is revealed by the example of a shipyard in Bremen, whose personnel files for the period between 1954 and 1980 were evaluated. The authors of the study come to the following conclusion: "Dismissals for personal or behaviour reasons are becoming an increasingly important instrument of employment policy, and in periods of recession are to a certain extent replacing the traditional lay-offs caused by a lack of work. Since 1967, during downturns, lists have been compiled of workers who are to be dismissed, usually for poor time-keeping or 'a lack of suitability'..., these dismissals fulfil two purposes: firms can shed jobs made superfluous by the state of the order book, and at the same time engage in a process of selection and 'clearing out': they can select workers with those characteristics and behaviour patterns which do not correspond to the standards of discipline and efficiency required by the firm ... the potential for conflict surrounding dismissals is also decreasing: since they are now decided on an individual basis, neither the reduction in jobs nor the process of selection is any longer a subject for debate. The destruction of jobs is transformed into personal fault. Selection is no longer politically negotiated as it was in the 1950s; social criteria for selection are becoming less important than yardsticks such as discipline and efficiency" [Dombois et al., 1982, p. 19].

[18] Of the OECD countries, the Federal Republic of Germany has by far the largest share of industrial workers, which means that, in contrast to many neighbouring countries, the mobility of industrial workers there still very closely follows the classic model of a transfer to other comparable industrial firms (see pp. 155-162).

employment in other industrial firms with similar wage structures and working conditions, as well as comparable social provisions; and as the economy grew and firms expanded, it also became possible to achieve rapid promotion. Today, on the other hand, the number of people employed in manufacturing industry is declining in all developed countries. Moreover, the division of labour both within firms and between firms is being changed by new forms of work organisation, while at the same time the general conditions of enforced mobility are being changed by government intervention in labour law (deregulation), partly in reaction to these structural changes, but partly also as a separate political process. Thus, workers who have lost their jobs are redistributed in the following manner:

(a)   The larger industrial firms are reducing their workforces, while at the same time demanding higher qualifications and greater flexibility from their smaller core workforces. Systematic selection processes are used in both dismissals and recruitment, at least to the extent permitted by institutional regulations. Against this background, the chances for

---

Individual Dismissals in the Federal Republic of Germany

According to the Law on Protection against Dismissal, every valid dismissal has to be "socially justified". It is "socially justified" if the dismissal is for the following reasons:

(1)   for personal reasons relating to the employee (e.g. loss of ability to work);
(2)   for reasons connected with the behaviour of the employee (e.g. persistent lateness, theft);
(3)   compelling economic reasons (e.g. loss of work due to loss of orders or rationalisation) (para. 1: Law on Protection against Dismissal, *Kündigungs-schutzgesetz*).

The dismissal notices are also valid only if the employees cannot be transferred within the workplace or within the firm, if the dismissal is contrary to a selection list agreed with the works council, or if another employee is less entitled to social protection and should have been dismissed instead of the person who was actually dismissed.

If there is a works council in the firm, it has to be consulted before the dismissal takes effect. But the works council may only object to the dismissal if:

(1)   the employer has not, or not sufficiently, taken into consideration his social situation in dismissing the employee;
(2)   the dismissal is contrary to the agreed selection list;
(3)   the employee who has been issued with a dismissal notice can be employed elsewhere in the same establishment or in another part of the firm;
(4)   the continued employment of the employee is possible after he has received retraining or further training; or
(5)   the continued employment of the employee is possible with an amended contract of employment and providing the employee has given his consent to such a course (para. 102, II: Law on the Constitution of Works Councils). The objection of the works council usually entitles the employee to continuation of employment up to the point when the decision of the court relating to the dismissal case takes effect.

various groups of workers of finding alternative employment have evolved in very different directions in recent years. Whereas for young people aged between 20 and 25, for example, the unemployment rate fell from 13.3 per cent in 1982 to 8.5 per cent in 1988, that for the 55-59 age group rose in the same period from 9.6 per cent to 12.7 per cent [cf. Adamy and Bosch, 1989]. Furthermore, since 1982/83 there has been a divergence between the evolution of the unemployment rate for unemployed people without formal qualifications and that for the unemployed with vocational qualifications. Between 1983 and 1987, the unemployment rate for workers without formal qualifications rose from the already high level of 16 per cent to 18 per cent, while that for workers with vocational training qualifications fell during the same period from 6.2 per cent to 5.9 per cent (see Figure 2). In the Federal Republic of Germany, the main method of "renewing" the workforce is through the firm-based apprenticeship system, which makes it possible constantly to reduce the age of the workforce (cf. also our case study of the mining industry on pp. 92-101); in other countries with less highly developed mechanisms for integrating young people, the restructuring of the workforce takes place largely by means of a direct exchange of labour involving dismissals and hirings [Ardenti and Vrain, 1988].

Figure 2:   Unemployment rate (%) for different educational categories

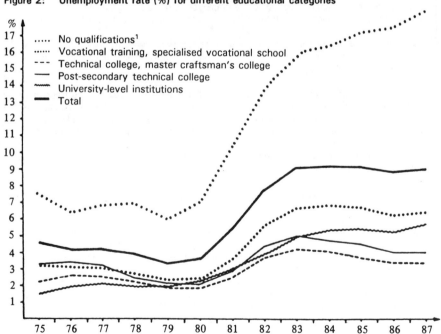

Note: [1] Excluding those in training; 1986-87 figures provisional.
Source: Tessaring [1988, p. 182].

(b) Within manufacturing industry, the proportion of workers employed in small and medium-sized firms is increasing at the expense of the larger firms. Large firms are reducing the scale of their manufacturing operations and are increasingly shifting production to subcontractors, partly in order to reduce their wage costs and partly in order to spread the risks associated with fluctuations in orders. Wages and social benefits are significantly lower in small and medium-sized firms than in larger firms, although the scope for divergence is limited in the Federal Republic by wage agreements covering whole sectors, so that extreme wage differentials cannot develop as they do in the United States of America and Japan (cf. Sengenberger [1988] and Table 3). Furthermore, transfer to a small or medium-sized firm entails a reduction in job security. Protection against dismissal is dependent in part on size of firm,[19] and is linked in part to the existence of works councils, which often do not exist in many small and medium-sized firms.[20] Because of tighter financial circumstances, lower product diversity with which to balance out fluctuations in demand for individual products and dependence on orders from large firms, the risk of dismissal increases as the size of firm decreases (cf. Table 4).

Table 3: Average wages by size of firm[1] (as % of the wage level in firms with more than 500 employees) in selected countries and years

Country	Year	Number of employees in firm		
		10-99	100-499	500 +
Denmark[2]	1978	93.2	97.3	100.0
FRG[2]	1978	89.7	92.2	100.0
France[2]	1978	82.9	86.3	100.0
Italy[2]	1978	85.4	92.7	100.0
Japan[3]	1982	77.1	82.9[6]	100.0[7]
USA[4]	1983	57.0[5]	73.8	100.0

Notes: [1] For the Federal Republic of Germany and Italy the data refer to size of establishment. [2] Hourly earnings for male employees in manufacturing industry. [3] Monthly earnings for regular employees in the private sector (excl. agriculture). [4] Weekly earnings for blue-collar and white-collar workers in the private sector (excl. agriculture). [5] 1-99 employees. [6] 100-999 employees. [7] 1000 +.
Source: OECD, *Employment Outlook*, September 1985, p. 78.

---

[19] Protection against dismissal does not come into force until there are 5 or more employees and social plans cannot be agreed in firms with fewer than 20 employees. A number of wage agreements also provide protection against dismissal and rationalisation, but again only if the firm has a minimum number of employees.

[20] Social plans can be negotiated only by works councils, and many other collective rights can only be exercised by works councils acting on behalf of individual workers (e.g. opposition to dismissals).

Table 4: Frequency of dismissal and estabishment size in the private sector

Establishment size	Percentage share in number of:		Dismissals per 100 employees
	Employees	Dismissals	
Up to 20	25.7	48.4	135
21 - 100	22.2	25.4	82
101 - 300	16.3	17.7	60
301 - 1000	14.5	6.6	32
1000 +	22.3	6.9	26
Total	100.0	100.0	74

Source: Falke [1983, p.16].

(c)   Because of the fall in the importance of those industrial sectors with strong trade union organisation and relatively high average wages, displaced workers are increasingly obliged to seek employment in the service sector. Because their skills relate largely to manufacturing industry, these workers have access only to simple service sector jobs, which are significantly less well paid than their previous jobs. Moreover, an increasing number of workers are making the double change to small and medium-sized firms located in low-wage sectors. The change in the sectoral structure is now aggravating the consequences of redundancies, whereas in the 1950s and 1960s it tended to cushion their impact because employment in large firms in the core sectors of manufacturing industry were gaining in importance relative to agriculture and small and medium-sized independent firms.

(d)   Finally, there is now, in addition to the permanent, full-time employment contract (the standard employment contract), a multiplicity of new, more flexible employment contracts (temporary employment, fixed-term jobs, self-employment, various forms of part-time work) which are based both on changed legal regulations and a different use of regulations that already existed. These flexible employment contracts can gain acceptance only against a background of high unemployment. There is talk, for example, of a flight into self-employment. The increase in the number of company start-ups has virtually paralleled the increase in unemployment. A recent survey found that 9 per cent of the founders of new firms were previously unemployed, and a further 32.3 per cent considered their jobs insecure. "This would suggest that the 'growing readiness' does not always reflect an existing desire to pursue an entrepreneurial career. Rather it may in part be an attempt to find work in the absence of any other opportunities" [Weitzel, 1986, p. 7]. For some redundant workers, these employment contracts may in fact foreshadow their departure from economic activity. For others, however, they may represent a precarious step down the road to reintegration into standard

employment contracts, a lengthy trial period they have to complete successfully in order to earn an offer of secure employment. In this case, some of those made redundant have to reckon with an *extended phase of instability*, which is something new, at least compared with the 1960s and 1970s. Such a differentiated analysis of mobility processes is based on the assumption that the consequences of mass redundancies cannot really be understood simply by means of purely statistical snapshots; rather, the dynamics of their development can only be fully comprehended in the context not only of the restructuring of workforces, industries and sectors but also of the forms of regulation of employment relationships. In any event, the structural changes outlined above are aggravating the already serious social problems caused by redundancies, which are made even worse by the decline in the influence of trade unions. Because of the low level of trade union organisation in small and medium-sized firms and in the service sector and the deregulation of labour law, they are increasingly less able to guarantee social standards in the event of enforced mobility, or even to establish new ones. In consequence, it is becoming increasingly difficult for the trade union movement to pursue constructive strategies towards the shaping of structural change - unless the reduction in social standards associated with current structural change is resisted by means of an active employment policy which at the same time maintains or even extends the trade unions' room for manoeuvre.

(7) *Labour market and employment policy*: Government labour market and employment policy has a fundamental structuring effect on the consequences of redundancies. Retraining can make the transition to a new job easier for workers affected by redundancy. Adequate financial compensation makes it possible for them to systematically seek work and reduces the pressure from the external labour market to accept the first job offer they receive, particularly if it represents a significant demotion. Finally, unemployment in the affected areas can be reduced by the creation of new jobs. However, the reduction of unemployment benefit in many countries has now increased the pressure of the external labour market. For those of a conservative persuasion, the supply of cheap labour thus created becomes an effective source of new demand for labour. The lowering of wages and the deterioration in working conditions are interpreted as preconditions for the successful reintegration of disadvantaged workers. In practice, such a philosophy - which is currently dominating policy-making in the Federal Republic of Germany - leads to increased unemployment in structurally weak regions and the elimination of older employees, unskilled workers, women and foreign workers from the labour market, or at least from its more stable segments. Only in few countries have attempts been made to provide better financial compensation for workers in the event of redundancy, while at the same time retraining them and creating new jobs.

One example of such a strategy "against the trend" [Heseler, 1989] is the restructuring of the Swedish shipbuilding industry. As late as the 1970s, Sweden had one of the largest shipbuilding industries in the world. By the mid-1980s, all the Swedish shipyards had been closed, without the closures leading to unemployment. When the Uddevalla shipyard near Gothenburg was closed, with the loss of 3,000 jobs, the Swedish government, in 1985, introduced a package of employment policy measures that included labour market policy measures, government investment, investment grants, assistance for Volvo to relocate, support for regional development corporations and regional technology consultancies as well as the establishment of additional further training facilities. The government estimated the whole package to be worth about 1,482 million Swedish kronor (around £138 million) [Larsson and Sigfridson, 1989].[21] This ambitious employment programme was developed with the active participation and advice of all the regional actors involved. Under this programme, unless the offer of early retirement was taken up, each former shipyard employee was offered a new job, for which retraining was given.

III.   From social plans to employment plans

The first social plans in the Federal Republic of Germany were agreed at *establishment level* in the coal and steel industry, in 1957 in the case of the mining industry and in 1963 in that of the steel industry [Vogt, 1974; *Autorengemeinschaft*, 1977]. There were mass redundancies both before and after in other sectors, but they did not result in comparable socio-political arrangements.[22] Social plans are the outcome of a specific set of labour market and political circumstances associated with the crisis in the coal and steel industry; it was a question not of the closure of isolated plants, but of industry-wide crises that heralded further redundancies. The industries were regionally concentrated and structured the local labour markets; they had hitherto been successful in preventing new firms from locating in the region, and the workers were very much tied to their firms or industry, both in terms of their skills (company or sector-specific) and of their private circumstances (e.g. because they lived in company housing).

As a result of these circumstances, a change of employer resulted, at least temporarily, in integration problems and loss of income, despite the high growth rate of the 1950s and 1960s. Trade union membership was much higher than

---

[21] The actual amount is even higher. Tax relief, the sale of land to Volvo at a reduced price and other measures were not included [Storrie, 1988].

[22] In 1961, after the car manufacturer Borgward went bankrupt, more than 15,000 employees were made redundant without being covered by a social plan. Government labour market policy was limited to a placement service intended to find jobs for the unemployed as quickly as possible, although it was not possible to prevent many workers being de-skilled.

average, and the works councils and the trade unions exerted particular influence on personnel policy through the co-determination arrangements that prevailed in the coal and steel industry; finally, virtually all redundancies were accompanied by mass protests, which gave rise to fears of political radicalisation in the Ruhr region. The demands made by the works councils and trade unions did not really challenge the decisions already taken by the companies: they were merely seeking to alleviate the hardship the redundancies would cause their members.

Most of the first generation of social plans provided financial compensation for loss of income and any relocation expenses that might be incurred, etc. The success of this social plan policy depended on the favourable situation in the labour market at that time, which enabled virtually all the workers made redundant to find another job fairly quickly. The wide variety of arrangements agreed by different companies persuaded company managements to develop uniform standards. Thus in 1968, for example, a social plan covering the whole of the coal mining industry was agreed [*Gesamtsozialplan, 1968*].

From the end of the 1960s until 1974, the rapid growth in employment ensured that displaced workers had no difficulty finding alternative employment. However, in view of major upheavals in technology and work organisation, it is by no means certain that they obtained comparable employment. During this period, the trade unions tried to intervene actively in the consequences of labour market processes, rather than simply obtaining financial compensation in order to cushion the blow of redundancy. And as a consequence of the debate on protection against rationalisation, a much-discussed issue at that time [Böhle and Lutz, 1974], social plans increasingly made provision for retraining programmes, in order to prepare workers for technological change and, for victims of rationalisations, transfers to other jobs.

During the period of reform, legislation was introduced to make the arrangements pioneered at firm and industry level more generally applicable. In 1972, the new Law on Labour Relations at the Workplace made it compulsory in firms with more than 20 employees to negotiate a social plan with the works council in the event of changes to the firm. Also during this period, it was established that transfers, and any necessary training measures, should take precedence over redundancies.[23] Thus "retraining not redundancy" has long been a legal norm, although only in a very restricted sense: at the time of dismissal, an actual opportunity for transfer within the firm must already exist. Possible employment opportunities in the more distant future, associated perhaps with the manufacture of new products or sections of the firm yet to be founded, are not generally included. In crisis situations, such long-term training measures are not generally considered reasonable from the firm's point of view; as a consequence, the best that can be expected under this legislation is short-term training measures, but certainly not the elimination of more significant skill deficits.

---

[23] In accordance with § 102, para. 3 of the Law on Labour Relations at the Workplace, a works council can object to a dismissal with notice if it is possible for the worker to be re-employed after undergoing a reasonable retraining or further training programme.

The social plans and measures protecting against dismissal implemented during the 1970s clearly emphasised dismissals and transfers at the expense of the training component. Two investigations of the contents of social plans show that both at the beginning of the 1970s and in the 1980s only the procedures for dismissals and transfers were regulated to any great extent. In general, the 1980s saw an increase in the diversity of provisions contained in social plans. In the 1980s, slightly more social plans provided opportunities for further vocational training than was the case in the 1970s (see Table 5).

Table 5: Personnel measures contained in social plans

Personnel measures	Investigation by Ochs: Number[1]		Investigation by Hase et al.: Number[1]	
	(N = 299)	%	(N = 350)	%
Redundancies	261	87.8	335	95.0
Transfers/continued employment	144	48.2	202	57.7
Early retirement for older employees	52	17.4	80	22.9
Vocational training measures	51	17.1	64	18.3

Note: [1] Multiple inclusions.
Source: Ochs [1976, p. 82] and Hase et al. [1988, p. 12].

Empirical investigations of rationalisation measures and cuts in staffing levels actually implemented tend to show that only in isolated cases did social plans drawn up in the 1970s lead to retraining programmes [Schultz-Wild, 1980, p. 135]. A survey of works councils, mainly in large firms, reveals that only 22 per cent of them objected to redundancies on the grounds that re-employment would be an option after a period of further training. This low percentage is explained as follows: an objection "requires more involvement from those affected [works councils - G.B.] and more planning. Further training and retraining cannot generally be implemented in the short term" [Kohl, 1978, p. 228].

With the beginning of mass unemployment from 1975 onwards, the limits of the social plan policy developed up to that point became evident. The chances of redundant workers finding another job were becoming more and more uncertain, and as a result the financial compensation available was becoming an increasingly inadequate means of making up for the loss of a job. In the coal and steel industry in particular, pressure from workers and their representative organisations led to a shift in strategy, with early retirement becoming the main plank of social plans (see Table 6).

Table 6: Measures taken to adjust manning levels in the steel industry in North Rhine-Westphalia between 1976 and 1986

Adjustment measures	Hoesch Stahl AG	Krupp Stahl AG	Krupp Klöckner Forges	Mannesmann-röhren-Werke AG	Thyssen-Stahl	Total
No. of employees transferred to other group companies, including those at other locations	809	2 969	96	6 400	5 200	15 474
Placement in other firms	98	-	-	-	-	98
Early retirement	11 864	10 700	850 [1]	7 630	19 783	50 827
Other cuts in manning levels						
(a) dismissals for operational reasons	-	-	-	-	-	-
(b) severance agreements and/or redundancy payment schemes (departure from labour market eased by social plans)	1 500	-	118	-	4 849 [2]	6 467

Notes: [1] Since 30 September 1983.
[2] Including foreign workers who departed under the terms of legislation introduced on 28 November 1983, and was intended to encourage foreign workers to return home.

Source: Parliament of North Rhine-Westphalia, circular 10/2135, p. 13.

Early retirement for older workers would not have been practicable without substantial government subsidies (59 rule,[24] Law on Early Retirement, etc.). Direct dismissals were avoided, and were even completely ruled out in some company agreements (such as in the Saarland, for example, cf. Judith et al. [1980]). However, sometimes foreign workers were subjected to considerable moral pressure, accompanied by financial inducements, to return home [Schäfer, 1986]. The rejection of mass dismissals made it possible to prevent direct protests against reductions in manning levels. These cuts were to a large extent tolerated, since the well-organised trade union members in large firms who could have resisted them remained well protected from redundancy. However, the negative consequences of the social plan policy for individual regions became difficult to ignore. Critical voices within the trade union movement began to make themselves heard: by negotiating social plans, they said, the unions were giving their blessing to the bleeding dry of whole regions and the loss of trade union influence over structural changes.

Shop stewards and works councils set up working parties which drew up proposals for alternative production [Bosch, 1985a; Mehrens, 1985]. The aim was to develop new products in order to avoid the need for reductions in staffing levels in the firm. These working parties formulated numerous concrete ideas for products, and some product development work was even carried out, albeit on a small scale. The product proposals were for the most part intended to encourage additional demand from government (e.g. for new energy supply systems); however, despite the existence of a genuine need, restrictive financial policy meant that the proposals were never brought to fruition. There was also resistance from management, which did not extend its product range at certain locations, preferring instead to rationalise its operations by discontinuing certain product lines and closing establishments. Finally, the development of new products, and thus the creation of new jobs, proved more difficult than had been anticipated, because of competition in the market place and a variety of research and development activities already undertaken by the firm.

Individual firms which were experiencing a collapse of demand wanted to diversify their product range in the medium term, and were looking for ideas "to tide them over", i.e. for ways to retain their skilled workforce until the firm had been successfully restructured. At the Howald shipyard operated by Deutsche Werft AG, the concept of a labour pool was developed, inspired partly by Swedish models. With assistance from the Federal Labour Office, employees were to be retrained in order to take up a new and different job in the restructured firm. At the request of the company, with the agreement of the works council and with support from the Project on the Humanisation of Work, this notion of a labour pool was developed to include further proposals for individual training measures [Drewes et al., 1982; Pellul et al., 1983]. However, the concept was not implemented, because the company management changed its

---

[24] The 59 rule provides for the early retirement of unemployed people who have reached the age of 59.

strategy; it gave up its plans for diversification and sought instead to shed labour rapidly in order to "retain a smaller but efficient and cost-effective nucleus of the shipyard, in order to remain competitive in the long term in the continuing difficult situation in the world shipbuilding market" [Drewes et al., 1982, p.21]. However, other, less ambitious variations on the pool concept were put into practice. Thus Arbed in Luxembourg used its surplus labour to form a so-called "anti-crisis department", which took over maintenance and other building work previously contracted out, and also loaned workers to other firms or for public works. At times there were more than 4,000 employees in this pool. The surplus labour was retained for a longer period, and when vacancies arose in the core workforce, members of the anti-crisis department had the chance to take over the jobs [Kohl, 1982; Deeke, 1983].

The experiences of the working parties on "alternative production", and also those of the Howaldt shipyard, had clearly revealed the limits of action restricted to firm level. For economic reasons, firms in crisis sectors are usually forced to make rapid decisions about shedding labour; moreover, as a result of inadequate planning for diversification in the past, they are not usually in a position to rapidly develop new company strategies. This requires new skills and structures, for which additional human and financial resources are a prerequisite.

In the view of the trade unions, the limits on action at plant or company level should be overcome by an active structural and regional policy, as in Sweden. The IG Metall union suggests the establishment of *employment companies*[25] in crisis-hit industries. A "steel employment company", for example, would be set up with government assistance as a subsidiary of a steel company. It would be financed by employment promotion funds channelled through the steel company. The employment companies would take on those employees unable to find an acceptable replacement job within the company. They would draw up proposals for replacement jobs both within and outside the company, and link them to specific training measures [IG Metall, 1987; GEWOS, GfAH, WSI, 1988]. The success of employment companies would be backed up by regionally specific government programmes aimed at stimulating demand [Löwe and Wand, 1987].

At the beginning of the 1980s, the debate within the trade union movement on the creation of new jobs in periods of crisis for firms and industries, which had advanced considerably, came up against harsher economic conditions and changes in companies' strategies. When several industries (steel, shipbuilding, coalmining, consumer electronics) were hit by new job losses, the limits of the strategies for shedding labour outlined above were reached. So few older workers were still employed in these industries that it was increasingly difficult

---

[25] Employment companies are legal personalities of private or public law, usually limited companies or registered associations, founded for the primary purpose of carrying out training measures, job creation schemes and to help redundant workers find a new job within or outside the company. They act as an employer on a fixed-term basis for the period of wage subsidy granted by the Federal Employment Office, by social plans or by other public or private funds.

to reduce staffing levels through early retirement alone. It is true that some companies temporarily implement, and repeatedly consider, rigorous exclusion policies against foreign workers, but for reasons of labour market policy (firms are very interested in hiring foreign workers) and over-riding foreign policy considerations (European integration, relationships with NATO partners) such strategies can hardly be pursued in the long term. Furthermore, government is increasingly withdrawing from the financing of early retirement schemes, since they are relatively costly.[26] The retirement age is being raised again in the medium term, and the provisions of social plans have deteriorated.

Moreover, firms no longer view the slump in employment as a temporary *cyclical* crisis, as they did in the mid-1970s, but rather as a long-term *structural* phenomenon [*Beschäftigungsrückgang*, 1985]. As a result, they have become less willing to retain workers within the firm for as long as possible by adopting short-time working, further training or other "bridging" measures. The aim of company strategy, and that of government policy, is rather to make rapid cuts, which in any case seem unavoidable in the longer term. A return to mass redundancies in large firms in the core manufacturing sectors, in which the maxim "no dismissals" determined personnel policy in the 1970s, seems unavoidable. The parallel political debate on deregulating the terms of social plans, on the grounds that they are too costly, indicates that there is the risk of a break with earlier policies. Policy is no longer based on a *model of socio-political progress*, which in times of structural change generalised tried and tested arrangements designed to protect both jobs and wages. Rather, a *flexibilisation model* now dominates, in which attacks on standards of legal protection pave the way for the imposition of less favourable terms in wage negotiations and company agreements.

This contradiction between, on the one hand, new trade union ideas for dealing with crisis and, on the other, redundancies, their incalculably negative consequences for employees in a period of high unemployment and the concurrent public debate on flexibility created the *explosive material for increasing conflicts over cuts in manpower levels* in the crisis sectors, out of which the first employment plans were born. Without the development of well thought-out alternatives to traditional social plans in the 1970s and the mobilisation of workers in the firms and sectors hit by crisis, the conclusion of the first employment plan in 1985 at Grundig AG and, soon afterwards, a number of other employment plans, also investigated here, would not have been conceivable.

It is worthy of note that even individual firms showed themselves receptive to these new ideas at an early date, since they were no longer able to use social

---

[26] The Law On Early Retirement expired at the end of 1988. Since 1984, companies have been obliged to reimburse the Federal Labour Office for unemployment benefits paid to older workers whom they have made redundant and who are waiting to take early retirement at the age of 59, unless this would be a "particular hardship" for the company in the light of its precarious economic situation.

plans to implement redundancies without conflict, and, moreover, as they were also seeking to diversify in any case. The debate about employment pools, employment companies etc., which has been going on for ten years, has softened firms' initial resistance, in principle, to new ways of managing both company and structural crises.

IV. Interim result

Relative to the United States, for example, firms in the Federal Republic of Germany internalise more of the costs involved in structural adjustment. Nevertheless, *German approaches to mass redundancies, based on the development of social plans, have been largely defensive or reactive*; they do not intervene directly in the mechanisms of the labour market in the event of redundancies, but have mainly been focused on promoting external mobility, which at most cushions the negative effects. Similarly, the Federal Labour Office, as we will see in Chapter 3, has not traditionally "intervened upstream" (meaning pre-lay-off) in promoting retraining as a way of preventing dismissals. They do not intervene in the labour market until workers have already been dismissed. *They represent a qualitative departure in that they attempt to internalise adjustment in a forward-thinking rather than reactive way.* In contrast, employment plans - according to the claim formulated at the beginning of the 1980s - are intended, by means of training and diversification measures, to act on the "root of the evil" and remove the need for redundancies. However, only time will tell whether this aim of a predominantly internal structural change can in fact be realised.

Numerous investigations into the consequences of redundancies confirm some of the notions on which employment plans are based. Vocational training can be a means of entering or remaining in occupational labour markets; this provides good protection in the event of enforced mobility both within and outside the firm. And although this is not included in the claim made for employment plans, training also opens up opportunities for mobility in the external labour market. However, these investigations also expose the limits of the protection afforded by training in the event of external mobility. Women and foreign workers come up against particular lines of discrimination, which cannot be eliminated by training measures alone.

Without geographical mobility or an active regional economic policy, any training strategy will come up against constraints in geographically isolated labour markets. And it is precisely here that pressure for internal solutions will presumably be strongest. Finally, a crucial role is attributed to selection processes in the choice of workers to be made redundant, since the criteria for selection for dismissal differ markedly from those for successful further training measures. This discrepancy will play an important role in the following chapter.

Chapter 3

Labour market policy and employment plans

I.   The eye of a needle: the German Employment Promotion Law

There are many different ways of envisaging government participation in the financing of employment plans. Federal or *Land* governments could, for example, establish a fund for training programmes in firms undergoing a period of restructuring. Such funds could also be set up on a regional or sectoral basis. However, the Federal Government only provided financial assistance for the coastal regions affected by the crisis in the shipbuilding industry; topped up with funds from the *Land*, this money was also used for training shipyard workers (see pp. 61-71 and pp. 109-113). There were, however, no other nationwide struc-tural policy programmes on which company employment plans could be based.

Consequently, employment plans were relegated to be treated as a part of the regular programmes for the promotion of further vocational training sponsored by the Federal Labour Office. This shift was reinforced by the additional funds made available by several *Länder* (e.g. the Saarland and Hamburg), since from the outset the only assistance they provided was to top up the subsistence allowances paid by the Federal Labour Office. Only in Hamburg were further resources made available to fund diversification programmes in the shipyards. Against this background, the precondition for all employment plans was that the Federal Labour Office would provide subsistence allowances and pay the teaching costs incurred in the planned training programmes.

Thus the implementation of employment plans is completely dependent on the support of the Federal Labour Office. Consequently, the training programmes they include have to conform to the provisions of the Employment Promotion Law. This gives rise to many problems and difficulties created by the *conceptual differences between employment plans and the Employment Promotion Law.*

The aim of *employment plans* is to train whole *groups of workers* threatened by redundancy, irrespective of their individual characteristics; the group in question is identified by negotiations within the firm, and the criteria for selection differ from case to case, depending on the situation in each individual firm. The Law on Labour Relations at the Workplace makes provision only for the procedural aspects of social plans; the subjects for negotiation and the outcomes of those negotiations arise out of these procedures, and are thus open-ended and malleable.

The aim of the *Employment Promotion Law*, on the other hand, is to support *individuals*, who have to fulfil certain requirements. Unlike in France or Austria, for example, the law does not provide for the support of whole groups of workers in particular sectors or firms. Therefore, it has not been possible for any individual employment office to give an undertaking to support planned training measures. In general, the employment offices declared that they would investigate each individual case and treat it in exactly the same way as any other individual request from an unemployed or employed person. Thus the groups of employees in question were disaggregated and offered interviews and advice on an individual basis.

These individuals had first of all to fulfil the personal requirements for training. These include: suitability for successful participation in a training programme; an intention, within a four-year period after completion of the training programme, to work for at least three years in compulsorily insured employment; the appropriateness in terms of labour market policy of the programme (likelihood of employment after completion of training);[27] and a certain amount of experience in the job (in order to distinguish further training from apprenticeship programmes, for which firms are responsible). The payment of subsistence allowances to workers on further training programmes proved on occasions to be very problematic. Federal legislation on employment promotion, which is the basis for any action taken by the Federal Labour Office, is part of a policy framework that has developed over time and which restricts the responsibility of the Federal Labour Office in the area of further training (see Figure 3):

-   *The training of apprentices* in the dual vocational training system is the responsibility of firms and the vocational schools.

-   The Federal Labour Office can support further *vocational* training but not general education, which is the preserve of a multiplicity of institutions (adult education centres, private agencies, etc.).

---

[27] Prior to training, the immediate possibility of a job renders an individual ineligible for support (DA A 6.04). However, a broad definition of appropriate further training measures has been drawn up under the heading "Training for the Future". This definition states: "An unfavourable labour market situation and the associated difficulties in finding employment should not have a negative effect on the promotion of vocational training. Even in difficult times, training increases the chances of finding or keeping a job. And even in a tight labour market it can be assumed that participants who, on the basis of a realistic assessment, are suited to the aim of the training programme, will find a job consistent with that aim. Under the terms of the above regulation, a period of time can be considered reasonable if the opportunity for employment following a proposed training programme can be expected to arise only in the longer term and in association with an economic upturn" (DA A FuU, 1987, Chapter 6.04, Section 2).

Figure 3:   The role of the Federal Labour Office in the further training system

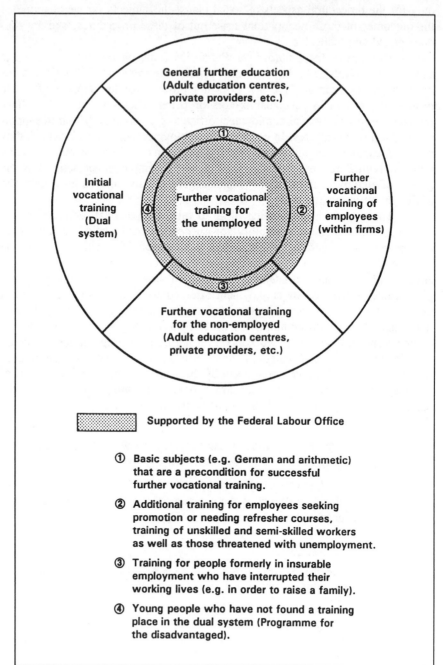

- Further vocational training for employees *within a firm* is the firm's responsibility, since such measures are primarily in the firm's interests.

- Payments made by the Federal Labour Office, at least as far as the payment of subsistence allowances during a course of further vocational training is concerned, are to a large extent based on the *insurance principle*. Therefore, unemployed persons cannot be assisted unless they have been in insurable employment for the required period of time.

In this sphere of conflict between various areas of responsibility, institutions and even systems of financing further training, the Federal Labour Office concentrates on the *further vocational training* of *individuals* who are insured, whom they assist, however, only if it serves the interests of labour market policy. This is defined primarily from the point of view of individuals whose mobility in the labour market is to be improved, rather than from that of institutions (firms, etc.) or geographical entities (efficiency of regional labour markets). By defining the interests of labour market policy in this way, the Federal Labour Office differentiates its role in further vocational training from that of other institutions. There is an important contradiction, for example, in the distinction between the interests of labour market policy and those of firms with respect to further training. At present, high unemployment means that the main focus of labour market policy is the provision of *further occupational training for the unemployed.*[28]

However, the borders between the various areas of further training are extremely flexible, and in the last two decades, since the Employment Promotion Law came into force, they have been constantly redrawn. Today, for the long-term unemployed and foreign workers, general education courses are also being authorised, since in these groups the main obstacle to successful participation in further training programmes has proved to be a lack of basic skills. By integrating the programme for the disadvantaged into the Employment Promotion Act, the Federal Labour Office took over some responsibility for the initial training of young people who have been unable to gain access to the *dual vocational training system.*[29] Access to further training programmes has been made somewhat easier for people not presently in employment who have taken

---

[28] In 1987, 64.2 per cent of all participants in further training programmes had previously been unemployed. In a period of full employment, on the other hand, the corresponding figure was only 5.8 per cent (1973); at that time, therefore, the mobility of employees was considerably improved [*Förderung der beruflichen Weiterbildung*, 1988, p. 12].

[29] The dual vocational training system is the traditional (and basic) system of vocational training in the Federal Republic of Germany. Under this system, a young person on a training contract or apprenticeship receives appropriate vocational training in the firm with which the contract is made and also, by law, has to attend a vocational school one day a week for the requisite theoretical instruction, over an apprenticeship period of three to three-and-a-half years. At the end of compulsory schooling, about 60 per cent of young people leave to take up a vocational training contract.

a break from work in order to look after children. This should help women who wish to return to work outside the home. With the subsistence allowance from the Federal Labour Office, many workers take part in further training programmes, in order to keep pace with technological and economic change, or to improve their chances of promotion.

II. Assisting employees in crisis-hit firms

Under certain circumstances (given below), it is also possible to provide assistance to *employees*; this includes the payment of subsistence allowances. The individuals who can be trained under the provisions of employment plans fall into one of the following four groups:

(1) Employees who are *directly threatened by unemployment*, in order to prevent them becoming unemployed (Employment Promotion Act § 44, section 2, clause 2, no. 2): assistance may not be provided if those affected can find employment in the "foreseeable future", since in this case they would not become unemployed. The threat of unemployment must also be "direct". Such a threat is assumed to exist:

- if notice has already been given or the firm has already gone into receivership;

- if a short-term employment contract is about to expire;

- if the employment office is aware that redundancies are likely because dismissals for operational reasons are anticipated [DA A FuU, 1987, Chapter 10.12].

Clearly, there is scope for each employment office to interpret the regulations. On the one hand, there is the question of how to define a worker's chance of finding alternative employment, which will depend to a certain extent on conditions in the local labour market, while on the other it is necessary to establish the criteria for defining what is understood by "expected" dismissal. The Federal Labour Office suggests to local employment offices that in examining applications they should distinguish between two cases: firstly, when an individual approaches the employment office, it should be sufficient that notice of mass dismissals has been given and that the applicant can reliably confirm (possibly with corroboration from the works council) that he belongs to the segment of the workforce likely to be affected. Secondly, when the firm approaches the employment office, it must submit a list of the names of those to be made redundant. If the firm is the applicant, detailed substantiation of the threat to the individual is requested; this is intended to prevent the firm passing on its further training costs to the Federal Labour Office.

(2) Employees who do not have a *vocational qualification* and can now acquire one (Employment Promotion Act § 44, para. 2, clause 2, no. 3): this also

includes employees who have worked twice as long as their training period in a trade other than their own. It does not include employees about to be made redundant. The only other stipulation is that the measures should not be primarily "in the firm's interests". If the programme is conducted within the firm, it must lead to a recognised vocational qualification (order FuU 1987 § 9, para. 2).

(3) Young employees who have not yet reached their 26th birthday and who work a mimimum of 12 and a maximum of 24 hours per week and are also attending a part-time training course. They receive a part-time subsistence allowance if the training course is necessary in order to take up a full-time job. This measure was a short-term one and was in force only between 1.1.86 and 31.12.1989 (Employment Promotion Act § 44, para. 2a, clause 1).

(4) Employees who are dismissed but are given a promise of re-employment by their old firm at a specified date (the *waiting-loop model*). This case differs considerably from the others, since the aim is not necessarily retraining and it is accepted that the employees in question may be unemployed or temporarily employed elsewhere. For the time being at least, they are no longer employed by the firm, but unemployed; to that extent, the same conditions apply as to all other unemployed people when an opportunity for retraining is being investigated. However, problems may arise with unemployment benefit. As far as the Federal Labour Office is concerned, a promise of re-employment raises "doubts about availability" to take up a reasonable offer of employment and may result in withdrawal of benefit. Those affected in this way must "dispel this doubt in individual interviews" (Federal Labour Office, circular 123/87) and it must not be reinforced by other pieces of circumstantial evidence (passive attitude towards careers advice and employment service) (circular instruction 61/87 from the Regional Employment Office, North Rhine-Westphalia). Lack of willingness to work is always suspected when the promise of re-employment is accepted in the event of placement in alternative employment (circular 123/87, Federal Labour Office).

If the applicant has a vocational qualification or is not under immediate threat of dismissal, the law states that training is not "necessary" but merely "advisable". In this case, only course fees are paid, with the subsistence allowance being advanced in the form of a loan. Very little use has been made of this provision in the context of employment plans: the individuals in question would only have ended up owing large sums of money to the Federal Labour Office, without any guarantee that they would be able to secure their jobs.[30] If they were unemployed, however, they would most probably receive the full subsistence allowance while attending a similar course.

---

[30] In exceptional cases, e.g. at Grundig and Thomson, the loan was repaid in whole or in part by the company.

The subsistence allowance paid to workers on training programmes can be topped up by the firm, up to 100 per cent of the amount laid down under the terms of the Employment Promotion Act. This includes gross pay without overtime and shift allowances as well as single payments (Christmas and holiday pay). In practice, the extra money made available by firms ranges from 27 to 37 per cent of the prescribed amount.

Finally, the Federal Labour Institute pays only the "essential" costs of the training programme itself. The estimated cost to firms implementing the training programmes themselves must be in line with those for comparable courses. Moreover, if the Federal Labour Office fails to provide financial assistance, the firm cannot be obliged to pay the costs itself, whether as part of a wage agreement, an agreement on protection against rationalisation or even an employment plan. Thus, finding solutions to the problem of redundancy, even with assistance from the Federal Labour Office, is not a priority concern for firms.

If new products are to be introduced or developed, retraining, according to this interpretation of the law, is primarily in the "firm's interest". In this case, which from the point of view of employment plans is an ideal situation, a subsistence allowance is not paid unless unskilled and semi-skilled workers will thereby obtain a vocational qualification. Only in this case will it be accepted that the training programme is largely in the interests of labour market policy. In the firms investigated, however, this problem did not arise, since in no case were the ideas for new products sufficiently far advanced; moreover, the training programmes were relatively broadly defined and not orientated towards specialised new activities.

To summarise, it would seem that assistance to unskilled and semi-skilled workers can be provided with little difficulty through employment plans, provided those workers are thereby acquiring a vocational qualification. Thus, the Employment Promotion Law makes definite provision for preventive assistance to unskilled workers, who are particularly disadvantaged in the labour market.[31]

However, the more highly qualified the employees are, the weaker this preventive element in the Employment Protection Law becomes. In accordance with the Federal Labour Office's restrictive interpretation of the Law, assistance is granted only if a dismissal has virtually taken place. When interviewed, an official from the Federal Labour Office stated that "such high demands are made that unemployment actually occurs". The contradiction between the preventive philosophy of the Employment Promotion Act and protection from dead weight is resolved here at the cost of "prevention". The fear of the Federal Labour Office, which certainly cannot be dismissed out of hand, is that costs which have

---

[31] This preventive component has also been used in practice. 9.1 per cent of all people starting vocational training programmes in the first nine months of 1988 (32,823 individuals) were on essential courses for employees. The greater proportion of them were unskilled and semi-skilled workers. A maximum of one in 2,000 cases fell into the category of "threatened by unemployment".

hitherto been borne by firms will be shifted on to the FLO (DA A FuU, 1987, Chapter 9.01).

However, it must be stressed that both the wording of the Act and the instructions for implementation issued by the Federal Labour Office would have allowed a broader definition of a "threat of unemployment". For example, a reduction in the labour force in the three years preceding the application, or an already finalised rationalisation project which will lead within a given period of time to job losses, could be accepted as an indicator of a threat of unemployment.

The restrictive interpretation of the Federal Labour Office, together with anticipated difficulties in encouraging employees to participate in training programmes as well as in organising and financing them, may induce firms to go down the route of putting employees into the waiting loop for unemployment (case 4 above). This strategy relieves the firm of many obligations, ranging from the need to clarify the legal position with the Federal Labour Office to the provision of training programmes. The preventive element of the employment plans can be privatised, i.e. left up to the individual. This route seems to fit best into the funding and organisational structure of the West German further training system, which is based entirely on the individual's initiative, motivation and willingness to pursue training opportunities. Since those affected are not tied to a firm, at least temporarily, the *fiction* of a purely individual approach to labour market policy can be preserved. However, this fiction can lead in practice to an abuse of the preventive training component of the Employment Promotion Act which will be likely to disadvantage unskilled employees. Of the workers in the waiting loop, the most highly qualified are the ones most likely to opt for further training, with the less qualified being left to their own devices, as their under-representation in the further training programmes sponsored by the Federal Labour Office indicates.

Because of its fear of dead weight in firms, which gives rise to the over-restrictive interpretation of the "threat of unemployment", the Federal Labour Office runs the risk of encouraging waiting-loop models with the negative consequences already mentioned, or even preventing employment plans altogether. The more difficult it is to assist the *not-yet unemployed*, the more difficult internal structural change in firms becomes; the concentration of resources on the *already unemployed* amounts to an attempt to impose external structural change, which is clearly more suited to the current institutional structures of the West German further training system and the Federal Labour Office's conception of its own function than the philosophy of the employment plans, the main aim of which is to avoid unemployment.

This outline of the options for promoting training open to the Federal Labour Office shows the difficulties of combining employment plans with the provisions of the Employment Promotion Act, as well as some possible unforeseen consequences of restrictive interpretations of legislation. The practical problems that may arise as a consequence will become clear from the case studies presented in Chapter 4.

Chapter 4

Employment plans in practice

Between 30 and 40 employment plans have been concluded in the Federal Republic of Germany since 1985, and they have probably been responsible for the training of between 2,000 and 3,000 employees. Most of the cases analysed below come from sectors in crisis (cf. Table 7):

- Employment plans were agreed in three *shipyards* in Hamburg and two in East Frisia, since both the Federal and *Land* authorities topped up subsistence allowances through the shipyard assistance programme. Without this external assistance, provided as part of government structural policy, there would probably not have been any training programmes. Other examples - not investigated here - can be found among the shipyards of Schleswig-Holstein.

- There are a number of different agreements in the *steel industry*, e.g. for the maintenance of training capacities (Hattingen, Oberhausen, Rheinhausen) and for promoting transfers both within and beyond the firm, as well as undertakings to create new jobs (Krupp Stahl, Rheinhausen). In these agreements, Saarstahl and Krupp introduced the waiting-loop model (see pp. 42-45), which the steel industry was the first to develop. The outline agreement developed at Krupps has not yet been implemented; this will probably happen shortly when the Krupp Rheinhausen plant finally closes. With the Saarland Steel Foundation on the other hand - and this is one of the characteristics of this case - one of the greatest personnel reductions was achieved in the shortest possible time. This was possible only with additional help from the *Land* government.

- Because of its traditional problems in recruiting young workers, which will become even more acute in the 1990s as the low birth rate leads to fewer young people entering the labour market, the *coalmining industry in the Ruhr* has concentrated above all on part-time training programmes for young people. The intention in the industry is both to reduce the volume of work for companies in the short term, and in the longer term to ensure the integration of trained young people into their firms. By far the most applications for part-time training programmes in North Rhine-Westphalia came from Ruhrkohle AG. And as the mines began to shed labour, firms supplying the mining industry also began to get into difficulties. To that extent, it is no accident that in virtually all the larger firms supplying the mining industry, employment plans have been the subject either of discussions or of negotiations. And in one case, Klöckner-Becorit in Castrop-Rauxel, a waiting-loop model was implemented.

- Finally, employment plans have been introduced in firms in the *consumer electronics industry*, which of all the "modern" sectors of the economy has experienced the sharpest reduction in employment levels as a result of the transition from precision engineering to electronics. While the consumer electronics manufacturers Grundig and Thomson (perhaps forewarned by the dispute that accompanied the closure of Videocolor in Ulm) agreed to employment plans, both in order to protect their brand name and to avoid jeopardising their employees' ties with the firm through a "hire and fire policy", attempts to negotiate similar arrangements at the capital goods manufacturer Berthold met with failure, although this producer of photocomposition machines had experienced a similarly profound technological change. However, because of its small size and precarious financial situation, Berthold had significantly less room for manoeuvre in its personnel policy than Thomson or Grundig.

- The two remaining firms were both *mechanical engineering* firms. The Klöckner subsidiary Becorit had already introduced a waiting-loop model, and a similar, though considerably less generous agreement (fixed-term contracts only during training period) was reached in the Klöckner-Humboldt-Deutz mechanical engineering group.[32] Prämewa is an example of a small firm in which an employment plan was agreed despite resistance from management, who then succeeded in preventing its implementation.

This chapter will describe in detail and assess a few of the larger and more complex cases such as Grundig, the Hamburg shipyards, Saarstahl, Thomson and Ruhrkohle AG (sections I-V below). There then follows a survey of the distinctive features of the employment plans in the other firms investigated (see section VI). The same evaluative framework was used in all the casc presentations in order to ensure comparability. Thus the presentations all contain information on the origin, objectives and financing of the employment plans, their relationship to traditional social plans, the implementation of plans for diversification, the content of training programmes, the selection of participants and their reintegration. The distinctive features of each individual case are highlighted: this information is essential, particularly if false generalisations or conclusions are to be avoided.

---

[32] Time restrictions did not permit the investigation into the implementation of these agreements.

Table 7:   Main characteristics of the employment plans (as at June 1989)

Plant/Firm	No. of employees	Total no. of jobs lost	Aims and provisions of the employment plan	Individuals on training programmes	Compulsion or entitlement to participation
1) GRUNDIG AG Nuremberg	1988 ca. 19,500	1985-88: 5,000	- Retraining and restructuring to be given priority over personnel reductions - Annual information on company and personnel planning and on training requirements - Joint "new products" committees at headquarters and plants - Manufacture of new products at endangered plants - Assessment of feasibility of retraining instead of short-time working - Joint committee on "work structuring and retraining" and Joint "further training" project teams at plants - Redundancies only if other measures fail - Compulsory offer of further training for all employees to be made redundant	107 from No. II Works in Nuremberg	a) Right to place on current retraining programmes by arrangement with firm b) Those to be made redundant must be offered further training
2) BLOHM & VOSS Hamburg	1986 4,500	By end of 1987: 630	- Operational redundancies to be avoided through the use of retraining programmes, provided that 180 employees are on further training programmes sponsored by the Federal Labour Office - About 400 employees to be retrained on the rolling programme by end of 1989 - No operational redundancies until the end of 1988	About 500	- Retraining for employees on company's redundancy list - Volunteers
3) HDW ROSS Hamburg	2/88 ca. 1,300	Plant to be closed by end of 1988 959 employees to be taken on by Blohm & Voss	- Retraining programmes by end of 87 on basis of the Blohm & Voss agreement. 100 employees to be on training courses at any one time. A total of 200 people to be trained during the rolling programme. - Approx. 300 jobs to be lost from 1988 onwards; redundant employees to be offered severance pay or a fixed-term employment contract for the duration of a training course and redundancy pay from B&V - 2.5 M DM available for the establishment of an employment company (Öko-Tech)	a) 59 in accordance with the 1987 settlement b) 81 in accordance with the 1988 settlement c) 100 workers on job creation schemes in employment company	a) Voluntary participation by end of 1987 b) From 1988 onwards, possibility of choice for approx. 300 employees between immediate redundancy pay or training with subsequent redundancy pay

4) Sietas shipyard Hamburg	1988 ca. 2,000		- Avoidance of operational redundancies through retraining - No operational redundancies until the end of 1988	80	Voluntary, approached by personnel department
5) Jansen shipyard Hamburg	4/88 ca. 340	Closed by end of 1989	- Retraining programmes as a means of avoiding the dismissal of 150-200 employees after the announcement of mass redundancies in 1987. - After the breakdown of survival plans, additional retraining programmes introduced to delay redundancies	280	- Half the participants were chosen by management - the other half volunteered
6) Sürken shipyard Papenburg	8/88: 400	- 70 since 1987	- Retraining in order to prevent redundancies - Workforce set at 239 for 1988 and additional training programmes agreed - Management and works council to try to implement a local employment initiative based on job creation schemes for former Sürken employees (unsuccessful) - Quarterly talks between management and works councils on ideas for new products	170	- Participation voluntary in 1987. Minimum number must be attained. - 1988: 50 planned redundancies withdrawn because of participation in retraining programmes.
7) KLÖCKNER-Becorit Castrop-Rauxel	12/87 ca. 1,400	Loss of 350 jobs by 9/89	- Loss of 350 jobs through: - Early retirement - Severance agreements or waiting loop with retraining programmes lasting 18 to 24 months with recoverable entitlement to reinstatement. - After return from waiting loop, rotation procedure to be used if necessary to send other employees into waiting loop	Approx. 70-80 on training courses; ca. 40 will return to firm.	- Redundant workers offered retraining in the waiting loop or redundancy pay
8) Klöckner-Humboldt-Deutz Cologne[1]	Loss of 2,322 jobs in 1988		- General agreement for whole group - Establishment of joint committee to discuss new products and group restructuring - Assessment of economic efficiency of order allocations		- Redundant workers offered training in order to improve chances of placement

[1] Based only analysis of agreement - no case study conducted.

Table 7 (contd.): Main characteristics of the employment plans (as at June 1989)

9) KRUPP STAHL Bochum	2/88 4,200	Loss of 600 jobs by end of 1988 - not carried out because of upturn in steel industry	- 1987: conclusion of three group-wide agreements, on early retirement, redundancy pay and a waiting loop model - Workers whose jobs cease to exist, whether directly or indirectly (multilateral exchange), and leave the company for 24 months are offered retraining - If on their return jobs still need to be shed, other employees are sent into the waiting loop	No current training programmes because of staff shortages	- Redundant workers are offered retraining, but they can also remain unemployed
10) Saarstahl Völklingen	12/86 ca. 13,200	Loss of 2,800 jobs in 1987	- Agreement between German TUC/IG Metall and employers' association - Agreement on the founding of a steel foundation to take over about 1,800 Saarstahl employees - The foundation's tasks are to ensure the supply of retraining programmes, to maintain initial training capability, to create alternative jobs and to top up unemployment benefit	a) 201 Saarstahl employees b) 106 from the steel foundation (1987)	a) Recruitment by management and works councils b) The criteria of reasonableness laid down in the Employment Promotion Law apply
11) PRÄWEMA Eschwege	12/87 370	Composition/takeover by Rothenberger 130 dismissals at end of 1987	- Agreement to uphold 25 training contracts - Founding of a training company, provided 50 former employees remain for further training - Redundant workers given opportunity of retraining in training company, provided employment office pays subsistence allowances and no reasonable job offer is forthcoming	10 former employees 35 to be trained	
12) Berthold Berlin	1/88 994	1986-88 240 jobs lost	- In the event of company restructuring, retraining programmes to be introduced, provided there is both need and opportunities within the company	20-30 in on-the-job training. Only 4 on basis of employment plan; released for 1 month for external training	Volunteers only
13) Thomson Brandt-EWD Villingen	5/88 1 047	371 jobs lost	- Plant remains open - Priority given to transfers and retirement - Establishment of an employment company for up to 350 employees; will organise further training, retraining, short-time working and job creation schemes - Development of an industry and technology park; establishment of new firms to be encouraged	158 severance contracts 60 employees transferred to employment company, incl. 30 on training courses 58 internal transfers 107 early retirement	Management offers transfer to employment company

Status of trainees	Financial support during training from firm	Deduction of financial support on departure	Training providers	Procedure on completion of training programmes	Consultation with employment office
1)a)Employee b)Suspension of employment contract	a) Wages paid, based on normal working hours b) On dismissal, subsistence allowance topped up to a max. 100% of previous average net wage	a) None b) If the extra support exceeds the possible redundancy pay, the extra money is reduced on a sliding scale to 85%. The extra support is offset against any redundancy pay	External/internal, depending on the programme	a) Right to job and grading corresponding to training b) Those successfully completing courses given priority when vacancies arise. If course is not completed successfully through no fault of the trainee, new offer of further training is made	Employees in the segment from which workers are to be made redundant are considered at risk of unemployment
2) Employment contract suspended	Subsistence allowance topped up by *Land* to 90% of net wage; holiday and Christmas money still paid by company	No deduction - subsistence allowance topped up by *Land*	Mostly external	Re-employment on completion of training	Agreement between *Land* and Blohm & Voss. Agreement approved by employment office
3)a) Employment contract suspended b) Fixed-term contract until end of training programme up to maximum of 2 years	as above	as above	as above	a) Re-employment b) Assessment of possibility of re-employment; Blohm & Voss employees take priority over those from Ross	as above Disputes over whether training was additional to normal provision, public interest and individual requirements for job creation schemes in employment company
4) Employment contract suspended	Subsistence allowance topped up by *Land* to 80% and by Sietas to 100% of net wage	as above	External	Re-employment on new product lines	as above

Table 7 (contd.): Main characteristics of the employment plans (as at June 1989)

5) Employment contract suspended	Topping up to 90% of net wage by state of Lower Saxony	as above	Mainly external, receiver did not want to commit company resources to training	- Dismissal because of bankruptcy	Bankruptcy agreement between state of Lower Saxony and regional employment office
6) Employment contract suspended	as above	as above	Partly internal, with use of a training provider in order to make full use of training capacities, partly external	- automatic re-employment - early talks on future personnel decisions - if the order book improves, priority to be given to former employees who have completed a course of training	as above
7) Unemployed with agreement to re-employ after 18-24 months	DM 150 per month on top of subsistence allowance or unemployment benefit, up to maximum possible redundancy pay	Offset against redundancy pay on departure from firm	All external, in order to loosen ties with firm	- Re-employment after 18-24 months; if retraining ends earlier, unemployed until taken on again	
8) Fixed-term employment contract suspended until completion of training. Contract automatically revoked if trainee leaves before end of course	Subsistence allowance topped up to 85% of previous net wage/ If offer of training is refused, redundancy pay reduced by 8.3 to 20%	Extra support offset against redundancy pay. In the event of re-employment, extra support becomes 2-year loan repayable if the employee leaves before the end of that period.	Offer to become provider of training programmes	- Automatic departure from the firm - Obligation on company to re-employ trainees if suitable vacancies arise	
9) Unemployed, employed in other companies, retraining	Topping up of subsistence allowance or unemployment benefit to 90%	Deducted from redundancy pay on departure. No redundancy pay if worker quits 12 months after initial departure from firm		Right to re-employment after 24 months. Employment in other companies does not nullify claim	Circular directive from Federal Labour Office: the unemployed must clear up doubt about their availability

10)a) Employment contract suspended b) unemployed	a) Company tops up wage b) Wage-related topping up of subsistence allowance or unemployment benefit by the *Land* until 1989 to 85% of previous net income	No deduction, since extra support provided by the *Land*	a) internal, in order to guarantee jobs b) external in isolated cases	a) will be re-employed subsequently b) given priority when vacancies arise at Saarstahl	- Saarstahl employees were not considered at risk of unemployment because of the IGM/DGB agreement - Programmes rejected because of high cost relative to other providers - Programmes for semi-skilled workers rejected because they had no vocational qualifications and because the firm's interests predominated - Disputes over "Zusätzlichkeit" and public interest of planned job creation schemes
11) Unemployed	Subsistence allowances topped up for former employees on retraining courses to 80% for maximum of 1 year	No redundancy pay if extra support is paid	External providers only; employment office assigned trainees to external providers. The number required for the employment company (50) was not reached.	Priority given when vacancies arise	The employment office considered - there was little need for retraining because of the high skill levels - there was no need for a new provider because of under-utilisation of other providers and block on resources for job creation schemes
12) Employees	- Time for training split equally between company and employees; 50% of course and exam fees paid by company	If employee resigns, grants may have to be repaid	External	When vacancies arise, priority given up to 2 years after departure provided qualifications are equal.	Employment office considered threat of employment did not arise until redundancies announced. It thought those to be made redundant too old for retraining
13) Dual employment contract, with EWD and the employment company; employment contract suspended during training	Subsistence allowance topped up to 80%	Extra support slightly offset against redundancy pay	External	Re-employment at EWD or new companies. Dismissal if neither training nor employment is possible	

I.   The Grundig employment plans

1.   The crisis in the consumer electronics industry

Compared to most of the other sectors hit by the crisis, the consumer electronics industry is a very young industry. Its first period of expansion was after the Second World War, due to the increase in the demand for radio and television sets, tape recorders and record players. The number of employees in this sector in 1950 was just over 20,000; by the mid-1970s it had risen to over 120,000 (see Figure 4). However, in the years that followed, market saturation, increasing international competition and a rapidly accelerating rate of rationalisation (that resulted in annual productivity increases of more than 10 per cent) were the factors that caused dramatic job losses [IG Metall, 1984]. Between 1978 and 1984, 51,000 of the 127,000 jobs in the sector were lost.

Figure 4:   Employment in the consumer electronics industry

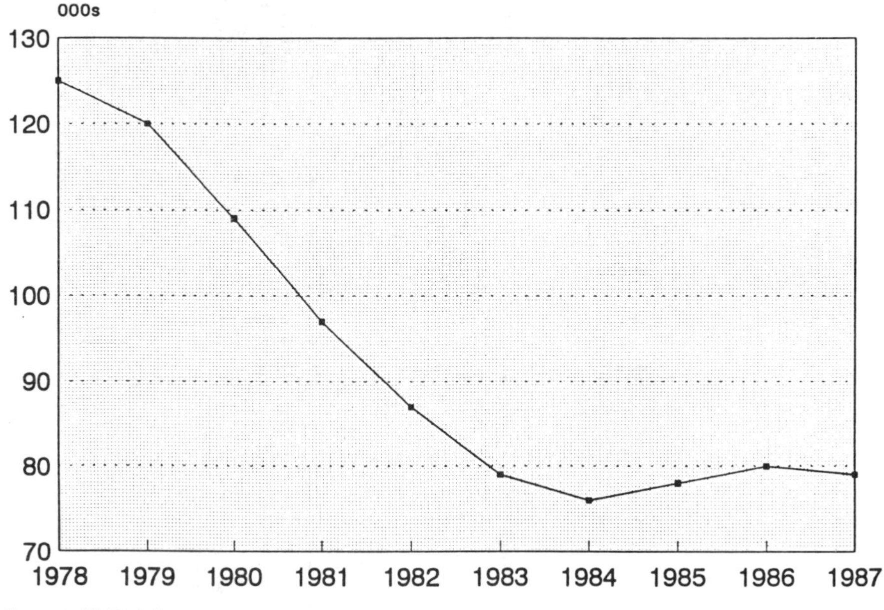

Source: IG Metall.

2.   The 1985 employment plan

Grundig, the largest German manufacturer of consumer electronic goods, had 37,449 employees in 1977. By 1984, this figure had fallen to 23,246. The reduction in the labour force was achieved primarily through natural wastage and early retirement. The firm was faced with a new crisis in the financial year 1983/84, when a loss of almost 300 million DM was recorded; losses were also forecast for the following year. Subsequently, Grundig was taken over by Philips and a cost-cutting measure was imposed through a rapid reduction in the workforce, particularly those not directly involved in the production process. Five thousand jobs were to be lost in this effort to return to profitability. Early in 1985, the employment office in North Bavaria was notified of the dismissal of 2,530 workers; entire plants were said to be faced with the threat of closure. Opposition to this devastating blow began to grow, and there were protests in all Grundig plants. IG Metall proposed that an employment plan should be drawn up in order to avoid redundancies. Management at first rejected this proposal, since it was feared that labour costs could not be reduced at the desired rate. Moreover, there was considerable doubt about the willingness of the Federal Labour Office to contribute financially to any training programmes.

After several discussions with the Federal Labour Office and the regional and local employment offices, IG Metall won a general declaration on the opportunities for financial assistance. This had proved difficult, since the Federal Labour Office was also breaking new ground with respect to labour market policy. Since they were afraid of creating a precedent that would give rise to unforeseeable costs, they were initially very reluctant and did not drop their opposition until several rounds of negotiations had been held. As a result of these negotiations, and since Grundig did not want a bitter conflict to damage their public image, the company management agreed in March 1985 to sign the first employment plan in the Federal Republic of Germany.

It contained most of the basic elements of the original proposal put forward by IG Metall. In order to avoid dismissals, employees over the age of 55 were offered either an "older workers' plan" (unemployment or supplementary benefit to be topped up to 85 per cent of net wage until early retirement) or a severance agreement. However, not all the job cuts required could be made in this way, and a so-called *transfer list* was drawn up, with employees being selected for inclusion on the basis of social criteria. Those on this list were to be given a choice between redundancy and a training programme. The company undertook to top up the subsistence allowance paid by the Federal Labour Office to 100 per cent of the previous net wage. However, if these payments then exceeded an individual's possible redundancy payment, the supplement was to be reduced in stages to 80 per cent of net earnings. The employment contract of employees on training programmes was to be suspended. Those who completed a training programme were to be given priority when applying for jobs in the company. However if jobs were unavailable, therefore making dismissal necessary, the extra financial assistance was offset against redundancy payments. The use of a higher multiplier (for age and seniority) in calculating redundancy pay than that applied to the subsistence allowance paid during training programmes provided a financial incentive to accept the former.

The company undertook to make available the necessary planning information and to formulate its training requirements. A joint committee was set up to oversee the implementation of the training programmes and to develop ideas on the humanisation of work; the committee met during working hours[33] and was able to call on experts if necessary. Moreover, it was agreed that the company had to diversify its product structure, and to this end a second joint committee was set up to make proposals for new product lines.

Staff cuts were implemented almost exclusively through the traditional instruments of the social plan, i.e. the older workers' plan and severance agreements, and through the closure of plants established abroad (e.g. in Portugal). The 1985 employment plan led to only a few training measures being introduced. The company had had a transfer list drawn up by its senior managers; it was composed mainly of older and less productive employees, who would certainly have opted for redundancy pay rather than a training programme. However, the works council did not agree to this method of selection and demanded that social criteria be applied to the choice of employees; in this instance, the greater weighting given to age and seniority would have ensured that mainly younger workers would have been selected, thus causing the management to reject the works council's request. No voluntary training measures were needed, because the level of qualifications among employees not directly involved in the production process - the only ones to whom the 1985 employment plan applied - was already very high.

The joint committee met on seven occasions up to the end of 1985. The company managements' intention was to formulate its further training requirements in a very selective way, putting the emphasis on the need for high technical skills. The requested survey of the skill structure of the workforce was never carried out, despite several reminders, and the company was equally dilatory in the final presentation of its training requirements. The committee's work petered out when it became obvious that no training programmes would be established. In a paper on the implementation of the employment plan, IG Metall states that "at least as far as the further training component of the employment plan is concerned, the halting of mass redundancies removes the necessity for further training" [IG Metall, 1986].

The committee on new product lines met a total of 16 times up to the end of 1986. At first management pursued a policy of pure obstruction. In the words of an employee representative, "They leant back and challenged the employees' side to put forward proposals for new products, which were then declared to be impracticable". After a change of management representatives, the atmosphere of the discussions became more co-operative. Management divulged selective insights into their innovation structures. It became clear that in the past all the company's development capacities had been concentrated on consumer electronics and that the industrial electronics sector had been neglected. On the initiative of the employees' representatives, discussions were held with market experts on the sales potential in the area of technology used for measuring environmental damage, particularly for detecting pollutants in waste water. The

---

[33] The scheduling of meetings during working hours emphasises the notion that training activities form an integral part of work.

committee's work resulted at least in the establishment of a board-level working party on product diversification and the initiation of a review of the outdated innovation structures, which had hitherto concentrated almost exclusively on consumer electronics. However, IG Metall sees this initiating function as the basic task of this committee [IG Metall, 1986].

3. The 1987 employment plan

The 1985 employment plan had been drawn up expressly to implement cuts in staff not directly involved in the production process. In 1987 further major rationalisation projects were implemented. The reason behind the negotiations on a new employment plan (which was to be extended to include production workers), was the cessation of the production of drive mechanisms for video recorders at the No. 11 Works at Nuremberg-Langwasser. The result of co-operation with the Japanese manufacturer Matsuhita since 1986 was that about 600 of the 1,300 jobs at the plant have been lost.

Management refused to sign the new employment plan that had already been negotiated with the labour director,[34] since in their view the codetermination rights and financial obligations to which it would give rise were too far-reaching. However, the works councils and the workforce were not prepared to give up what they had gained during negotiations. And, as management could not have diluted the proposed plan without endangering internal labour relations, they finally signed it in April 1987.

In the new employment plan, which goes beyond the 1985 one, management committed itself to forward-looking production and personnel planning. It states that proposals for extension of the product range can be formulated by joint project teams located at plant level that meet during the day and can call on expert advice. The company will draw up an annual training plan. Gaps in training are to be eliminated by further training programmes leading to a recognised qualification. Women, older workers, foreign workers and unskilled workers are to be particularly encouraged to take part in these training programmes. Joint project teams will be set up to implement these training programmes. If subsidies are not available from the employment office, the company agrees to bear the costs. If the employment office will only grant a loan, this will be paid back by the company. The new agreement makes the same provision for the topping up of subsistence allowances as the 1985 plan. Unlike the older plan, however, the multiplier for the calculation of individual redundancy payments to be made after completion of a training programme is higher than that for a severance contract. So there is now a financial incentive to join a training course, particularly since those who successfully complete a

---

[34] Under German laws of worker codetermination, the labour director (*Arbeitsdirektor*) is a member of the company's executive board, being charged with handling personnel and social affairs. He/she is appointed by the Supervisory Board. According to the codetermination law in the coal and iron and steel industry, the appointment has to be approved by the worker members of the Supervisory Board. In other sectors, the labour director normally has their confidence.

training course have to be offered a job commensurate with their new qualification. If there is no job available, dismissal can take place only after a process of selection based on social criteria.

At the end of 1987 the central works council signed a somewhat less generous employment plan covering the whole group. For example, if there is no finance available from the Federal Labour Office the company pays only the tuition fees for a training course, and no subsistence costs. However, the more generous provisions still apply to the No. 11 works at Nuremberg-Langwasser.

By May 1989 a total of 107 Grundig employees had joined training programmes supported by the Federal Labour Office. Of the 600 workers at the No. 11 Works who lost their jobs only about 18 went on training courses. The rest were transferred within the group or left the company, either under the terms of the "older workers' plan" or with redundancy pay (particularly skilled workers or foreign workers). This leaves about 200 workers who either do not wish to take part in training programmes, or who are unable to do so because of their age or chronic illness, and who could not for the same reasons be transferred in the short term to vacant positions on shifts in other factories. They are reduced to doing small service jobs for customers, or "otherwise twiddle their thumbs". They were not dismissed, because the works councils at all sites declared their opposition to any such move. By mid-1989 about 100 of them had taken early retirement or had been transferred within the group. The board has now decided that each site should make a sacrifice in the name of solidarity and take a few of these workers who are difficult to place.

A further 80 workers were accommodated on training programmes through an exchange scheme, which involved the redundant workers being transferred to other sites to perform the jobs of employees there who wanted to attend training courses. Thus, after completion of the rationalisation progamme at the No. 11 Works, there were only a few training courses left to be provided. The employment office accepted the exchange scheme. It no longer insisted on having a dismissal list, as it had in 1985, but accepted a statement from the works council that these employees belonged to that section of the workforce threatened by dismissal. As a result of this scheme, most of those who went on training courses did so voluntarily, thereby increasing the chances of the programmes' success. However, a few of the training measures failed because the employees did not meet the requirements or were felt to be difficult to place.

There are two types of training courses. In the first case, unskilled workers are trained to become mechanics in industry or office workers. Some of them are taking part in the "Mechanics in Industry" model scheme administered by the Centre for Work, Technology and Environment (*Zentrum für Arbeit, Technologie und Umwelt*), which consists of a three-month pre-training course (with general educational components, advice and practical exercises) followed by a two-year retraining programme. In the second case, skilled workers are given further training in order to become technicians or master craftsmen. As already mentioned, the company repays loans granted by the employment office for these retraining courses.

Most of the participants are under 40 years. This low average age reflects the high degree of voluntarism among the participants. In individual interviews they were given advice by the works council and directed towards specific courses. The degree of willingness to undertake further training was greatest in those in whom it had "already been developed" in the past. Since 1985 there has been a debate at the No. 11 Works about the need for further training. As a result, expectations developed among some of the unskilled workers who wanted to get away from the production line. During a period of *short-time work*,[35] female production line workers were offered a one-week course covering their area of work and basic electronics. Some of the workers displayed their enthusiasm by voluntarily attending evening classes in basic electronics and later expressed interest in the further training measures provided for in the employment plan.

The training programmes all take place outside the firm, some of them at the Grundig *Akademie*. Ties with the firm are maintained to a certain extent by practical work in the company. In addition, the works council maintains regular contact with the participants. Their aim is to return to the firm; their willingness to participate in further training can be explained by the fact that further training does not carry the stigma of possible redundancy. Before redundancies are announced, there has to be a process of selection based on social criteria; the probability of being dismissed decreases with participation in further training programmes.

At the time of writing (May 1989), the favourable economic situation meant that the workforce at Grundig had stabilised at around 19,000 employees. No further reductions are planned, at least in the short term, so that in the foreseeable future only a few individuals will embark upon the training courses provided under the terms of the employment plan. The first participants in such courses (graduates of master craftsman programmes) have already gone back to work in the company. They are either working as senior craftsmen or are on course to be promoted to that position.

The project team at the No. 11 Works is now helping to determine the content of and the selection of the participants in virtually all further training programmes; each rationalisation measure is examined for its possible effects on employee numbers and training, and there is now a better match between the training courses on offer and employees' needs. For example, the increasing proportion of employees alternating between two shifts meant that the Grundig *Akademie* had to run certain courses twice over a period of two weeks. In one contested case, the labour court established that in respect of the employment plan the works council enjoyed a right of codetermination that went beyond the provisions of the Law on Labour Relations at the Workplace.

---

[35] The term *short-time work* refers to the introduction of arrangements for working fewer hours than normal in periods of business slack or plant rationalisation. In return for public subsidies, employers agree to avoid impending redundancies and use short-time work to divide the available work.

In order to curb the dynamics of codetermination in further training programmes and hence limit the ensuing costs, management put off the development of a group-level training plan covering each individual site, and for a long time the general works council played into their hands by not demanding action in this area. It was not until 1989 that the central further training committee began to meet again and advise on the effects of the long-term investment and company organisation strategy known as "Scenario Grundig 2000".

The committee on new product lines had also ceased to be active, both because the personnel situation was less strained and because the works councils involved were overburdened with other tasks. However, the works council wants to revive this committee. At the No. 4 works in Fürth the new products working committee distributed a questionnaire on possible ideas for new products. But the management there has challenged the right of the committee to distribute such a questionnaire, and the controversy is to be settled in court.

4. From employment plan to long-term personnel strategy?

The Grundig employment plan was something of a pioneering effort, as much for the trade unions and works councils as for the company management and the Federal Labour Office. Without the results achieved during the 1985 negotiations, both within the company and with the Federal Labour Office, many of the subsequent plans would not have come into existence. The Grundig plan was so symbolic for IG Metall that on some occasions the limited extent to which the agreements had actually been implemented was not realised.

However, when it came to the implementation of personnel reductions, the further training measures played less of a role in both management strategy, and that of sections of the works council, than the traditional provisions of the social plan. When the company was unable, as it had intended, to bypass the process of selection based on social criteria, it refused to implement any training measures at all. Management's attempts to obstruct the work of the committees and its refusal to provide information and plans as had been agreed show the extent to which the far-reaching ideas contained in employment plans can be boycotted when implemented. Only with great expenditure of effort and support from IG Metall - and support on this level can only be given to a limited number of companies - was it possible at least to initiate the re-analysis of the company's innovation structures.

Both in content and practice, the employment plan negotiated in 1987 represented a great step forward. The works councils at the No. 11 Works now have a greater say in further training and have initiated several measures, particularly for skilled and semi-skilled workers; under the terms of the employment plan they are empowered to *force through an extension of Grundig's in-firm further training programme beyond what is necessary in order to manage the actual situation out of which the need to shed labour arises.* However, a precondition for this was a corresponding readiness on the part of employees to take part in training measures, an attitude that had already been fostered by smaller programmes carried out in previous years.

In several Grundig plants the employment plan is not currently in use. In these plants the further training programme is in that familiar static situation, in which the works council does not press for change because, in its view, the workforce "is not interested", and employees do not approach the works council because they do not feel themselves capable of undertaking further training and do not expect any support or advice in this respect from the works council. Since no jobs have been lost in these plants in recent years, it was not considered necessary to use the instruments made available by the employment plan. However, rapid technological change and new concepts of work organisation are changing the skills required in the company so drastically that management has been forced to improve its planning for staff development. The Grundig employment plans contain many pivotal rights on access to information and on codetermination, which are not limited in time or tied to concrete rationalisation projects. It is becoming apparent that the works council is coming to grips with this agreement and will begin to exploit its rights to codetermination in the next few years. There is a chance, therefore, that the Grundig employment plans will not come to an end with the completion of a precisely defined programme of personnel reductions, as has been the case in most other companies, but will mark one step along the road towards long-term personnel planning, in which the works council will be a player. It is this key factor that distinguishes the Grundig employment plans from most others.

II. The Hamburg shipyards

1. The Hamburg Economic Action Programme

The worldwide recession in the shipbuilding industry left deep marks on the Hamburg shipyards. Between 1957 and 1980 the number of people employed in the shipyards fell from 35,000 to 14,100, and from 1980 to 1986 a further 5,000 jobs were lost. Most of these job losses were implemented through the standard instruments of personnel policy: dismissals, severance agreements, early retirements and transfers to other firms.

As long as the region was continuing to prosper to a certain extent as a result of the expansion of the service sector, this social plan policy was accepted. However, as mass unemployment began to increase and become a permanent feature of economic life from the end of the 1970s onwards, works councils, trade unions and local politicians became increasingly critical of the traditional social plan policy in the shipyards and began to look for alternatives to job losses. At Howaldt Deutsche Werft (HDW) in the early 1980s there were well-developed plans to diversify and retain the workforce by establishing a labour pool, providing training programmes and developing new product lines. However, they were not implemented because the company decided to reduce its short-term wage costs by dismissing large numbers of workers. At both Blohm

& Voss and HDW, shop stewards and works councils set up working groups to investigate alternative products; these groups drew up proposals for new products, in order to prevent further job losses [*Zukunftsperspektiven*, 1985]; the shipyard companies and the Hamburg Senate described them as unworkable (see pp. 18-30).

By 1986, however, when a new round of job losses looked likely, things had changed: these well worked-out alternatives to the traditional forms of labour force reduction, the political discussions and actions (by the HDW workforce) that accompanied them and the forthcoming senate elections persuaded the government in Hamburg to be more receptive towards new initiatives.

The chief ministers of the federal states along the coast had requested 500 million DM for the creation of new jobs and 350 million DM for restructuring measures in the shipbuilding industry, the money was to be made available as part of a special programme. Instead of the 850 million DM that had been requested, in October 1986 the federal government agreed to give 300 million DM for the years 1987 and 1988, together with an increased amount of 120 million DM in funding for the joint project on improvement of the regional economic structure[36] for the years 1987 to 1989.[37] "In addition, the federal government requested the Federal Labour Office to activate those instruments of labour market policy available under the terms of the Employment Promotion Act, particularly in those areas affected by the adjustment measures being implemented in the shipbuilding industry" [*Hamburger Aktionsprogramm Wirtschaft*, 1986, p. 2]. The state of Hamburg supplemented the 60 million DM of federal aid with 30 million DM of its own resources, thus making a total of 90 million DM available for the Hamburg Economic Action Programme.

The companies immediately announced that they needed support for the implementation of social plans. The Coastal States Guideline on the granting of aid in the event of capacity adjustments provided for subsidies up to a maximum of 50 per cent of the total cost of social plans. Unlike the government of Schleswig-Holstein, however, the Hamburg senate decided, not least at the insistence of the trade unions, that only in exceptional cases would they assist in the financing of social plans and exceptional write-offs. New ways of stimulating the economy had to be found. "In addition to modernising the shipyards to meet the demands of the future, the aim of all measures must be to improve the economic structure in Hamburg. Since the economic restructuring process must not be carried out on the backs of the workers, the aim of all measures must be not only the preservation of jobs and/or the creation of new and replacement jobs, but also training and the acqusition of new skills. The Senate therefore intends, in co-operation with companies, chambers of commerce, works

---

[36] This joint project provides subsidies for regional investment [cf. Bosch et al., 1987, p. 82 et seq.].

[37] The granting of federal assistance was tied to an agreement between the states concerned about the use of the funds in the so-called "coastal states guideline".

councils, trade unions and the public employment service, to couple the necessary financial assistance for the Hamburg shipyards with an active structural policy that will improve the local economy in the medium and long term" [*Hamburger Aktionsprogramm Wirtschaft*, 1986, pp. 5-6]. To this end, new technologies for ecologically sensitive modernisation, the founding of new companies, the diversification of the Hamburg shipbuilding industry and the retraining of shipyard employees were all to be encouraged.

The aim of the training programme[38] is to prepare employees for a change of job within their shipyard or in another firm, and to ease the burden of personnel costs for firms in a difficult period of restructuring. The *Land* provided funds to supplement the subsistence allowances paid by the Federal Labour Office to around 400 shipyard employees, topping them up to around 90 per cent of their last net wage. According to the programme, the crisis in the shipyards was only the immediate reason for the training initiatives, and regional plans for further training went well beyond these initial concerns. Shipyard workers were not the only people to be offered further training. In addition, the agencies providing further vocational training received funding for the development of new training programmes, also aimed at shipyard workers, as well as for the further training of trainers themselves. Money was found for the modernisation of training centres, as well as for the setting up of a new training centre to train workers in the use of computer numerically controlled technology (CNC).[39]

The area employment office initially expressed reservations about the training of shipyard employees. It originally considered it necessary to have proof of the threat to each individual's job in the form of a dismissal notice. These reservations disappeared, and the area employment office declared itself willing to support the programme.

The Senate had suggested that the implementation of the training programmes should be overseen by a co-ordinating body made up of representatives of the relevant official bodies, the chambers of commerce, the trade unions and other institutions of importance for the successful realisation of the scheme. This proposal "caused a great deal of annoyance in the employment office" and was seen as an unwarranted attack on the autonomy of the Federal Labour Office. Moreover, the employment office rejected the notion that

---

[38] The retraining programme is the subject of a research project being conducted by Siegfried Bergner in collaboration with the Office of Vocational and Further Training in Hamburg and with support from the Hans-Böckler-Stiftung. The preliminary results of this research have been taken into account here on a number of occasions [cf. Bergner, 1987; 1988].

[39] The establishment of this CNC centre has been the subject of much criticism. It has been pointed out there is already sufficient capacity in Hamburg for CNC courses. The planned CNC centre would not be able to raise finance from commissions from industry and would necessarily be in competition with existing training agencies for programmes sponsored by the Federal Labour Office. This demonstrates many of the difficulties of targeted regional further training policies.

structural policy considerations should be taken into account in the planning of the training programmes. The starting point should rather be individual cases and the evolution of vacancies and placements. Thus it soon became clear that it would not be feasible either to incorporate structural policy considerations into the training programme or to link the programme with strategies for diversification. The training and diversification components of the Hamburg Action Programme were subsequently developed in a totally unco-ordinated way by two separate Hamburg authorities. The scheduling of the two parts of the programme could not be synchronised: the training programmes had to be introduced quickly in order to relieve firms of the burden of costs, whereas the diversification component had to be preceded by preliminary conceptual studies. At a very early stage, the Hamburg authorities abandoned the original objective of linking the various parts of the programme and spoke of the value of training in its own right as a way of enhancing the individual's position in the labour market.

2.   The implementation of the training programme

After the Economic Action Programme had been adopted, negotiations on the implementation of the training initiative were begun at the company level.

A.   Blohm & Voss

At the end of 1986, Blohm & Voss announced the loss of 630 jobs out of a total of around 4,500. Some of these jobs (about 450) had already been shed through natural wastage and redundancy agreements, so that by the spring of 1987, when negotiations began, the problem of the labour surplus had already been resolved to a certain extent. This somewhat less tense personnel situation, as well as the fear of Blohm & Voss, a Thyssen subsidiary, that mass redundancies would damage their image, increased the company's willingness to implement the type of training programmes included in the Hamburg Economic Action Programme.

In March 1987 a company agreement was signed. Under the terms of this agreement, 420 employees whose names appeared on a list drawn up by the board and included in the agreement were to be offered further training. Dismissals for operational reasons were ruled out, so long as 180 of these 420 workers were taking part in training programmes supported by the Federal Labour Office. Any other people leaving the firm would be included in this figure of 180. The company was to pay those taking part in further training programmes both holiday and Christmas money, so that in total they would be receiving about 97 per cent of their net wage. The employment contract was to be suspended durng the training period, and those completing the courses would be re-employed. The *Land* and the area employment office both confirmed in writing their support for the company agreement.

The first list of 420 people was drawn up by the company. It included many workers unpopular for a wide variety of reasons (e.g. refusing to do overtime). The employment office was given a list of 440 names, 250 of which were those of employees over 45 years of age, while a further 100 were Turks, most of them with few qualifications or skills; according to the employment office these were not the company's best employees. The works council advised those thus identified to take part in the training programme, since otherwise there was a risk of redundancies. The first list undoubtedly looked like a dismissals list; those included felt singled out and recognised the danger of being squeezed out of the firm as a consequence of their participation in the programme. When advice on the training programmes began to be given, however, the first applications came from employees who feared that when the trainees returned they would be disadvantaged by their own lack of qualifications; other employees were advised by their supervisors to do something for themselves if they wanted to have a future with the company; some others had their own plans for training, in some cases with a view to a new job. These voluntary applications significantly increased and thereby reduced the average age of the potential participants.

The employment office interviewed 700 Blohm & Voss employees over a period of only a few days. Training courses for 490 people were proposed during these interviews; individuals were given very little time to come to a decision, and older workers in particular felt themselves unsuited for the programmes on offer and accepted redundancy payments instead. The stress generated by the situation became evident from interviews with subsequent participants in further training courses. One group of interviewees reported, "They were told by superiors that they had to go on the training courses, or face immediate dismissal". Another group declared, "We had no choice. We were told that otherwise we would all lose our jobs" [Bergner, 1988]. By exerting pressure in this way, the company was able almost completely to circumvent the selection process and to shed significantly more jobs than had originally been planned. The lack of information provided by the firm makes it impossible accurately to assess the number of workers who took early retirement or accepted redundancy payments.

As a result of these selection processes almost two-thirds of all participants in training programmes were less than 30 years old. The older employees took part mainly in shorter courses. About 30 per cent of all courses lasted up to three months, while a further 36 per cent lasted more than 18 months. The shorter courses mainly provided training in welding, CNC machine tool operation, hydraulics and pneumatics. The longer courses mostly provided training for those seeking promotion as technicians or for semi-skilled and unskilled workers, including foreign workers who also required a preliminary language course.

The company did not involve itself in the planning of the training programmes, since it considered its workforce sufficiently well trained. Outside the company, however, it was stressed that the company survived largely on "one-off" orders. Consequently, in contrast to firms engaged in mass production, it was not possible to offer training programmes that would keep the entire workforce abreast of the latest technical developments. At certain intervals, therefore, it became necessary to exchange part of the workforce for new workers qualified to cope with the demands of the new technologies [Bergner, 1988]. One indicator of the low level of interest within the company in internal structural change is the rudimentary character of its staff development policy. For example, the supervisory staff described a section of the workforce as incapable of integration. The company's main interest in the training programmes was as a means of getting rid of the employees on the first list they had drawn up. And in order to weaken ties with the firm, the training courses were organised externally. Those involved were not to be trained in self-contained groups, but were to have contact individually with other people, training institutions and firms (through practical training), in order that they "should begin to think about the possibility of working elsewhere". Furthermore, the labour director did not want any "underemployed groups of employees stirring up political unrest in the plant".

In the end, because of the voluntary applications for training courses, management did not get its way in the selection of participants. This is probably the reason for the decidedly negative assessment of the retraining programme by the management of Blohm & Voss. Of the 500 company employees who took part in the courses (plus the 130 HDW-Ross employees who also participated), most were already well-trained skilled workers receiving further training. "Most of the individuals whom the company would actually have liked to release and who most needed training were unwilling to participate. The programme protected them completely from dismissal, but the company no longer had any use for these people. As a result, consideration must be given to ways of restricting voluntary participation" [Bergner, 1988].

B.   HDW-Ross-Industrie

HDW-Ross-Industrie formerly belonged to the Howaldt Deutsche shipyard; it was taken over by the Thyssen subsidiary Blohm & Voss in 1986. By offering attractive early retirement and redundancy schemes, the new owners reduced the workforce from 2,500 to around 1,800 in 1986. In June 1987 a company agreement on training programmes was signed; its content was the same as that concluded at Blohm & Voss and provided for the training of 300 employees in total. In contrast to Blohm & Voss, the works council did not accept the list of names submitted by the company as an element in the company agreement, but canvassed from the beginning for volunteers, without, however, being able to rescue all employees from the predicament of having to decide between training or redundancy.

In the middle of 1987 it was decided to wind up Ross-Industrie; the yard was to be closed and production transferred to Blohm & Voss. At the same time management and works council at Blohm & Voss reached an agreement that there should be no dismissals for operational reasons until the end of 1988; consequently, all job losses were to be borne by Ross-Industrie. This agreement at Blohm & Voss led to a split between the two works councils and workforces, giving rise in turn to considerable tensions and eventually to legal proceedings. After the decision to close the yard, management refused to offer any more Ross employees a place on a training course under the terms of the company agreement that had already been signed, since this contained a right of re-employment in the firm. The Ross agreement was revoked and training courses that had been planned but not yet begun were cancelled. The first company agreement at Ross had led to training being offered to 59 employees.

Under the terms of the agreement reached at the beginning of 1988 between Blohm & Voss and the Ross works council, 936 of the remaining 1,277 employees were to be transferred to Blohm & Voss, while the other 341, whose jobs were listed in detail, were to be dismissed. These 341 workers were offered either a severance agreement or a fixed-term employment contract that would run for the duration of a training programme (up to a maximum of two years). At the end of the training programme they would either be offered a job at Blohm & Voss (although the company only committed itself to "investigate" this possibility) or - if they could not find employment elsewhere - they could enrol in an *employment company* (see footnote 25, p. 35), for the establishment of which Blohm & Voss made available 2.5 million DM to the City of Hamburg. Despite considerable reservations, the Ross works council signed this agreement in order to rescue the idea of an *employment company* which it had supported.

After the closure of HDW-Ross, 81 individuals on fixed-term contracts embarked on training courses provided under the terms of the 1988 agreement; almost half of them are receiving further training as technicians and are hoping to find employment at a corresponding level. Initially only about 30 of those taking part in training programmes declared an interest in joining a new employment company. In this closure period the works council did not necessarily insist on training for all redundant workers, but decided rather, in view of their age structure and seniority and the failure to implement a selection process based on social criteria, to initiate unfair dismissal proceedings. The small number of people taking part in training programmes seemed to endanger the establishment of the employment company, since the 1988 agreement defined it only as an extension to training courses. Consequently, the company initially refused to make available the 2.5 million DM it had promised. However, in a survey of the 400 employees who had left the company, 230 of them, mostly older ones, expressed an interest in it.

A barrage of publicity brought the controversy over the establishment of the employment company into the open. Those supporting the company included the Departments of Labour, Youth and Social Affairs. Those hostile to it included the Department of Economics, the FDP (Free Democrat) group in the Hamburg Senate and the Chamber of Crafts. A state subsidised employment company was seen as a distortion of competition, to the detriment of craftsmen, and an unacceptable extension of state intervention. Furthermore, the company feared that the establishment of a successful employment company would give rise to similar demands in its steel companies.

However, the employment company, known as Öko-Tech, was eventually set up in mid-1988, after Blohm & Voss finally accepted that Ross employees who had not taken part in training programmes could also join the new company. The Senate decided that three of the seven members of the board of the new company should be representatives of organisations opposed to it (the Chamber of Crafts, FDP and the Departments of Economics, Agriculture and Transport) and that all major decisions had to be taken with a majority of 5 to 2. Öko-Tech was set up for a period of two years by the Senate and financed with the aid of the 2.5 million DM from Blohm & Voss and 1.4 million DM from the Hamburg Economic Action Programme. Additional funds for employment creation schemes were provided by the Federal Labour Office (8 million DM) and the City of Hamburg (2 million DM). Öko-Tech has started to function with around 100 people on job creation schemes; initially they were composed of only former Ross employees.[40] Eighty per cent of the wage bill is paid by the employment office and the remaining 20 per cent by the City of Hamburg. Ten permanent employees are funded by the company's own resources. Those on job creation schemes were "made aware of ecological issues" during six-week courses financed by the City of Hamburg and organised by the Centre for the Reintegration of the Unemployed. The first project is a commission from the planning department for 4,000 cycle parking spaces at Hamburg underground stations, which are intended to form the basis of a "bike and ride system". An outline agreement will be signed with the Technical University of Harburg for the provision of equipment for the special research unit that is being set up to investigate ways of cleaning up environmental hazards. In addition, there are a number of ideas for individual projects. There is obviously a market for smaller environmentally-friendly products which large firms consider to be too small-scale and which established small and medium-sized firms do not (yet) have the necessary foresight and skills to develop and produce. In the long term, the development of succesful new products, e.g. in the area of *Altlastensanierung* or waste management, is to provide the basis for the establishment of new firms. However, the contradiction between the push for innovation on the one hand, and the skill and age structures of workers on such job creation schemes on the other, should not be overlooked. In order to strengthen its push for innovation, the employment company will in the long term have to change the balance between permanent workers and those on job creation schemes or increase its potential for development by seeking external support.

---

[40] According to management there is no room in the short term for other unemployed people. Blohm & Voss threatened to withdraw its funding, which it wants to reserve exclusively for former Ross employees. The works council denied that this had been agreed. In the medium term other unemployed people will probably be included. Otherwise, the employment office would have difficulties in providing financial support, since it would be funding a private company project rather than a public one.

C.   Sietas

The training programmes developed at Sietas progressed in a completely different way from those at Blohm & Voss and Ross. There were no job losses. Until 1989 the shipyard had been working at full capacity on two orders, one for six trawlers from Morocco and the other for six freighters for Finland. At the same time, the yard was extending its product range. It has now started to produce gas containers, in which perishable goods can be conserved by the use of inert gases. The manufacture of these containers requires workers skilled in working with light gauge steel sheet as well as in advanced welding techniques. The workforce did not possess these skills to the extent required. Consequently, 80 Sietas employees were recruited by the personnel department for training courses in these welding and metalworking skills. For the duration of the training courses, which were held outside the firm, funds provided by Sietas and the City of Hamburg enabled their full normal wage to be paid, which significantly increased their willingness to retrain. The training programmes were oriented towards the new products, and as a result those involved knew what jobs they could expect after they returned to work. They also declared they would use their newly-acquired skills on the job when they returned to the firm.

From the point of view of the employment office, the threat of unemployment for these workers lay in the possibility that the company might, under certain conditions, dismiss them or other, similar, workers and replace them with workers who had the specific skills they needed. It was also accepted that the scheme would to a large extent serve the interests of labour market policy and not just those of the firm, since the training programmes would lead to recognised qualifications, or to certificates that were also accepted in the labour market (see Chapter 3).

However, there is no doubting the ambivalence of the Sietas training programmes. On the one hand, public funds were used to support the internal diversification of a firm in a shrinking sector, a strategy which did not succeed in the other shipyards. On the other hand, the deadweight effect[41] could not be predicted. It is by no means clear that training and diversification can be closely linked elements of structural policy without giving rise to considerable deadweight effects.

D.   New curricula

The further training agencies in Hamburg proved to be only partly prepared for the implementation of the training programme. The start of the courses was delayed by bottlenecks in the training agencies. There were also deficiencies in the curricula. At one organisation, shipyard workers spent four weeks doing simple filing work which they had learnt to do 20 years earlier. A number of foreign workers took morning language classes at one agency and

---

[41] This term reflects the fact that some of the subsidy goes to firms which would have increased their employment anyway.

vocational courses in the afternoon at another agency, the two programmes being entirely unco-ordinated. Although the criticisms cannot be applied to all training agencies or courses, there was an obvious failure, on the one hand, to integrate the general education components with the vocational elements and, on the other, to adjust the level of the courses to the differing needs of the trainees.

New curricula, particularly further training courses targeted at specific groups of workers, were developed as part of the Hamburg Economic Action Programme. A foundation set up to provide vocational training for the unemployed was given funds to develop a curriculum for preparatory courses for foreign workers in which general education (including German lessons), theory and practical work are integrated. In the German course, for example, grammatical points are illustrated by means of technical expressions to be used in the next practical session, while the mathematics course uses examples from the theoretical component (e.g. areas). The precondition for an integrated curriculum of this kind is that the various teachers should work as a team, that they should be obliged to be present and that they should also attend parts of the course given by their colleagues. These preparatory courses for foreign workers are based on a modular system: those who speak almost perfect German attend only the final stage. Only a small number of the shipyard workers have been able to benefit from these new curricula, since most of the courses had to be started very quickly.

3.   The decoupling of training and diversification

The Hamburg Economic Action Programme is certainly noteworthy for its attempt to combine the resources available within the framework of regional structural policy with those from the Federal Labour Office and the social plans drawn up by several companies. However, the original plan to couple strategies for retraining and diversification could not be implemented. One major shipyard was closed (HDW-Ross) and another (Blohm & Voss) tried to consolidate at a lower level. The training programmes at these two shipyards were intended solely to implement labour force reductions. In fact, all those responsible for the Hamburg programme tacitly accepted this situation. The training courses were organised outside the firms only in order to loosen the ties between them and their employees.

A total of 790 employees from all Hamburg shipyards were retrained under the terms of the programme. Because of the plans for dismissals, the various interested parties at Blohm & Voss and HDW-Ross could not agree on the criteria for selecting those to be retrained. Management wanted to draw up what were virtually redundancy lists in order to circumvent the selection process based on social criteria. A number of employees with very poor qualifications were made to choose between "training or dismissal", and left the company resigned to their fate. This strategy made it more difficult for works councils to make a full contribution to the initial phase of the programme and to convince employees of the need for training courses. Only through voluntary applications for training courses could the selection process be altered and some of the poorly qualified workers be protected. At HDW-Ross the implementation of the programme was affected by the closure decision, which meant that any notion of equal treatment for those to be trained was abandoned. From that moment onwards, employees taking part in training courses were divided into two groups: those with a chance of employment at Blohm & Voss and those on fixed-term contracts who had of necessity to look to the external labour market for employment.

Both Blohm & Voss and HDW Ross wanted to shed labour and also had underdeveloped personnel planning policies; as a result, they gave no encouragement or assistance in the planning of the training programmes. Only Sietas, with its strategy for diversification, put forward concrete proposals for the content of the training programmes. For those affected in both the other companies, all decisions on courses were made by the employment office during individual interviews. Various government departments in Hamburg criticised these interviews, saying that the employment office assumed, wrongly, that people "move completely freely in the labour market and are able to choose virtually any course of vocational training. Issues are not yet being formulated in terms of structural policy".

As a result of the retraining programme, several hundred workers at Blohm & Voss and Ross have been guaranteed a job at Blohm & Voss, provided they had begun a training course by the autumn of 1987. It remains to be seen whether, and how, Blohm & Voss will integrate these people whose new skills are said to be unnecessary. Many poorly qualified employees were protected from dismissal by the voluntary participation of younger workers in training programmes. In Hamburg this is seen as a positive development in terms of labour market policy, since the number of long-term unemployed would otherwise have risen. Furthermore, the establishment of Öko-Tech created a means of gathering together redundant older workers whose skills were specific to the shipyards. For Blohm & Voss, on the other hand, the lack of rigour in the selection of employees for training programmes is one reason for a rather negative assessment of the retraining programme.

III.   "The Saarland Solution"

1.   The restructuring of the Saar steel industry

The steel industry in the Saarland was the first of the West German steel producing regions to be hit by crisis; the factors contributing to this include its inconvenient location, its fragmented ownership structure, which inhibited technological modernisation,[42] and the relatively late emergence of co-operation between the various steel producers in the region.

In 1978 Arbed-Luxembourg began to restructure its Völklingen, Burbach and Neunkirchen plants. In 1982 the various companies were merged to form "Arbed-Saarstahl". At the end of the 1970s, it was decided to set up a joint pig iron production plant (Rogesa) in Dillingen and, in conjunction with the Saar coalmines, a central coking plant (Cogesa) that would supply the required blast-furnace coke. When the new pig iron plant came on-stream in 1985/86, it was planned that the other works should cease to produce pig iron and coke. In addition, Arbed embarked upon a comprehensive programme of modernisation and concentration of its steel making, rolling and processing activities. The entire restructuring process led to considerable rationalisation effects in the Saarland steel industry.

Saarstahl reduced its workforce from over 30,000 in 1974 to around a third of that figure (11,300 employees) by the middle of 1986. This drastic reduction met with little political resistance because the social consequences were to a large extent cushioned. A restructuring agreement reached between Arbed-Saarstahl, the *Deutscher Gewerkschaftsbund, DGB* (the German TUC) and IG Metall prohibited redundancies for operational reasons during the technical restructuring of the Saarland steel industry [Judith et al., 1980]. The job losses were largely implemented through early retirement schemes and by not filling vacancies that arose through natural wastage.

The Dillingen steelworks remained largely unaffected by the dramatic crisis in the Saarland steel industry, and even increased its workforce slightly in the 1980s. It produces relatively inexpensive heavy plate steel for the French market, where it has regular supply contracts both independently and through its French parent company (Usinor-Sacilor).

When the steel crisis worsened again at the beginning of the 1980s, the industry began to lose more jobs. Faced with this situation, Arbed-Luxemburg sought to withdraw from any responsibility for the consequences. The newly elected SPD (Social Democrat) government in the Saarland favoured a local solution to the problem that would also cover the Dillingen works. Ideas for co-operation with one of the steel groups in the Ruhr were rejected. It was feared that these groups would concentrate closures in the Saarland because of their regional ties with North Rhine-Westphalia. The Saarland Investment and Credit Bank, in which the Saarland has a 51 per cent stake, took over Arbed-Saarstahl and in 1986 transferred its management to the Dillingen works. In 1989 it was agreed that both companies should be united under the umbrella of a holding company; Usinor-Sacilor took 70 per cent of the shares, with the remainder

---

[42] Before 1971, the four steelworks at Dillingen, Völklingen, Burbach and Neunkirchen were owned by six major shareholders from three European countries, who could not agree in time on a policy of co-operation and modernisation because of their differing national and company interests [JHK des Saarlandes, 1982]. In 1971 the Burbach steelworks and the Röchlingen iron and steelworks merged, but continued to maintain two integrated steel plants.

being divided between the Saarland (27.5 per cent) and Arbed-Luxemburg (2.5 per cent).

The transfer of the management of Arbed-Saarstahl to the Dillingen works in 1986 was linked to the need to make savings of 320 million DM in the following year, 150 million of which was in personnel costs alone. This was equivalent to the loss of 2,800 jobs.[43]

2. The 1987 job losses

The earlier personnel reductions had already exhausted the possibilities for shedding labour through early retirement. It was obvious to all involved that further personnel reductions could not be managed with the resources hitherto available and that new solutions had to be found. Management considered issuing dismissal notices and/or negotiating redundancy agreements. Lengthy negotiations led to the signing, in July 1986, of a new agreement which prohibited dismissals for operational reasons, with only limited exceptions. Instead, the personnel reductions targeted for 1987 were implemented in the following way:

(1) The Dillingen works had an age structure completely atypical of the steel industry. Unlike virtually all other steelworks, this plant had not had jobs lost through early retirement schemes; consequently, there were plenty of workers aged 55 or over. This time, 400 older workers were offered early retirement and their places taken by 400 workers from Saarstahl[44] (Table 8).

(2) Two hundred Saarstahl employees aged 55 or over took early retirement. Their unemployment benefit was topped up to the level of the early retirement pension by a fixed-term company pension (Figure 5).

(3) A further 200 jobs were lost through natural wastage.

(4) Two hundred Saarstahl employees began a longer-term programme of retraining or further training. Their employment contracts were suspended during the training period.

(5) It was agreed that the employment contracts of the remaining 1,800 employees should be suspended without notice and that they should join the steel foundation, which in terms of personnel policy is the innovative element of the "Saarland solution".

---

[43] The number of jobs to be lost was decided in a somewhat schematic way: the figure of 150 million DM was divided by the average annual income of a company employee, which produced a total of 2,800 jobs to be lost.

[44] The early retirements at Dillingen and the corresponding transfers from Saarstahl are still continuing, since jobs are still being lost at Saarstahl.

Table 8:   Job losses at Saarstahl in 1987 [1]

(1)	Early retirements at Dillingen and transfers to Dillingen (exchange scheme)	400
(2)	Early retirements at Saarstahl	200
(3)	Natural wastage	200
(4)	Retraining and further training at Saarstahl	200
(5)	Transfer to the steel foundation	1 800
	Total	2 800

Note: [1] Rounded figures. The actual figures are slightly different. In addition there were, and
            still are, flows between the individual categories, e.g. from retraining to the foundation.
Source: Saarstahl.

Figure 5:   Saarstahl early retirement scheme

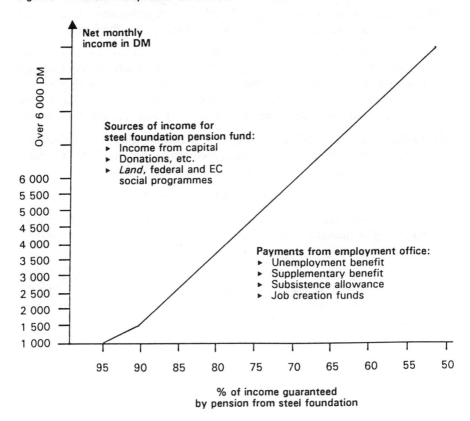

Source: *Das soziale Konzept Stahlindustrie. Die saarländische Lösung 1987.*

The steel foundation is a non-profit-making organisation. Its advisory board is composed of representatives of management, the works council, IG Metall, the Ministry of Economics of the Saarland and the area employment office.

The foundation has been set some demanding goals. It is supposed to serve the interests of its members, offer them training courses or job creation schemes, create replacement jobs, support employment initiatives and set up a "non-profit-making employment and retraining company" to put these activities into practice.

The former Saarstahl employees whose interests the foundation now represents have been made redundant and are unemployed. Their unemployment benefit is topped up by the foundation to between 50 and 90 per cent of their previous net income, depending on the level of that income (see Figure 5). On average foundation members receive 85 per cent of their previous net income.

This so-called *fixed-term company pension* was guaranteed until 1989. However, the foundation will probably be financed for a further two years. If the foundation cannot pay the fixed-term company pension, the company has to make up the shortfall.

The company has undertaken to give priority to foundation members when jobs fall vacant or are newly created. However, there is no formal guarantee of a return to employment in the company, because if such a guarantee had been given the employment office would have refused to pay unemployment benefit on the grounds of non-availability for work.[45]

The foundation's expenditure is financed from many sources. In 1987 and 1988 the company contributed 538,000 DM from its house-building association. A promotion association, whose members are mainly company employees but also include pensioners and suppliers, contributed 288,000 DM in 1987 and 800,000 DM in 1988. Payments from the Commission of the European Communities made under the terms of the Treaty on the Establishment of the European Coal and Steel Community totalled about 5.1 million DM in 1987 and 5.4 million DM in 1988. The *Land* contributed 78.5 million DM, which guaranteed the foundation's expenditure for five years. These sums are sufficient to cover the foundation's remaining expenditure (4.8 million DM in 1987 and 5.1 million DM in 1988). However, the main burden of the cost falls upon the Federal Labour Office, which pays unemployment benefit, subsistence allowances for people on training courses and the wages of foundation members on job creation schemes (the costs amounted to about 60 million DM in 1987).[46]

---

[45] This is an obvious case where the Federal Labour Office has not acted consistently. Krupp Stahl and Klöckner-Becorit gave guarantees of re-employment without the employment office in North Rhine-Westphalia questioning the availability of workers in the waiting loop (see pp. 106-109).

[46] In 1988 this expenditure was estimated at about 50 million DM, since more than 400 foundation members found alternative employment, at least for a time.

In order to achieve the manpower reductions said to be necessary, a comprehensive restructuring programme had first to be implemented in order for the required number of jobs to be cut, and then workers had to be selected for the different programmes. Since the middle of 1986, up to 1,000 workers from the shut-down blast furnaces, coking plants and molten phase had been on permanent *short-time work* (see footnote 35, p. 59). These closures had been decided on ten years previously as part of the restructuring programme. As a result, no younger workers had joined these departments, where the average age was about 50. Virtually all of this group was transferred to the foundation.

In addition, the company's procedures were examined and changed. The meagre allowances for personnel policy measures available at Dillingen were transferred to Saarstahl, which created a certain degree of conflict. Thus, on the apprenticeship training programme, the trainee-instructor ratio was 1:15 at Dillingen and as low as 1:7 at Völklingen. The sickness rate at Dillingen was significantly lower than at Völklingen. As was the case at Dillingen, regular one-to-one interviews are now conducted at Saarstahl in cases of frequent absence from work. Partially disabled people are employed in the newly created personnel deployment department.

The Dillingen works placed "great demands on the professional skills and state of health of the workers" who were transferred there. In addition, however, a contract was offered to workers who lived in Dillingen or who travelled past Dillingen on their way to Saarstahl.

Unskilled and semi-skilled employees were given prority when it came to applying for training programmes. This resulted in 200 people starting training courses. Everybody who eventually joined the foundation was also offered the opportunity to retrain. The self-confidence to embark upon a course of further training is not very widespread in the typical steelworking environment, as several interviews revealed; this meant that fewer employees than expected were willing to take part in training courses.

Some of these training courses (about 50) were aimed at trades specific to the steel industry, such as process engineering. The remaining 150 courses are in trades not specific to the steel industry, such as lathe operator or control engineering. The chances of these people finding employment in their new trade seem to be relatively good. To a certain extent "the Saarstahl works are waiting for them to fill gaps in their workforces".

The remaining "superfluous" employees were transferred to the foundation. With the support of the works council, each individual was interviewed with the aim of reaching agreement on termination of the employment contract. Agreement was reached in 95 per cent of cases, and employees were transferred to the foundation without the required period of notice being given. This high level of voluntariness could be achieved only on the basis of the company's "moral commitment to re-employment", which could only be made credible to employees with the help of the works council. Without the support of the works councils, neither the concept of the foundation nor the control over redundancies would have been possible.

3.   The steel foundation in practice

A total of 1,957 people joined the foundation (cf. Table 9). Of these, 1,295 (66 per cent) were over 50 years and 74 per cent were unskilled or semi-skilled.

Those aged over 50 were to take early retirement. However, the regulations in this area differ according to age. Under a new regulation approvedby the European Coal and Steel Community, workers over 52 can take early retirement at 56 without having to return to work. Those aged between 50 and 52 are assumed to have little chance of re-employment. In accordance with its moral commitment to re-employment, the company has to find work for these people; if they lose their jobs again after their return, giving rise to what the guidelines in the European Coal and Steel Treaty term an "adjustment case", they can take early retirement at the age of 55. Current legislation does not allow this group of workers to leave the foundation and immediately take early retirement.

The remaining members of the support scheme were under 51 years of age. Even in this category, there were a number of obstacles to their placement in the labour market, caused in part by lack of qualifications and health problems; in addition, the female members of the foundation have experienced great difficulty in finding employment because of the very small number of jobs that are available for women in the traditional coal and iron region of the Saarland.

Most members of the foundation "did nothing during their time on the support scheme". This was problematic from all points of view. In the case of those under 51, the main fear of both works council and management was that their skill levels would deteriorate, leading to problems with their reintegration; management was worried that it would have to keep its promise to re-employ these people without obtaining adequate performance from them. For the *Land*, the financial burden was set to rise, because eventually unemployment benefit would cease to be paid, and when that happened the Saarland would have to top up the less generous unemployment assistance or even, in the case of those ineligible for benefits, pay the entire subsistence costs.

Thus it was in the interests of all the parties represented on the foundation's advisory board not to allow this inactivity to persist. All members of the foundation were approached on several occasions about participation in training courses. To date, however, only 106 individuals have taken part in a training course during their time with the foundation. Some of these were courses for individuals, such as training in CNC machine operation, but there were also group courses in building trades and metalworking. There are several reasons for this low participation rate, despite the considerable expenditure on publicity. There was virtually *no financial incentive to enrol in a training course*; in some ways participants on such courses were worse off because of the additional expenditure they incurred. The older workers were waiting to take early retirement and could no longer be persuaded to retrain. Many of the younger ones did not meet the requirements for participation in a training course

Table 9: Membership structure of Saarstahl steel foundation (as at 31.5.1989)

Age-group	Joined foundation up to 31.5.89	Left foundation	Re-employment			Retraining			Total	Not available	Numbers available 31.5.89[3]
			Saar-stahl	Other[1] firms	Job creation schemes	On courses	Completed training	Before foundation[2]			
Up to 30	118	26	25	49	-	14	29	74	117	3	1
31-40	175	34	61	58	4	7	16	81	104	-	11
41-50	369	60	181	62	4	9	22	43	74	-	53
51 +	1 295	62	119	25	8	6	3	3	12	4	1 071
Total	1 957	182	386	194	16	36	70	201	307	7	1 136

Notes:

[1] Mostly Saarstahl subsidiaries.
[2] Retraining at Saarstahl instead of joining foundation. Not foundation members.
[3] Foundation members minus those re-employed, on training courses and job creation schemes and those who have left.

Source: Saarstahl Steel Foundation.

because of a lack of aptitude. Finally, questions have to be asked about the selection process. The most capable workers were not chosen for membership of the foundation, and each person who joined the foundation had already turned down the chance of a place on a training course. Two hundred people had opted for training courses at the point of joining the foundation.

This reluctance on the part of most of those joining the foundation to undertake further training, coupled with their lack of aptitude, threatened to undermine the resolve of the 200 people taking part in training courses in the company, who were no better off financially despite the efforts they were putting into their courses. A number of them wanted to opt out of the courses, which they found onerous, and join the foundation. About 10 or 12 of them were removed from training courses for health reasons. In order to prevent the whole training programme from collapsing, however, the others were given a choice between redundancy and continuing with their training courses.

Plans to help individual employees - e.g. engineers - set up on their own account seem to have come to nothing. The company was going to assist in the birth of these new businesses by making available equipment and helping to establish contacts with potential customers. One example cited was the setting up of a laboratory for environmental analysis which would find ways to reclaim areas of land that had previously been the sites of industrial plants.

By mid-1988 about 400 members of the foundation were transferred back to Saarstahl or Techno-Stahl. These transfers were made possible by the improvement in the market for steel. In addition, in the same year, no temporary staff were taken on during the summer break; their place was taken by foundation members on fixed-term contracts, some of which were later converted into permanent contracts.

However, Saarstahl and the Dillingen works had only limited capacity to absorb new staff in 1987 and 1988. Thus, for many foundation members the only option open was in government job creation schemes. By 1988 most of the foundation members had been unemployed for more than a year and thus fulfilled the individual requirements for participation in a job creation scheme (unemployed for at least six months). As a result, a number of ideas for job creation schemes was developed by the foundation; however, they were either abandoned or delayed because of financial restrictions at the Federal Labour Office and fundamental objections from the area employment office. Places on job creation schemes run by the foundation and the municipality of Völklingen, which were intended to develop ideas for the use of former industrial sites, were not approved because this was seen as an area of "statutory responsibility". A "prospecting group" was to draw up a sort of contamination map for the former industrial sites. This scheme was rejected on the grounds that ownership of the land was unclear, making it difficult to determine the eventual beneficiary of such activities. After a lengthy tug-of-war, a job creation scheme with ten places was approved; the plan was to maintain the compressor building and the old blast furnace complex - the oldest of its kind in the Federal Republic of Germany - and possibly convert them into a museum. The initial reservations expressed by the area employment office, namely that this was part of the statutory responsibilities of the *Land* conservation department, have obviously been overcome. However, the area employment office did ensure that the scheme was opened up to other unemployed people, which enabled the office to "maintain its autonomy" by allocating workers on job creation schemes to the project.

In addition, an application was made to the European Social Fund for a grant for a job creation scheme that would deal with the decontamination and reconversion of a former hydrocarbon plant. Eighty older and semi-skilled former workers in the Saarland were to carry out this decontamination work and be trained for it as part of a model project. A planning group made up of former engineers was given the task of preparing for this work and the training that would be required. The EC agreed to this. Managers at the Federal Labour Office mobilised all their numerous bureaucratic braking mechanisms and manoeuvres in an attempt to thwart these schemes. Their main argument was the lack of public interest in the reclaiming of contaminated former industrial sites, since the benefit would accrue to the private owners of the land. However, the tripartite committees of the Federal Labour Office in Nuremberg eventually approved the scheme. The schemes are to provide job creation places for 80 people, but very few of them will be from the steel foundation. The area employment office will give most of the places to the long-term unemployed, so that the "non-profit making employment and training company" set up by Saarstahl will become a *job creation agency for the general labour market and cease to be an employment company for the steel foundation.*

The resistance of the area employment office to the promotion of job creation schemes by the foundation is an indication of reservations about the very concept of such foundations. Because the ideas had been formulated externally and publicised in advance, the employment office felt it had been presented with a *fait accompli*. It pointed out that it did not wish to create two classes of unemployed, those backed by the foundation and those who had no lobby to support them.

Similarly, the relationships between the area employment office on the one hand and the foundation or the steel company on the other, were problematic when it came to support for further training schemes. Thus, because of the 1986 agreement between the company and IG Metall and the DGB, which more or less prohibited redundancies for operational reasons, there was not considered to be any threat of unemployment at Saarstahl. On its own admission, the employment office "withdrew to a very formal position. The company, the works council and the trade union made a great deal of fuss in public about there being no redundancies, but at the same time requested financial support from the employment office. The contradiction evident in this meant that, despite the threat of bankruptcy, it was the agreement, loudly trumpeted in public, rather than the company's actual position, which was decisive for the employment office". It could not be assumed that there was a threat of unemployment unless the agreement was rescinded. Since neither the works councils nor the unions were willing to agree to this, the employment office refused to pay subsistence allowances to skilled workers on training courses as long as they continued to be employed by Saarstahl.

The quality of the training courses was also a source of friction. The employment office refused to pay subsistence allowances for semi-skilled workers on individual training courses, since these courses were not intended to lead to a recognised qualification and also because there was little visible distinction between the training and normal work. In this case, the deadweight effect was not balanced by adequate training programmes and the objections of the employment office were justified.

4. The steel foundation: perspectives and evaluation

The sustained recovery in the steel industry and the implementation of the agreement on shorter working hours increased the need for labour at Saarstahl and the Dillingen works in 1989, making it possible for those foundation members under 50 to return to the company more quickly than originally anticipated. By June 1989 all but 117 of this group had been transferred back to the company. Individual plants were allocated a share of foundation members in proportion to the size of their workforces to be reintegrated. In the case of manual workers, the existence of the personnel deployment departments provided mechanisms for the integration of entire groups of workers; in the case of white-collar workers, reintegration proved more difficult, since individual jobs had to be sought and found. As a result, the larger part of the 117 individuals who have not yet found a job are white-collar workers. Fifty-two people from this group are still on training courses or job creation schemes. A few individuals aged over 51 were also transferred back to the company, some because they had skills that were in demand and others (those aged between 50 and 52) because temporary employment would make their eventual retirement easier.

Only about 70 workers left the foundation on their own initiative and found a job with another employer. Thus, in comparison with workers in the waiting loops set up by other companies in our survey, foundation members are particularly inward looking and are comparable in this respect to the workers threatened by unemployment in the East Frisian shipyards (see pp. 109-113). As in East Frisia, this attitude has its origins in the unfavourable situation in the local labour market, but also in the considerable wage differentials between the steel companies and the alternative sources of employment in the region, which are widened still further by the shift bonuses paid in the steel industry. Finally, foundation members were the responsibility of the personnel deployment departments at each plant, which were of course able to provide information on jobs within the company but not on any external vacancies. This gave the placement process a decidedly inward-looking perspective, strengthening the dependence of foundation members on the company and underlining the relevance of its moral commitment to reintegrate former employees.

The foundation model is not easily transferable. Its purpose was not, in essence, to develop innovative training or job creation programmes or to create new job opportunities, but rather to relieve the company in the short term of 150 million DM of its annual personnel costs. The concept emerged from the particular situation in the Saar steel industry and probably helped to ensure the survival not only of Saarstahl but also of many associated jobs in the coal mines and other sectors. One in two jobs in this region is dependent on the steel and coalmining industries; however, despite this initiative, unemployment remains higher than average. Only in this particular industrial and regional context was it possible to obtain the agreement of the works councils and IG Metall to the setting up of the foundation. IG Metall considers the Saarstahl foundation to be an exceptional case. Transfer of the model to other companies would imply tolerance of those companies' withdrawal from their obligation to implement social plans at the expense of the *Länder* (taxpayers) and the Federal Labour Office (payers of social security contributors). In other cases (e.g. at Krupp Rheinhausen and Grundig) IG Metall has called for companies to take greater account of regional policy considerations and to make greater financial commitment when shedding labour.

The area employment office tried in vain to prevent any takeover of structural policy. Another reason for this hostility was undoubtedly a fear of establishing a precedent. However, since there is currently no watertight way for area employment offices to resist the establishment of waiting-loop models in regions hit by crisis,[47] the area employment office has reserved most of its criticism for the planned training and job creation schemes. This is presumably also connected with the expenditure cuts at the Federal Labour Office. Since 1988, each training and job creation measure for a foundation member has been charged to the budgets of the local employment offices, thus reducing their scope for developing programmes for other unemployed people; unemployment benefit, on the other hand, is a statutory obligation which is paid irrespective of the state of the budget.

The conclusion to be drawn from this, depressing though it may be for labour market policy, is that in the next few years the opportunities to establish waiting-loop models in which those affected - mainly older people or those with health problems - are without work, i.e. remain passive, will be greater than those for models involving training or work creation schemes; the fact that the economic costs are virtually identical seems unlikely to change this situation.

Digression: the Austrian steel foundation

The foundation model has now been copied and extended in Austria. Over a period of five years starting from 1988, the Austrian steel company Voest-Alpine is reducing its workforce by 10,000. Some of the redundant workers will join a steel foundation. Just as in the Saarland, the employment contract will be rescinded on entry into the foundation. However, the Austrian

---

[47] It is precisely in these regions that area employment offices will not succeed in finding jobs to offer to workers, usually older people or those with health problems; hence they will be unable to test their availablity for work during their time in the waiting loop.

steel foundation is more oriented towards the external labour market. In order to manage this in a way that is reasonably socially acceptable, the foundation prepares workers for external mobility in a variety of ways. A six-week course of training gives all those affected the opportunity to go through a "process of clarification", during which they can formulate their plans for the future. They then have opportunities to embark on an intensive job search, assisted by the foundation, to go on further training courses and to develop ideas that may lead to self-employment. All these options are organised and monitored by the foundation. The maximum stay in the foundation is two years, but this can be extended if further training is successful. If the training course is not completed successfully, membership of the foundation ceases. On leaving the foundation or when joining another company, members receive their redundancy payments in full. The foundation makes every attempt to find employment for members, preferably with Voest-Alpine but also in other companies, but placement is not guaranteed. The foundation organises its own training clubs at the various company sites. The workforce also contributes to the financing of the foundation with a monthly subscription of 0.75 per cent of their wages or salaries. Foundation members themselves contribute the interest earned on their redundancy money during their time with the foundation. Subsistence allowances paid by the employment office for further training measures and unemployment benefit paid during the development of projects for new businesses are topped up to a maximum of 80 per cent of the previous net income. The foundation also funds a scheme to encourage the exchange of ideas for the development of new products or individual projects and monitors the progress of members. Each supervisor is responsible for 12 people [Dolleschka et al., 1988].

IV. The Thomson training and employment company

1. The agreement that established the training and employment company

In the late 1970s and early 1980s, the French electrical group Thomson took over a number of German companies in the consumer electronics business (Saba, Videocolor, Nordmende, Dual, Telefunken); as a result of specialisation at individual sites, concentration of production, transfers of production and the rapid pace of rationalisation in the consumer electronics industry, many jobs were lost at these plants and Videocolor in Ulm was closed down completely (Table 10). The long struggle against the closure of Videocolor made the Thomson group's personnel strategies known to a wide public [*Projektgruppe Videocolor*, 1987]. The company was popularly known as a "job killer".

Since 1983, the parent company Thomson had been shedding labour in France and at the same time implementing reconversion programmes roughly equivalent to, or in some cases more extensive than, the West German employment plans (see Chapter 5). The group wanted to use the experience it had gained in France to deal with the personnel reductions in the Federal Republic of Germany, in order, on the one hand, to avoid confrontation and take the spotlight off the company and, on the other, to restrict the negative consequences of the company's rationalisation policy on particular groups of employees and individual regions.

Even before the first German employment plan was concluded at Grundig, a group of personnel managers who had had personal experience of the French reconversion programmes was campaigning for the implementation of new training models in companies in crisis situations. In their view, a programme of retraining and diversification measures implemented in conjunction with personnel reductions was "a more intelligent policy which makes sense in business terms and also has benefits for the employees involved". An initial agreement on retraining at the Villingen-Schwenningen works was not accepted by IG Metall, since the group was not prepared to guarantee that the works would not be shut down. The union feared that such an agreement could be used principally to legitimise a closure.

Table 10:   Acquisitions by Thomson and effect on employment

Year	Company	No. of employees on acquisition	Workforce reduced by		Measure
1977	Nordmende	4,000	1,700	= 2,300 [1]	Job losses
1978/79	Videocolor	2,400	2,400	= 0	Job losses/ closure
1980	Saba	5,300	2,400	= 2,900 [1]	Job losses
1982	Dual	2,000	600	= 1,400 [2]	Job losses
1983/84	Telefunken	10,500	3,154	= 7,346 [3]	Job losses

Notes: [1] = 1982 figure; [2] = 1983 figure; [3] = 1983/84 figure.
Source: *Projecktgruppe Videocolor* [1987, p. 61].

It was not until 1988 that the protracted preliminary negotiations led to a concrete agreement. A further 1,000 job losses spread over all the West German plants were announced. In the worst affected plant, the Thomson subsidiary Electronic-Werke Deutschland (EWD) in Villingen-Schwenningen, 470 of a total of 1,050 jobs were to be lost as a result of the transfer of colour television chassis production to Celle and the closure of several central departments. This time management guaranteed the plant's survival. As a result, IG Metall and the works council were prepared to co-operate in the restructuring of the company. In May 1988 negotiations led to the establishment of an *employment company* for the redundant workers at Villingen-Schwenningen.

The details of the agreement were as follows:

- The future of the Villingen-Schwenningen works was to be secured by additional investment for the modernisation of conductor plate production and the introduction of new products. This would ensure the retention of 582 jobs.

- Older employees would be able to take early retirement after the age of 53.

- A maximum of 350 employees would be offered a transfer to the new training and employment company *Ausbildungs- und Beschäftigungsgesellschaft* (AuB).

- Private investors were to set up a company, *Industrie- und Technologiepark Management-Gesellschaft* (ITM), specialising in the management of industrial and technology parks which was to promote the establishment of new companies on the former Thomson site (Figure 6).

Figure 6: Villingen Industry and Technology Park

Source: *Der Gewerkschafter 6/88*.

In management's view it was necessary to separate AuB and ITM, because the chances of attracting new companies if IG Metall were involved would be "precisely zero". The company's view, as declared in the course of the negotiations, was that "the merest hint of social cushioning is seen in many quarters as unworthy of support; a management company seems to inspire greater confidence in private investors". Neither the *Land* nor the local municipality felt able to contribute to the funding of the project. They both supported the scheme, but did not initially want to take any responsibility for structural policy, although such a commitment was indeed necessary in a region that had hitherto specialised in precision engineering and had now to change over to electronics.

The innovative element in the Thomson agreement was the setting up of the AuB. However, transfer to the new company was to take place only after other measures, such as transfer to other plants and early retirement, had been tried. Thus the company was conceived as a safety net for those unable to benefit from any of the other measures.

When workers join the AuB, their contract of employment with EDW is not terminated, but it is replaced by a dual employment contract which maintains the ties between workers and the company. This dual employment contract facilitates the implementation of *short-time work* (see footnote 34, p. 59) and transfers between firms and the employment company, and also maintains an integrated system for the representation of interests, which simplifies future negotiations. For these reasons the company accepted this innovative dual employment contract.

It is the job of the AuB:

- to offer its employees further training or retraining courses;

- to employ them within the company, at EWD or elsewhere under their previous conditions of employment;

- to secure their employment contract through *short-time work*, if necessary;

- and to place its employees in jobs with third parties.

If employees refuse reasonable offers of training or employment or if there is a lack of employment opportunities, they can be dismissed. Contrary to most press reports, therefore, dismissal was by no means excluded. The company had in fact built in a safety valve in order that the costs of the employment company could be calculated. And it was made abundantly clear during the negotiations that a specific sum of money was being made available for the employment company, and that under no circumstances could the budget be exceeded.

Those on training courses receive a supplement equivalent to 12 per cent of their net income in addition to the subsistence allowance paid by the Federal Labour Office; however, all trainees receive a minimum of 80 per cent of their previous net income. A corresponding supplement for those receiving *short-time work* allowances has also been agreed during wage negotiations.

On leaving the company, employees receive redundancy pay; the amount paid varies considerably depending on the circumstances of the departure, but it clearly favours those who would find it most difficult to find a new job. Those employees who are dismissed because of a lack of employment opportunities receive 100 per cent of the redundancy payment with only minimimal deductions, even if they have been with the employment company for a long time; on the other hand, anyone who has refused two reasonable job offers receives only 50 per cent (see Figure 7). The potential expenditure per employee to which this agreement might give rise is considerably higher than that incurred under the terms of a traditional social plan. However, the risk of the cost actually exceeding that of a social plan was felt to be extremely small. The company assumed that virtually all those who successfully completed a training course would find employment, and that two years was a long enough period for the other employees to be placed in suitable jobs.

2. The employment company in practice

The reduction in staffing levels did not take place as quickly or on the same scale as the company had planned, both because actual personnel requirements had been underestimated and also because there were delays in the implementation of the rationalisation plan. In March 1989 EWD still had 676 employees. Fifty-eight workers - more than originally expected - were found places in other Thomson companies. This was partly because the personnel department contacted other firms in order to block proposed hirings, preferring instead to transfer employees internally.

One hundred and seven people took early retirement. Around 237 people were initially offered a transfer to the AuB. The works council had little influence on the selection process, since all the provisions contained in the agreement are voluntary. The company itself made offers to those who had been selected for transfer to the employment company or for early retirement. Initially, therefore, there was *no process of selection based on social grounds*. The most highly-skilled workers from the departments to be closed down were transferred, in order to form the basis of the workforce required for the company's plan to develop new products. The rest were initially offered a place in the AuB.

During the negotiations it had been agreed that the employment structures of EWD and of AuB should be broadly similar, in order that a negative selection should not from the outset rule out the possibility of building up new employment opportunities outside the company with EWD employees. This agreement was initially not honoured by sections of management, who tried to push a disproportionately high number of "problem cases" into the AuB. After several rounds of negotiations, during which the works council was supported by the personnel department, a better "mix of age structure and disability quotas was achieved in the AuB".

Figure 7: Procedure for individual employees

Procedure for individual employees

1,047 employees at present	**EWD**	Electronic Werke Deutschland GmbH	

	Agreement on risk limitation of 9.5.1988

Offer of transfer to TEC

Worker accepts — NO → **80% of scheduled benefits**

350 employees ↓ YES

Training and Employment Company (TEC)

Training	for a limited transitional period
▸ Further training ▸ Retraining	Short-time working	Employment (with EWD and a third party)

Continued employment with a new employer New job	→	50% of scheduled benefits + 20% in the event of failure (2 years)
Worker gives notice of his own accord	→	80% of scheduled benefits up to 31.12.1988, then a 3% reduction per month, but not less than 50%
Worker has already turned down two offers	→	50% of scheduled benefits
Lack of employment opportunities	→	100% of scheduled benefits up to 31.12.1988, then a monthly reduction of 1.5%, but not less than 80%
Continued employment at EWD		
Hardship cases	→	To be dealt with individually

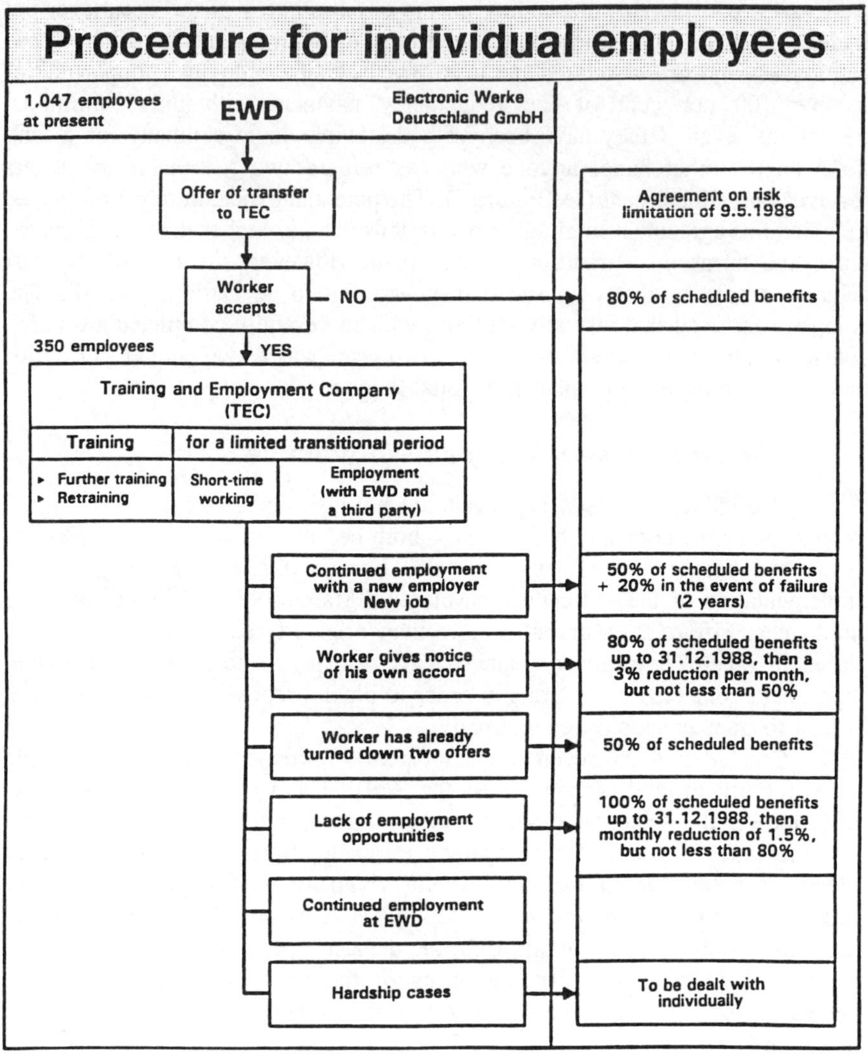

Source: Der Gewerkschafter 6/88.

The personnel department had already been preparing for the task of counselling those selected for the employment company. It was for activities like this that the Thomson Foundation had been set up several years earlier in order to foster innovative schemes for mitigating the consequences of large-scale job losses. As part of a job creation scheme, the Foundation employs several social workers who have been trained for this counselling work. However, it was not possible to put the counselling plan into practice, both because of the need to implement the personnel reductions as rapidly as possible and also because the annual holiday period was approaching.

All those involved are agreed that pressure of time and inadequate skills meant that a great deal of poor advice was given, which did nothing to diminish people's reservations about the agreement, but simply served to reinforce them. The employees - who for years had been taken by surprise by the company's constantly changing plans - obviously did not trust the company to fulfil the commitments which it had undertaken. As late as the autumn of 1987 the closure of the entire works had been expected. Insensitive workforce reductions in the past had obviously undermined the credibility of the company in the eyes of its own employees, so that the AuB was seen as little better than a prelude to dismissal. The workforce was gripped by a mood of panic, best summarised in the motto: "Get out while the going's good". The employees "persuaded each other to leave the company".

As a result, a total of 158 employees, including many younger and skilled workers but also some intended for the AuB, signed severance agreements. Some of them had already found new jobs. Local firms helped themselves from the Thomson labour pool. Furthermore, the capacity of the regional labour market to absorb labour proved to be greater than had been feared, both because of a general economic upturn and the reduction in working hours that came into force in the early summer of 1988. However, around 50 of these former Thomson employees are now unemployed again and regret their hasty decision to quit the firm.

These departures gave rise to considerable movements of personnel within the company. People who were originally destined for the AuB were required again in the company. Negotiations over the groups of workers from which potential candidates for the training and employment company were to be drawn also led to alterations in the personnel lists. The works council can no longer state how many people were offered a transfer to the AuB because there are 12 different lists.

In the end, approximately 70 people were actually transferred to the AuB. Most of them continued to work in their old jobs, since these did not disappear until chassis production finally ceased in the middle of 1989. Since the departure of employees opened up gaps in the company and, as mentioned, the personnel reduction did not take place at the planned rate, it was soon possible to transfer some of them back to the firm; about 35 people went to jobs in other firms. Not one of them is currently unemployed, since they were able to look for new jobs without being pressurised by time constraints. Only 30 people started training courses. Women without any vocational qualifications were trained as quality controllers, and six women are attending a two-year retraining course for managers. There were also data processing and CNC courses for skilled workers. Other training courses did not materialise as planned, because the employees either left the firm or were taken on by EWD under the terms of their original contracts.

Thus, in June 1989, there were only 18 people left in the AuB (six on retraining courses and 12 working in the factory). IG Metall is considering having the company wound up, at least as far as its function for EWD is concerned, because it should not be used permanently as a "personnel buffer for EWD". The works council also considers its activities to be virtually completed. However, the municipal authorities are now thinking of becoming shareholders in the company in order to be able to use it in the event of closures or rationalisation plans in other companies. If necessary, these companies could then become shareholders in the company, bringing their know-how to bear and using the company to implement training and placement policies. The AuB would then become a regional *employment company*, which could react in different ways to companies in crisis.

The pressure to set up new companies for former EWD employees has diminished considerably, quite apart from the fact that the establishment of new companies could not keep up with the reductions in personnel. The job losses were implemented rapidly, whereas a much longer lead time is required to build up the ITM and to make successful acquisitions. Thus everything pointed to a decoupling of the activities of the training company from those of the ITM, although according to the terms of agreement they were actually to be linked to each other. In the end the ITM became a shareholder in the AuB.

The ITM owns a private investment consultancy and has made efforts with five employees to establish new firms. However, the empty land is no longer available. Of the 40,000 m² of workshop space owned by the ITM, EWD initially wanted to rent only 17,000 m². However, the demand for space from many small, expanding Thomson subsidiaries increased so sharply that virtually all of the available space was rented by Thomson.

The municipal authorities had obviously not expected these Thomson subsidiaries to establish themselves in the region and were surprised by the ITM's success in attracting companies from within the group. They are now considering making more space available to the ITM and transferring a proportion of regional settlement policy to the company.

3.   A regional employment company in the making?

As a result of the reconversion policy that the group had pursued in France, new models for the implementation of personnel reductions [Laballe, 1985] had lost some of the terror for the company that they later inspired in the Association of Metal Industry Employees in Baden-Württemberg, which saw in them a systematic attempt to extend the system of codetermination and warned against further agreements of this kind [*Handelsblatt*, 30.6.1988]. Moreover, the disciplinary power that a German employers' association can exert over a French multinational company is strictly limited, which in this case turned out to be to the advantage of the affected employees.

This *transfer of knowledge and experience from France* has been barely noticed by the public in the Federal Republic of Germany. Management's primary motives in signing the agreement that set up the employment company were to avoid damage to the company's image; however, it was only through the commitment of a few personnel managers that these concerns were translated into new ways of dealing with job losses. In the words of the *Südwestpresse*: "The company can live with its reputation [as a jobkiller - G.B.] so long as nobody makes the connection between the unpopular parent company and its brand names. However, if the customers begin to associate names such as Saba, Nordmende or Telefunken with the antisocial behaviour of their parent company, then the alarm bells will start to ring".

Signing the agreement has turned out to be in the company's interests. The structural change has been accepted by both IG Metall and the works council. It is true that the *potential costs* are significantly higher than those of a "standard solution". As expected, however, *the actual costs have been significantly lower*. In the final analysis, the dynamism of the internal and external labour markets has meant that some of the important, innovative elements of the agreement have not been tested. These include not only the AuB's duty to find employees jobs in other companies and to guarantee employment through *short-time work*, but also the planning of a larger number of training courses and, in the medium term, possible links with the ITM's attempts to set up new firms. Moreover, the company was happy to have a pool of labour in reserve when the process of shedding labour became completely unpredictable because of the employees' lack of belief in a stable future in the company and the favourable evolution of the external labour market.

The establishment of the AuB created an additional reception mechanism for "superfluous personnel", which made it possible to avoid dismissals for operational reasons. From the employees' point of view, this is the most important achievement of the Thomson agreement. One weakness in the implementation of the agreement proved to be the great time pressure. The hectic and thus unsatisfactory counselling process increased employees' mistrust of the company together with the widespread fear of having to "return to school". As a result, many employees saw the new settlement as discriminatory rather than as one offering them new opportunities. Improved counselling and co-ordination and a less hectic pace would certainly have persuaded a number of inadequately qualified workers to embark on a training course rather than rushing to leave the company.

The AuB and the ITM seem to be freeing themselves from their exclusive links with the parent company and to be taking on functions in both the regional labour market and economic policy. This process is inconceivable without the close involvement of both organisations in local politics and policy-making. The fact that relations with the employment office in Villingen-Schwenningen were not as tense as in other areas is proof of such involvement.

Even if the full potential of the AuB has not been exploited, a model has certainly been created that could be transferred to other companies in the future. From the trade union point of view, the most problematic aspect was a plan to start loaning employees to other firms. Although the plan was never put into practice, the trade union will have to take a critical look at this trend towards loaning superfluous personnel, since a conflict may arise between trade union plans for employment companies and the aim of restricting flexibilisation of employment relationships through loaning arrangements.[48]

The risk of becoming unemployed is - as we have seen - significantly greater after redundancy than after a transitional period in an employment company. Despite this finding, the EWD employment company in Villingen-Schwenningen has not found widespread acceptance, even within the group. In the middle of 1989 the works council at EWD in Hanover insisted on a traditional social plan with redundancy payments, despite management's readiness to negotiate. This insistence by the works council can be explained by a combination of distrust of the company, the traditionalism of works councils and probably also a lack of confidence in their own ability to participate in determining the activities of an employment company.

V.   Part-time training for young people: the example of Ruhrkohle AG

1.   Part-time work for new entrants to the labour market

Ever since the mid-1970s, young people in companies that are reducing their workforces have been offered part-time jobs after completion of their training period. The companies' aim in doing this is to strengthen their ties with these young workers and thus to prevent both the loss of their investment in training and a continuous ageing of the workforce. Part-time work represents a form of reduction in working hours without any compensatory increases in wage rates.

During the period when the conflicts surrounding the reduction in weekly working hours were at their most bitter (1983-85), these forms of part-time work were seen as alternatives to collective reductions in working hours, rather than as a structural complement to such reductions, with a limited time frame. Moreover, it was thought they would replace other, more highly regulated forms of temporary reductions in working hours, such as *short-time work*. By introducing part-time work, companies gained flexibility at relatively low cost. They did not have to pay the extra *short-time work* allowances for which company agreements often make provision; frequently, only fixed-term part-time contracts were offered, which gave management scope to implement personnel reductions at low cost if the need arose. Finally - and this is undoubtedly one of the objectives of conservative flexibilisation strategies - such an entry into working life has a socialisation effect. The young generation is accustomed to the flexible employment relationships required by the company, in order to make

---

[48] Virtually all steel companies already have personnel deployment departments which organise a sort of labour loan scheme, both on a firm and a group basis. Labour directors in the steel industry have already made repeated attempts to loan workers to outside firms.

them more acceptable to older age groups (temporary conversion of full-time to part-time jobs, waiting loops in the event of unemployment, etc.). The trade unions were correspondingly critical and forthright in their disapproval, even though, when a crisis situation actually arose, works councils usually agreed to part-time work rather than to take the joint responsibility for the non-assimilation of young people after their period of training [Casey, 1984].

2. Part-time working or non-assimilation after training?

Between 1986 and 1989 the Employment Promotion Law offered an alternative to part-time work for young people in the age cohorts with high birth rates. Under the terms of this special provision, young people were able to combine 12 to 24 hours of part-time work per week with attendance on a part-time further training course. They received subsistence allowances from the employment office provided the training course was necessary to obtain a full-time job (see Chapter 3).

This part-time training scheme for young people was used mainly in the steel and mining industries, where it served principally as a means of reducing the volume of work in the short term, without losing well-qualified young people. By 1995, 25,000 jobs are to be lost in the mining industry, and there is an unwritten law - the result, as at Saarstahl, of the coal and steel codetermination system - that the cuts are to be made without dismissals. Past reductions in the workforce have more or less exhausted the scope for using early retirement as a means of shedding labour. Underground workers already retire at 50, and surface workers at 55. To reduce the age limit still further would be to increase the safety risk, since underground work requires years of experience: the feel for dangerous situations cannot be instilled solely by training. Because of the high training quota in the mining industry, the average age of the workforce has already been considerably reduced in the past ten years: one in every two workers at Ruhrkohle AG was recruited after 1970. Since then, with the workforce now standing at around 100,000, 130,000 people have left the company. The average age at present is just over 30 years. At some locations the oldest workers are just 28 years old and therefore lack the necessary experience.

Bringing training temporarily to a halt was ruled out as a means of effecting job cuts. Such a move would have been rejected by the trade union, since the regional concentration of the mining industry would have resulted in a drastic deterioration in the labour market situation for young people. In the 1970s, the mining and energy workers' union had been able to push through an increase in the industry's training quota, despite considerable job losses at Ruhrkohle AG and in other mining companies. In the mid-1980s the training quota was almost 10 per cent, twice as high as in 1970 (Table 11). Since many of the highly trained young workers left for jobs in other firms, the mining industry played a central role in the development of a *regional stock of skilled workers*. The agreement of the union to pit closures depended not least on finding a successor to take over the industry's responsibility to the region and the next generation.

However, the mining companies themselves did not wish to eliminate training altogether. Because of the tough working conditions and the enduring crisis in the coal industry, it had for a long time been difficult for the mining companies to recruit young workers for training. If training had been abandoned altogether, it would have been virtually impossible to persuade youngsters in the age cohorts with low birth rates that there was any future at all in the mining industry.

Table 11:   Employees and trainees at Ruhrkohle AG

Year	Employees	Appointment of new trainees	Total no. of trainees	Training quota[1]
1970	186 101	3 530	9 012	4.8
1975	145 101	4 603	10 438	7.2
1980	129 421	5 836	11 811	9.1
1985	113 907	4 525	10 996	9.7
1986	112 569	4 187	10 777	9.6
1987	107 134	3 503	10 128	9.5
1988	101 506	2 164	8 036	7.9

Note: [1] Number of trainees relative to the number of employees.
Source: Ruhrkohle AG.

These political conditions meant that thought had to be given to alternatives. The result was a package of measures. Part-time work at Ruhrkohle AG was to be encouraged; foreign workers were to be given longer periods of home leave, and were also offered bonuses to return home. Despite the problems mentioned above, the training quota was to be reduced temporarily to between 8.5 and 9 per cent. Finally - and this is our concern in this section - all those completing a training course were to be offered a part-time job lasting for a period of three to four years and secured by a collective agreement (Mining and Energy Workers' Union, Special Collective Agreement 1987). Until the end of 1989 - i.e. before the part-time training courses organised by the Federal Labour Office were discontinued - some 7,600 examination candidates (winter examination 1987 to summer examination 1989) were able to choose between part-time work alone and an additional part-time training course.[49] If they opted for part-time work alone, they were given a contract for 75 per cent of the

---

[49] The collective agreement has no time limit, but should not remain in force any longer than it takes to implement the planned job losses in the coal mining industry. When the special arrangements made possible under the terms of the Employment Promotion Law come to an end, it is probable that part-time work will be the only option left. However, trainees taking examinations after 1990 have already completed training for a reorganised occupation, so the courses currently available would not be suitable for them in any case.

agreed working hours for full-time employees. Alternatively, they could opt for a course of training (see Figure 8). After three years they would be offered full-time employment at Ruhrkohle AG, provided they had not been found another job. Under the terms of the agreement, the young persons' daily working hours were the same as those of full-time workers. In insisting on this, the Miners and Energy Workers Union was seeking to prevent those young people working 75 per cent of full-time working hours from being forced to do in a six-hour shift what their older colleagues did in eight hours. In underground work, the question of shorter shifts hardly arises because of the long distances to be travelled to the coal faces. Contrary to the agreement, however, six-hour shifts seemed to be common in office work.

3. Part-time training in practice

The company provided four advanced training courses for young workers, offering opportunities to progress from electrical fitter to electrician, from fitter to industrial mechanic, from miner and machine operator to mining mechanic (new occupational profile) and from machine operator to the same grade in the restructured occupational profiles. All these courses were intended to equip young workers whose initial training had been based on old job profiles with the skills needed for the restructured occupations. This reveals the transitional nature of the courses, and in a sense the part-time training courses were an attempt to eliminate the competitive disadvantage of one generation of trainees in relation to younger workers whose initial training had been based on the restructured occupations.

Another advanced course for clerical workers wishing to become computer operators was originally planned. However, the company was obviously only interested in using and maintaining its technical training capacities and thus did not pursue this plan. For smaller groups with two years' work experience, there was also the option of attending technical college on a part-time basis or completing a course at a higher technical school.

The advanced training scheme provided a total of 920 hours of training. On a part-time basis, this was equivalent to 1.7 years of further training. After the training period, the young people transferred to part-time employment, working 75 per cent of normal full-time hours. The company's personnel plan was originally based on the assumption that at least one-third of the young workers would accept further training. "We will be satisfied with one-third and are hoping for 50 per cent". If the lower target was not reached, the required reduction in work volume would not have been achieved and alternative measures would have to be taken.

Such a comprehensive training programme naturally had serious effects on the budgets of the employment offices in the mining regions of North Rhine-Westphalia. Since the first financial cuts had been made in 1988, there was considerable resistance from some individual employment offices to this part-time training programme; the offices feared they would lose their ability to support other groups of employees. It was pointed out that some of the young

Figure 8: Part-time work for those commencing employment

Part-time work for those commencing employment — at a glance

All those completing their vocational training with Ruhrkohle AG after 1 January 1988 will be employed part time.

Duration of part-time work: maximum 3 years.

Part-time model	75% model	50/50% model
Location and length of working time	3 weeks' work, 1 week off	1 week's work, 1 week's training
Location and length of training period		3 days' instruction in a factory, 1 day's instruction in a part-time vocational school, 1 day with a work group
Wage/salary	Pro rata	Pro rata
Subsistence allowance		Example: In accordance with Employment Promotion Law, about 450 DM per month for single persons in wage category 09 (tax free)
Holiday Holiday pay	30 or 33 days Pro rata	30 or 33 days Pro rata
Supplementary payments ▸ Annual payment ▸ Heating allowance ▸ Loyalty bonus	Pro rata	Pro rata
Miner's bonus Underground bonus	For every full shift underground	For every full shift underground

Source: Ruhrkohle 1/88.

workers, particularly electricians, could be placed in new jobs immediately, and that the provision of advanced training for those seeking to become mining mechanics was primarily in the interests of the company. However, following discussions with the area employment office and the offices in the affected local authority areas, it was agreed, in principle at least, that the planned training programme was indeed in line with general labour market policy.

Three to four months before the examination dates, the two options were discussed with the young workers. Works councils, youth delegations and representatives of the training department all took part in the discussions, which were followed by talks at the pit with representatives of the employment office. All the participants were ill-prepared for the first round of talks held at the end of 1987. Numerous questions were asked, to which no satisfactory answer was forthcoming. Could the young workers be placed in employment by the employment office? What happened if a person failed to complete a training course - would the subsistence allowance have to be repaid? Contradictory or unclear answers undermined the young people's confidence, and many of them withdrew their initial consent to the further training programme. After this experience, better preparations were made, at least in some pits, for the second round of talks with those who had completed their examinations in the summer. The legal questions were largely answered [Ruhrkohle AG, *Handbuch für Teilzeitarbeit von Berufsanfängern*, 1988] and significantly more young people were persuaded of the merits of further training, in so far as this was the intention of personnel managers and works councils at the individual pits.

However, the number of young people opting for further training fell far short of the target of 33 per cent. Of the 4,352 individuals who had completed a course of vocational training (winter examination 1987/88 to winter examination 1988/89), 826 (19 per cent) opted for part-time training. At the 1988/89 winter examination the proportion of part-time trainees was only 5.4 per cent (Table 12). This proportion rose slightly in the summer of 1989, although the target figures were not reached. In order to compensate for this, the company lowered the training quota further than originally intended. In 1988, for example, it was planned to take on 2,500 trainees. However, the company was so late in sending confirmation of a training place to many young people that they had already accepted a place on other courses; moreover, the proportion of foreign workers among the trainees was limited informally to 15 per cent, which reduced the number of potential applicants in mining regions and for mining occupations. As a result, only 2,164 of the planned 2,500 training places were filled. The outlook for 1989 was similar.

The low participation rate and, above all, the declining trend in participation is an indication of problems in the implementation of the training programme. It had been planned to implement the training programme on a rotational basis: the young people were to be divided into "pairs", who were to alternate between employment and training. The purpose of this was to allocate the young people to fixed groups. Significantly more problems with the deployment of labour had been anticipated with the part-time employment model

Table 12: Participation of apprentices in part-time further training courses at Ruhrkohle AG

	Winter examination 87/88			Summer examination 88			Winter examination 88/89			Total		
	Successful candidates	Participants in training	%	Successful candidates	Participants in training	%	Successful candidates	Participants in training	%	Successful candidates	Participants in training	%
Power plant electricians	255	37	14.5	113	44	38.9	274	18	6.6	642	99	15.4
Fitters	186	27	14.5	538	231	42.9	124	3	2.4	848	261	30.8
Mining engineers	399	73	21.5	973	318	32.9	284	23	8.1	1 596	414	25.9
Others	109	0	0.0	1 030	52 [1]	5.0	127	-	-	1 266	52	4.1
Total	889	137	15.5	2 654	645	24.5	809	44	5.4	4 352	826	19.0

Note: [1] Mostly miners and machine fitters (two-year shortened training) taking additional training courses to become mining engineers.

Source: Ruhrkohle AG/IG Bergbau und Energie.

in which 75 per cent of full-time hours were worked. The young workers do not work for one week every month; it was feared that they would be used as stopgaps or that others would have to do their work for that week. These expectations were purely academic. In practice, it was the participants on training courses who were used to fill gaps and who had little continuity in their jobs; other employees, supervisory staff and the trainees themselves had a correspondingly low opinion of their status. These problems were one reason why many trainees failed to complete their courses. For example, of the 645 individuals registered for a training course in the summer of 1988, only 515 were still attending courses in February 1989. The young people in part-time jobs were much more likely to remain in fixed working groups and considered themselves much closer in status to full-time employees than the other young workers.

The problems encountered in allocating young workers to jobs were tackled in very different ways from pit to pit. The rate of participation in training courses varied considerably between pits, ranging from less than 10 per cent in some pits to over 90 per cent in others. Low participation rates can be explained by the following factors:

- training managers feared themselves unable to provide the additional training or tried simply to avoid the additional work;

- works managers said that the efficiency of the young workers would be restricted by not working one week in four;

- many works council members, usually older ones, encouraged the young people's reluctant attitude towards training by advising them that: "You must get some practical experience, and show your face on the shop floor so that you really become part of the firm";

- the employment offices stated that they could find jobs only for certain groups;

- problems in putting into practice the first series of training courses increased hostility to the part-time training courses in the next series.

At some pits, all the parties involved promoted further training in order to guarantee their own training facilities by keeping them working at full capacity (the courses were all conducted within the company) and also to improve the young people's employment prospects.

Except in the summer of 1988, the participation rate for fitters and mining mechanics was higher than that for electrical fitters (Table 12). Many fitters see improved vocational training as a means of increasing their chances of changing jobs, even if the crisis in the mining industry deteriorates further. Mining mechanics see advanced training as a way of strengthening their position in the mining industry. The relative lack of willingness of electricians to participate in further training probably has something to do with the fact that they have already passed two tests of their acquired professional skill (after two years as an electrical fitter and after three-and-a-half years as an electrician): that level of vocational training means they already have very good chances of mobility in the external labour market.

Even after restructuring, the skill composition of a collier is still very specific to the sector. It would have been sensible to retrain these young workers as industrial engineers, which would have given them access to skilled jobs in other sectors. However, this is not possible, since the Federal Labour Office only supports part-time *advanced training* for young people without work experience, and not retraining.

Despite management's earlier assurances, it remained unclear for a long time whether the part-time courses would lead to a recognised qualification. The trade union demand was for a "slimmed down" test of professional skill, in which only the new elements would be examined. Not until the beginning of 1989 was it agreed that the further training courses would lead to a certificate awarded by the Chamber of Industry and Commerce. This belated decision on the nature of the qualification to be awarded on completion of training further reduced the young workers' readiness to take part in the scheme. The qualification was all the more important as an incentive since it was clear from the outset that advanced training would not lead to any additional payment.

Trade unions, management, personnel managers, works council members and youth representatives are all agreed that most young workers view part-time work and part-time training as something that has been forced upon them. According to statements by works council members and youth representatives in one pit, some of the young people doing part-time work do not really know what to do with their week off. Most of their friends and acquaintances are working during the week, so that the young part-time workers "regularly turn up in the works canteen", just to find some company.

On the whole, both part-time schemes are seen at Ruhrkohle AG as something of an "unloved child", that can nevertheless be justified as an alternative to the non-assimilation of new entrants to the labour market or a drastic reduction in the training quota. Part-time training is now seen at Ruhrkohle AG as a "discontinued model"; because of the low take-up rate and financial problems at the Federal Labour Office, and therefore candidates are no longer being actively sought out.

4.   Part-time training: precarious status
       or opportunity to retrain?

What distinguishes the part-time models for young people in the mining industry from comparable earlier approaches is that they form part of a collective agreement. Under the terms of the agreement, part-time work is obligatory for all those who have completed a course of training; this prevents young workers from being divided up into full-time or part-time employees, a division for which there cannot really be any objective criteria and which would therefore be discriminatory. Moreover, the collective agreement guarantees transfer to a full-time job and emphasises the exceptional nature of the part-time models, that will remain in place only for a transitional period. However, it proved impossible to prevent the part-time employees from being divided into two different groups. Contrary to initial expectations, managers, employees and young entrants to the labour market alike seem to have preferred the 75 per cent model to part-time training. By taking up this option, many young workers have obviously been pushed into a stopgap role, which lowers the status of all those on further training courses and weakens the resolve of the next group of young workers to embark upon further training.

The part-time training programme, which ceased at the end of 1989, was justified in training policy terms by the restructuring of occupations and the resultant need for the current generation of trainees to catch up on the new requirements. However, the low take-up rate shows how difficult it is to convince management, training directors, works councils and young workers themselves of this. Young workers' main aim, obviously, is to put an end to their precarious status as trainees and become properly integrated into the company. Because it has been conceived in such a short-term way, the alleged need for further training is, in their view, a specious argument advanced to justify job losses, particularly since their predecessors on training courses had been assimilated without difficulty and the training system at Ruhrkohle had always been described as exemplary and forward-looking.

The low take-up rate meant that the effect of the part-time training scheme was less to even out disadvantages caused by a lack of training than to widen inequalities between young people, which in the long term may have a negative effect on the employment and promotion opportunities for most of them.[50] Those who successfully complete further training courses certainly have better chances of promotion in the company and improved opportunities for mobility in the external labour market. The temporary acceptance of a precarious and unpopular status may in the long term prove to be a thoroughly sensible decision on the part of individuals. Finally, one negative effect of the relative failure of the part-time training model, as measured by its own criteria, is the unfavourable repercussions it has had on the hiring of trainees, which has in turn reduced the effectiveness of Ruhrkohle AG's attempts to ensure continuity in the supply of skilled workers in the region.

---

[50] The *Sozialforschungssstelle* in Dortmund has been commissioned by the Ministry of Labour, Health and Social Affairs of the *Land* of North Rhine-Westphalia to investigate the part-time training scheme at Ruhrkohle. A central issue in this research is the extent to which the training policy objectives of the part-time scheme were achieved and the subjective views developed by the young workers themselves. The retention rate among the young people is also being investigated, in an attempt to discover whether they are oriented primarily towards the internal or the external labour market.

VI. Some other employment plans

The remaining cases will be presented in significantly less detail than those above, since they also reveal many of the structural problems inherent in training programmes already described. However, the plans and the experience of their implementation, which ranges from success to outright failure, have a number of particular characteristics, investigation of which will increase our knowledge of the genesis, conception and practical implementation of training plans.

In the two medium-sized firms Präwema, in Eschwege, and Berthold AG, in Berlin, training plans were not implemented because of a lack of public support and acute financial problems within the companies. However, the conflicts surrounding the employment plans did, as far as can be ascertained at present, provide the impetus for the establishment of a training centre in Eschwege and the development of an in-firm further training system in Berlin (see pp. 103-106).

At Klöckner-Becorit and Krupp-Stahl, two further, widely differing waiting loop models were agreed. Klöckner-Becorit made their agreement to re-employ trainees dependent on an intermediate training course, probably in the hope of building in a selection threshold. At Krupp-Stahl, the agreement to re-employ trainees continues to stand even if they work for an indeterminate period in another firm, which allows those affected to accustom themselves to alternative jobs without incurring any extra risk (see pp. 106-109).

The two East Frisian shipyards, Jansen-Werft in Leer and Sürken-Werft in Papenburg, were able to benefit from the shipyard assistance programme established by the *Land* of Lower Saxony. In none of the other firms investigated was the percentage take-up for training courses as great as in East Frisia. The alternatives - redundancy or a voluntary move - were ruled out by the extremely difficult situation in the regional labour market; unlike in the other areas, retraining appeared to many to be the only alternative to unemployment. Consequently, neither of the two workforces was broken up by an absorptive labour market, and both were able to a large extent to preserve the notion of collective strength on which training plans are based. The precarious labour market situation certainly also encouraged the local employment office's relatively generous interpretation of the Employment Promotion Law, despite initial legal reservations (see pp. 109-113). Finally, Klöckner-Humboldt-Deutz (KHD) is the only case investigated in which a training plan was agreed not as a result of public debate and trade union pressure but largely on the initiative of the company. In this case, the main aim of the training courses is employment *outside* the company. Of all the plans studied, the KHD agreement is the one that most clearly reflects the interests of the employer; at the same time, however, it manages successfully to reflect those of employees as well, and also to take account of the wider public interest (see pp. 113-114).

1. Training plans without training

A. Präwema Eschwege

In August 1987 the management of the Eschwege machine tool factory announced they were no longer able to pay the wages of their 400 employees. The following month, insolvency proceedings began. Because of difficulties in determining the precise ownership structure and the outflow (in connection with an inheritance) of resources urgently required for investment, the company had not recently been modernised.

In order to avoid bankruptcy and the sale of the machinery, the factory was occupied for 125 days to demand government assistance. In the autumn of 1987 it became clear that a buyer would not be found for the company unless the workforce was reduced by half. IG Metall and the works council demanded that an employment and training company be set up, with the aim of preventing unemployment and giving employees an opportunity to retrain instead. Since at that time, the company had none of the CNC machines that were a precondition for modernisation, there was a great need for further training despite the workforce's high skill levels.

However, it soon became clear from initial negotiations with the employment office that official support for such a company would not be forthcoming. The employment office did not see its task as "the development or maintenance of an industrial structure in order to avoid unemployment, but rather to place the registered unemployed in suitable jobs. Moreover, the employment office does not support programmes that further sectional interests. Finally, the skilled workers at Präwema are sufficiently well qualified to be placed without difficulty in alternative employment, while the DGB's work in the field of vocational training would be jeopardised by the involvement of another agency".

At the end of 1987 Präwema was taken over by the Rothenburger company, on condition that the workforce would be reduced to 200. This company had already had experience of cushioning job losses with training programmes, and had set up its own training centre in South Hesse (the *Pittler-Lehrwerkstätten GmbH*). It offered to build a similar training centre in Eschwege. The *Land* agreed to finance the continuation of training for 25 trainees in this centre.

One of the provisions of the social plan that was finally agreed was the establishment of a training company. This company was to provide training programmes oriented towards the restructuring of the metalworking and electrical trades. Employees made redundant were to be offered a place on a training course, provided the Federal Labour Office supported their presence on such a course and no other reasonable job could be found for them.

After the social plan had been concluded, the works council agreed to the dismissal of 130 workers, in order to pave the way for the takeover by Rothenburger. The selection of employees to be made redundant was based on social criteria, as laid down in the Law on Protection against Dismissal. The works council was for the most part able to prevent the dismissal of older workers. Of the 3 million DM made available to fund the social plan, 2.4 million were earmarked for the training company. Before it could be established, at least 50 of the redundant workers had to enrol on training courses. The remaining funds were used to top up the unemployment benefit of the 58-year-olds leaving the firm to 90 per cent of their net wage, until the time at which they could take early retirement.

The employment office saw the dismissal of the 130 employees as a "vitamin injection for the labour market". Only 10 to 15 of them - mostly older ones, who would in any case soon be taking early retirement - had no training. Sixty-five of them were 30 years of age and under and 38 were between 31 and 49 years of age. By March, about half of them had found a new job. About 20 people were sent on further training courses by the employment office. Some took part in CNC courses put on by the DGB's training organisation. There was apparently no room for a new training agency, since the existing agencies were not working at full capacity and the cuts at the Federal Labour Office were already restricting the employment office's room for manoeuvre.

The company itself built a training centre with the funds made available for the social plan; by the end of 1988, only 11 of the 35 trainees were former employees. In future the centre will concentrate on providing training courses for apprentices or modules for such courses, on a commercial basis. The further training of redundant workers, which was the basis on which the training centre was financed and legitimised, played no role in the company's thinking. By mid-1988, several months after the redundancies, the company had still not contacted the employment office to discuss possible further training courses for former Präwema employees.

It is too early to estimate the future importance of the training centre for the region, so a final evaluation is not yet possible. However, it has to be put on record that a considerable part of the finance for this training centre was provided by the redundant workers, whose redundancy pay or compensatory wage increases (paid if they had taken a job with another company at a lower rate of pay) would have been significantly higher without this arrangement. The failure to put into practice the plan for a training company for the redundant workers is the result of several factors: the new owners did not feel bound by the social plan drawn up by the receiver and wanted to concentrate solely on developing a commercial centre for basic vocational training. The further training agencies in the region were not working at full capacity; as a result, competition developed between the trade union training organisation and the planned new agency. The redundant workers were very highly qualified and their average age was very low, so their chances of finding employment in the external labour market were fairly good. This was the result of using social criteria in the selection process, as insisted by the works council. In the works council's view, it was more important to protect employees at risk than it was to abandon the social criteria in order to create a "better clientele" for special labour market initiatives with uncertain results. Finally, the local employment office was very narrow in its interpretation of the Employment Promotion Act. And it is virtually impossible to check whether it gave preferential treatment to the redundant workers, in order to justify its interpretation of the law in practical terms.

B.   Berthold AG Berlin

H. Berthold AG developed the first photocomposition machines in the 1970s. On the basis of its technological advantage, the company expanded during this time and at peak periods employed more than 2,000 people. However, the ill-judged purchase of companies in difficulties and inadequate preparation for the technological change from precision engineering to electronic machines led the company into a severe crisis and for a while they stared bankruptcy in the face.

By 1988 the workforce had been cut by half. The works council wanted to implement the job losses without redundancies for operational reasons; as early as 1985, it was able to push through a training plan under the terms of which employees affected by rationalisation were to be offered opportunities to retrain, although only if the training envisaged matched the company's needs and capabilities, a stipulation that barely goes beyond the terms of the Law on Labour Relations at the Workplace.

The plan did not lead to any training being offered. The company wanted to make restructuring easier by replacing part of its workforce. Workers familiar only with mechanical equipment were to be dismissed and replaced by more highly qualified personnel with knowledge of electronics. The company exerted considerable pressure on individual employees, mostly older and less well-qualified workers, to accept redundancy payments. They were told that if they did not do so they would be dismissed. The employment office did not support the works council in its attempts to push through a training programme. One of its objections was that the employees likely to be dismissed were over 40 years and thus too old for the proposed training courses; furthermore, it held that the risk of unemployment would not exist until *after* the dismissals had actually taken place.

However, the deficiencies of the firm's further training system became glaringly apparent during the restructuring process. Moreover, the remaining core workforce, much reduced in size, was inadequately prepared for the new production processes. In their case, the works council was able to push through a number of training programmes, some of the finance for which was provided by the company on the basis of the 1985 training plan. With the assistance of the employment office, some employees obtained a certificate in electronics. Technical draughtsmen went on computer-aided design (CAD) courses, and a total of 40 employees took part in a basic course in personal computers organised outside working hours. On the initiative of the works council, one group of workers received instruction in the latest technological developments, while another acquired better knowledge of their own machines and area of work, all of which are important preconditions for later training courses. The company now has its own further training department and a budget for training courses for employees threatened by rationalisation.

The training plan, which was originally intended to help avoid dismissals, failed because of the danger of bankruptcy, the need to reduce personnel costs rapidly, earlier deficiencies in further training and modernisation programmes and the extremely hectic pace of and lack of preparation for technological change. In this situation, the company lacked the skill, the resources and the time to restructure the skills of its workforce by means of training courses that in some cases last several years. Now that the company has had time to consolidate its position, this agreement may possibly provide the impetus for the *long-term development of an in-firm system of further training* and the preventive further training that would be needed in the event of future rationalisation programmes.

2. Two waiting-loop models

A. Klöckner-Becorit in Castrop-Rauxel

Klöckner-Becorit is a supplier to the mining industry, which accounts for 90 per cent of its turnover. Because of the renewed crisis in the mining industry and a shortfall in orders from abroad (especially from Poland), turnover fell in a few years from 400 to 250 million DM. In order to save on wage costs, an increasing share of production was being subcontracted to outside firms. In 1982 the workforce was some 1,800 strong; by 1987 this figure had been reduced by 400, mainly through the departure of older workers and natural wastage. In November 1987 management announced that a further 500 jobs were to be lost by September 1988. Since there was no further scope for early retirement, there were now to be "real" dismissals.

The works council and the workforce reacted with six weeks of industrial action (stoppages, street blockades, demonstrations by employees in Bonn and Düsseldorf), which forced management to agree to a waiting-loop model and to limit the number of job losses to 350 through a reduction in overtime and a number of other measures.

An agreement was signed, under the terms of which:

- Employees of 55 years and over were to leave, with their unemployment benefit being topped up to 90 per cent of their previous wages until they were able to take early retirement.

- Severance agreements were to be offered, but only if the departure did not run contrary to the company's interests.

- Workers to be dismissed were to be offered further vocational training courses. Those who expressed an interest would leave the company to attend a course organised by the employment office. After 18 months at the earliest and 24 months at the latest, all these former employees would be re-employed (the company gave an "unconditional commitment to rehire" them) provided they had not found another permanent job. Employees who did not accept the offer of training would leave the company for good with redundancy pay.

During training or during the period of unemployment between completion of a training course and reappointment, workers receive a monthly allowance of 150 DM, which ceases, however, when they have received the amount of severance pay to which they are entitled under the terms of the social plan. This additional payment amounts on average to 80 per cent of previous net earnings. If a worker fails to complete a course, his right to re-employment is automatically lost.

In contrast to Krupp, re-employment is dependent on successful completion of a training course. In order to prevent this becoming a means of excluding certain individuals, the works council succeeding in having the so-called "41a courses"[51] for older and unskilled workers classified as training courses. And by winning the right to veto the dismissal of some older workers or "problem cases" who would certainly have been unable to cope with a training programme, it also managed to exert some influence over the processes leading up to the selection of workers to be made redundant.

The company took absolutely no part in the planning of the training programme, which it regarded as having been forced upon it. It also feared that any active involvement on its part "would give rise to hopes that we want to see these people again". The problem for the company was that if all the trainees returned, it might have to send more employees on training courses or offer more older employees early retirement, which would lead to a considerable increase in the costs of the social plan.

The loss of the 350 jobs was carried out in the following way. One-third were older workers who took early retirement, another third signed severance agreements and the remaining third were dismissed and placed in the waiting loop. A few in this last group did not take up the offer of training because they found a new job; they accepted redundancy pay instead. They were mainly younger employees and skilled workers who, because of the upturn in the economy, were welcomed with open arms by other firms. About 70 people embarked on a wide variety of different courses (welding, CAD courses, retraining as turners, etc.). Some of these people also found a new job after they had completed their retraining and accepted the remaining redundancy pay from Klöckner-Becorit.

At the beginning of 1989, Klöckner-Becorit also began to benefit from the favourable demand in the machine tool industry and took on 10 people from the waiting loop sooner than expected. A further 30 to 40 have not yet given up their right to re-employment. It is likely, however, that this group will begin to crumble as individuals find jobs in other firms. There will probably be a "hard core" of older and hard-to-place workers who do not give up their right to re-

---

[51] These are courses, lasting up to six weeks, designed to "improve employment prospects". Among other things, they are supposed to help workers "to maintain or improve their skills", to take up employment or take part in vocational training programmes.

employment; without this company agreement, these people would have become permanently unemployed. Because of the buoyancy of the local labour market, most employees were able to find a new job in another company. Klöckner-Becorit's commitment to take them back gave them the backing they needed to appear self-confident when applying for jobs, and accordingly they were successful. However, this backing was not always exploited to the full. Some employees gave up their right to re-employment, although they had only obtained a short-term contract. Several of them are now unemployed and regret their hasty decision.

Compared with the settlement at Krupp, the extra financial assistance given to those receiving unemployment benefit or subsistence allowances was not very generous and some employees, particularly those with families, got into financial difficulties and took up employment in a new firm. It was precisely this group that was most afraid of having to "go back to school" and decided against retraining. This relatively low level of extra assistance is now seen by the works council as the fundamental weakness of the Klöckner-Becorit waiting-loop model, since it exerted considerable financial pressure on employees to seek employment in the external labour market.

B.   Krupp-Stahl

Just a few years earlier, each Krupp-Stahl plant had its own social plans. In 1987 all these plans were amalgamated into three outline social plans, making provision for early retirement for older workers, redundancy payment and a waiting-loop model. This outline agreement both worsened the financial provisions of the old agreements and introduced new elements, namely the waiting loop.

In the event of personnel cuts being introduced at individual plants, the reductions were implemented through additional negotiated settlements. Thus at the Krupp plant in Bochum it was agreed that the waiting-loop model was not to be used until all other options had been exhausted.

When the waiting-loop model does come into play, employees are made redundant. At the same time, they are given an absolute right to re-employment,[52] which cannot be revoked even if an employee takes a temporary job in another company. Offers of training courses can be distributed among those made redundant. However, participation in such courses is voluntary. The company can re-employ any worker by giving one month's notice. If the job offer is not accepted, the worker is dismissed without redundancy pay. While employees are in the waiting loop, unemployment money or subsistence

---

[52] After negotiations with the Federal Labour Office the original term "guarantee of re-employment" had to be changed, because the Labour Office would not have paid unemployment benefit because of "doubts about availability for work". However, the change is merely cosmetic. It is possible that the Labour Office insisted on this cosmetic alteration simply to avoid contradicting itself. It was an objection from the Labour Office that led to the abandonment of a guarantee of re-employment for members of the Saarland steel foundation.

allowances are topped up to 90 per cent of the previous net wage. This extra assistance is deducted from any possible redundancy payment. The right to re-employment must be claimed in writing at the latest seven months before re-entry into the firm, otherwise the right is lost. On rejoining the company, the employee is entitled to a job of equal status to the one he had previously.

The waiting loop has not yet been put into practice; because of the upturn in the market for steel, the job losses planned for 1988 in Bochum did not actually take place.

In addition to the measures described above, Krupp also assented to an "agreement on the safeguarding and creation of jobs". Among other things, the company committed itself, in collaboration with other companies, the local authorities and central government, to providing replacement jobs. A working party, in which the central works council is involved, is supposed to be drawing up proposals in this area. This group has met twice; the company had put no resources into it, and it is undoubtedly little more than a front.[53]

However, the Krupp waiting loop has one new element. The distinctive feature of the Krupp model is that a permanent job in another company is not an obstacle to re-employment by Krupp. This may appear to constitute a very sweeping right to re-employment. In practice, however, the effect may be exactly the opposite. Employees may take new jobs shortly after entering the loop, since in so doing they neither lose the extra financial assistance that will be paid if their new earnings are less than 90 per cent of their old net wage nor do they jeopardise their right to return to Krupp. Depending on the capacity of the local labour market to absorb surplus labour, an apparently "generous" provision may in fact encourage workers to leave the company.

3. The East Frisian shipyards

Of all the companies investigated during the project, it was the two East Frisian shipyards, Sürken-Werft in Papenburg and Jansen-Werft in Leer, that implemented the most comprehensive retraining programmes. In Lower Saxony, just as in Hamburg, federal government funds made available as part of the shipyard assistance programme were used to top up subsistence allowances paid by the employment office to 90 per cent of usual net earnings. This assistance was granted on condition that the company made an application to declare mass redundancies, in accordance with the Employment Promotion Act. Such an application was considered by the regional employment office to be sufficient proof of a threat of unemployment. Thus the starting point in this case was a collective threat of unemployment, which was indeed an accurate reflection of the situation in these particular shipyards.

---

[53] In connection with the planned closure of the Krupp steelworks in Rheinhausen, however, the company committed itself "to direct its own efforts and those of third parties" towards the maintenance of 779 jobs and the creation of 721 new ones at the Duisburg-Rheinhausen works. To date 620 new jobs have been agreed at Rheinhausen; most of them are to be created by the establishment of a retraining centre and as a result of investment by various Krupp subsidiaries.

A.   *The Sürken shipyard in Papenburg*

In 1987, the Sürken shipyard in Papenburg had a workforce of around 470. Because of the crisis in the shipbuilding industry and a consequent lack of orders, redundancies were announced at the beginning of 1987. The works council and IG Metall proposed that a training programme, along the lines of that introduced at Blohm & Voss, should be set up instead. The employment office initially stipulated that employees should be declared redundant before the training programme could begin. This requirement was dropped because of the *Land* shipyard programme, which provided only for the retraining of employees and not of the *unemployed*; in other words, the programme was intended to contribute to internal structural change, and to this end resources were not to be concentrated on workers who had to leave the shipbuilding industry because of the severity of the crisis.

Since each employee at the Sürken yard was considered to be under threat of unemployment, the workforce could be addressed collectively at department meetings and then interviewed individually about possible training courses. It proved to be extraordinarily fortunate that the affected employees were drawn from such a wide circle, since it meant that the list of participants did not smack of a redundancy list. Many of the younger employees (under 40 years) volunteered for further training and took the pressure off the older workers who no longer considered themselves able to cope with a training course. This willingness to participate in training had been increased by a previous lengthy period of short-time work; those opting for training were significantly better off financially than they had been on permanent short time.

In 1987, 70 unskilled and semi-skilled employees embarked on 27-month courses designed to retrain them as fitters, turners, drill operators, etc. The first three months of this retraining period were spent on a preliminary refresher course in German and mathematics which was intended to prepare participants for retraining; 56 skilled employees then embarked on 9 to 12 months of additional training in data processing, CAD, CNC, hydraulics, pneumatics and welding.

At the beginning of 1988 a new crisis emerged. Management wanted to make 70 employees redundant. In collaboration with IG Metall, the employment office and the municipal authorities, the works council was able to prevent many of the redundancies. A further 30 employees began further training courses and 21 older workers left the company under the terms of a social plan. However, redundancies could not be avoided altogether. Individual workshops (e.g. the carpentry shop) were shut down completely, while some functions (e.g. cleaning) were subcontracted to outside firms; it was in these areas that workers were made redundant. Plans to establish an external employment company that would organise job creation schemes for former Sürken employees failed because the employment office was by now concentrating its dwindling resources on job creation schemes for the long-term unemployed.

The retraining and advanced training courses are held for the most part at the shipyard. However, as a sort of quality control measure, the employment office has commissioned an outside agency to provide the courses. Most of them are intended to provide workers with new skills, in order to reduce specialisation and increase the range of jobs to which they can be allocated. However, the welding courses remained specific to the shipbuilding industry. Since the employment office assumed that the shipyard would stay open, it agreed to these industry-specific courses, which do, nevertheless, lead to a generally recognised qualification.

At the beginning of 1988 the company was also planning its long-term future with a reduced workforce of 255. This would have led to redundancies after the end of the training courses. However, this pessimistic figure was overtaken by economic developments. As a result of the takeover of the dredger building activities of the bankrupt firm of Weser-Hütte, the diversification away from shipbuilding and the upturn in the shipbuilding business, the company was able without difficulty to re-employ both groups of employees who had completed advanced training courses. Other labour shortages were overcome by taking on temporary workers and overtime work, in order to create a situation in which it became possible by mid-1989 to re-employ those who had been on retraining courses as well. In 1989 the Sürken shipyard had a workforce of just over 430.

Of these 430 employees, more than one-third have taken part in a lengthy course of retraining or advanced training. This skilled workforce constitues a substantial base for product diversification and for the flexible deployment of personnel in the company's various departments. Only 11 of those who started retraining courses dropped out, either because they could not cope with the work or because they found alternative employment. Much of the success of the further training programme can be attributed to the preliminary courses and intensive supervision during training courses conducted in familiar surroundings. There is every indication that the Sürken shipyard constitutes a successful model for rescuing a company, maintaining a core workforce and even extending its skill potential in a structurally weak region. The successful restructuring of the company, combined with a favourable economic situation, made it possible, unexpectedly and with hindsight, *to link training to diversification*; small groups of workers, whose departments were shut down completely (carpenters, cleaners), were of course excluded from this process. Moreover, the Sürken shipyard is a model example of unbureaucratic co-operation between works council, management, IG Metall, employment office, training agencies and external management consultants, all of whom were concerned to preserve jobs and to implement the training programme as rapidly as possible.

B.   The Jansen shipyard in Leer

The starting position at the Jansen shipyard in Leer was completely different. In May 1987, this shipyard also had a workforce of about 460. Unlike the Sürken yard, however, it specialised exclusively in the building of new ships and was particularly severely hit by the collapse of demand. Bankruptcy proceedings began at the beginning of May 1989.

The commencement of the proceedings marked the start of an imaginative, well-organised campaign by the workforce, initially against closure and later against the cannibalising of equipment and the plant; the story of this two-year campaign has still to be written. The press reported on the campaign with the apt headline: "Asterix among the East Frisians. A small shipyard resists successfully and with good cheer" [*TAZ*, 17.8.88]. To begin with, the launching of a ship was made conditional upon the ship also being fitted out at the yard. This guaranteed employment for part of the workforce for a further six months. It was agreed with the receiver that between 150 and 200 employees would then be offered retraining, in order to avoid redundancies. The precondition for this was an assurance that the *Land* would top up subsistence allowances. It took a demonstration by the workforce in Hanover to force the *Land* to agree to top up the subsistence allowances paid to Jansen employees on training courses. Such extra financial assistance was originally restricted to employees of firms still trading, and was not given to those from firms in receivership. After the ship had been fitted out in the autumn of 1987, a further round of training courses was agreed.

By the end of 1988, a total of 280 Jansen employees had started a training course. About 100 employes left the firm on their own initiative; 40 apprentices were not taken on after they had completed their courses, and the remaining 40 people took early retirement.

Most of the training courses - except for one welding course - took place outside the company. The works council wanted to keep the workforce together at the yard "as a political force" in order to be able to exert pressure on the government to act as guarantor for new orders. The receiver, on the other hand, did not consider himself able to enter into binding, long-term agreements. Even the employment office planned the training offered to Jansen employees primarily with the external labour market in mind. In consequence, the proportion of retraining courses was greater at the Jansen yard than at Sürken, and there were virtually no industry-specific advanced training courses as there had been at Sürken.

The planning of the training programme was accompanied by a running battle between the receiver and the works council regarding the selection of participants. The receiver asked the foremen to select those people they wanted to be rid off. The employment office sometimes had to react at very short notice to constantly changing lists, but on the whole dealt with the matter in a very flexible way.

The yard has now been closed. The site was sold in December 1988 to a Hamburg company that is going to develop it as an industrial park and is hoping to attract firms from Southern Germany in particular. A sit-in by the workforce prevented plant and machinery from being auctioned.

The training programme came to an end at the beginning of 1989. The workforce - and this is surely unique in the Federal Republic of Germany - has continued to meet for "staff meetings without a company" [*Ems-Zeitung*, 28.1.1989]. With the support of IG Metall and several research institutes, a plan for a "regional workshop of the future" was drawn up. According to the plan, job creation funds and government subsidies are to be used to employ former Jansen employees to produce prototypes for wind-powered electricity generators, to build a floating museum and also to establish a regional labour pool in an attempt to cut back on the use of loan workers and overtime in other firms in the region. As a result of continuous pressure and good public relations work, the Jansen employees have already obtained job creation funds and subsidies for individual projects (e.g. for the building of the floating museum). A registered association has been set up to organise job creation schemes and some of these projects.

As a result of the training programme, the redundancies at the Jansen yard were postponed for almost one-and-a-half years. Many former employees were still involved in the programme in May 1989. The time thus gained was used to develop plans for an employment company, that will be able to absorb at least some of the former Jansen workers, and to exert political pressure for these ideas to be implemented. The unfavourable situation in the regional labour market meant that the workforce was less likely to be broken up by individual mobility in the external labour market.

The particular situation in the local labour market is also partly responsible for the extraordinarily high take-up rate for training courses in the two East Frisian shipyards. The capacity of the regional labour market to absorb labour is so low that redundancy payments and labour migration are not realistic alternatives. Moreover, the readiness of all those involved at the Sürken yard to co-operate shows that small and medium-sized firms with their roots in the region may be prepared in crisis situations to avoid redundancies by implementing imaginative new programmes.

4. Training plan without trade union pressure: Klöckner-Humboldt-Deutz

The economic position of Klöckner-Humboldt-Deutz has deteriorated considerably in recent years. Turnover fell from 4.6 billion DM in 1984 to 3.1 billion DM in 1987; planned turnover for 1988 was 2.9 billion DM. In the same year, a total of 2,332 jobs were to be lost at various sites.

The employment-cum-social plan signed by the works council at the beginning of 1988 is the least generous of all the agreements in the *large firms* that were studied. It makes a distinction between personnel reduction measures and redundancies. In addition to severance payments and special pension schemes, the measures agreed to include the offer of training.

This training programme has the explicit aim of improving employees' chances in the external labour market. If training cannot be offered - perhaps on the grounds of age - or if an offer is refused, then redundancy ensues. On completion of their training courses those affected leave the company. However, the company has promised to keep them on if a suitable job happens to be free. Subsistence allowances are topped up to 85 per cent of previous net earnings. The full amount of this extra financial assistance is offset against any future redundancy pay. If an employee is taken on again, the extra money is considered to be a loan for a further two years; if the worker is subsequently made redundant, it is offset against redundancy pay in gradually decreasing amounts.

There are considerable financial incentives for individuals to agree to a settlement. For an employee aged between 35 and 45 with 15 to 25 years' seniority and monthly earnings between 3,000 and 3,500 DM, redundancy pay ranges from 20,250 to 48,125 DM if a severance agreement or a training course is accepted. The amount paid on dismissal ranges from 18,000 to 43,125 DM, falling to between 15,750 and 39,375 DM if an offer of training is turned down.

Chapter 5

Reconversion in France

I. New elements in French personnel policy

In France, from the mid-1970s, personnel reductions in sectors and firms hit by crisis were made easier by government subsidies for early retirement schemes. Virtually no other OECD country concentrated the resources devoted to labour market policy so heavily on early retirement schemes established as a result of collapses in the labour market following economic downturns or structural changes. In 1987, France spent 1.07 per cent of GDP on such schemes, compared with only 0.02 per cent in the Federal Republic of Germany [OECD, 1988, p. 86]. As a result, the labour force participation rate for men aged between 55 and 64 in France[54] fell between 1975 and 1985 from 68.9 to 50.1 per cent; the corresponding reduction in the Federal Republic was from 68.1 to 56.2 per cent [OECD, 1987a]. This policy initially allowed French firms to shed labour quickly, but after the relevant age groups had been pensioned off (in the steel industry early retirement is now possible from age 50 onwards), it subsequently came up against both financial constraints and those imposed by personnel policy. Early retirement from 50 years of age costs the government between 1 and 1.2 million FF per person, thus far exceeding the cost of financial assistance for other labour-shedding measures.[55]

The expansionist employment policy and reductions in working hours introduced by the new socialist government at the beginning of the 1980s meant that French industry was no longer shedding labour at the same rate. With the following change of direction in economic policy and the consequent budget reductions, however, firms came under increasing pressure to adjust, particularly in the shipbuilding and steel industries, but also in other sectors (e.g. the motor and electronics industries). The number of people employed in manufacturing

---

[54] The participation rate for women cannot be used here for the purposes of comparison, since it also reflects differing trends in women's economic activity.

[55] For firms, however, early retirement remains by far the most financially advantageous way of shedding labour, with the cost estimated at between 80,000 and 140,000 FF per person [Burdillat, 1987].

industry fell by 3.3 per cent between 1983 and 1985, compared with 1.9 per cent between 1979 and 1983 and 1.0 per cent between 1975 and 1979 [OECD, 1988, p. 197]. The scale of the job losses far exceeded the reductions possible through early retirement. However, the experience of the militant resistance by Longwy steelworkers in 1979 against planned closures was still all too fresh in the minds of French politicians, making it impossible for the socialist government to contemplate mass redundancies, uncushioned by any special measures, in the (mostly) nationalised companies in the crisis sectors.

As a consequence, French labour market and personnel policy was supplemented by a package of measures usually described collectively by the term *"reconversion des salariés"*. Further vocational training is only one part of this package. It also includes information on job vacancies, guidance on work in other sectors, assistance in becoming self-employed, a placement service and a settling-in allowance to facilitate integration into employment. In many companies, so-called "conversion structures" were set up to implement these measures, to help individuals affected by redundancy find a suitable route into re-employment and to co-ordinate the activities of the various institutions involved (company, economic development agency, local authorities, training agencies, employment office, other companies, etc.). The aim of the reconversion programme is not to maintain employment relationships, but rather to terminate them; its goal is not internal but *external* structural change, although *the company issuing the redundancy notices retains responsibility*. The companies or government agencies try hard to attract new firms or to develop local small and medium-sized enterprises[56] and to uncover job vacancies in other firms that can be filled by their redundant personnel.

This reconversion policy increased the obligation upon French companies to not simply abandon redundant employees to their fate in the external labour market but to help them find alternative employment. As a result, large French companies have tended to replace simple dismissals with a package of reconversion measures. In ideal cases, reconversion is an instrument for avoiding industrial conflict and futile obstacles to personnel reductions, which make it more difficult both to introduce training programmes for employees and to restructure the company rapidly. In such cases, it also reduces the pressure of time when placing employees in alternative jobs, thus increasing their chances of success, and finally, by changing purely compensatory budgets (redundancy pay, unemployment benefit) into active employment policy measures, it makes it possible to operate in a way that is managerially more efficient, possibly cheaper, but in any event socially and economically more effective. However, this ideal case occurs only in a favourable labour market situation. The main constraints on reconversion policy are a lack of jobs and wage differentials

---

[56] For example, there were special grants available for firms setting up in steel-producing regions; like Thomson in Villingen-Schwenningen, individual enterprises set up companies whose purpose was to encourage new firms to establish themselves in the local region; when redundant steelworkers were taken on special settling-in allowances were paid.

between the old and potential new jobs in any given region. It proved impossible for companies to overcome these difficulties in the short term and in many cases they left their mark on the implementation of the reconversion package.

This often meant - as we shall see - that the main focus of the package was no longer on training, described by Chérèque, the French Minister for Industry and Reconversion, as an "entrance ticket" to a new job [Chérèque, 1988, p. 15]. Vocational training was in part replaced by the psychological preparation of previously well-paid core workers in key industrial sectors for new employment conditions with precarious contracts, unfavourable working conditions or low wages.

In contrast to employment plans in the Federal Republic of Germany, reconversion in France has been the subject of much political debate. It is seen as a key element in French industrial policy, which has been extraordinarily thoroughly investigated by both government and privately funded researchers and can therefore be characterised with precision [cf. Outin et al., 1988; Chaskiel and Villeval, 1988; Bellet and Boureille, 1986; Burdillat, 1987; Ardenti and Vrain, 1988].

Reconversion policy is undoubtedly most highly developed in the steel industry, particularly in Lorraine, where job losses were particularly severe (cf. section II below). The agreements in the steel industry, and also in other sectors (e.g. shipbuilding) and firms (e.g. Thomson), were the forerunners of legislation which incorporated the conversion period into the general provisions protecting workers against unfair dismissal. This is the subject of section III below, while the peculiarities of the French experience are investigated in section IV.

II.   Reconversion in the Lorraine steel industry

1.   The 1984 social agreement

In 1984, the French government decided that the nationalised steel industry would have to shed between 20,000 and 25,000 jobs by 1987; three works - at Pompey, Vireux and Longwy - were to be shut down completely. Shortly afterwards, all the trade unions involved, with the exception of the *Confédération générale du travail* (CGT),[57] reached agreement with the employers' association and the French government on a social plan for managing the personnel reductions (Convention générale, 1984). The social plan made

---

[57] The CGT did not sign the 1984 social agreement because the French government wanted to restructure the steel industry as rapidly as possible and was therefore forcing the pace rather than putting the brake on. The union wanted the steel industry to be restructured internally, with new jobs being created within the sector. The CFDT (*Confédération française démocratique du travail*), on the other hand, accepted the decline of the steel industry and sought above all to implement the new conversion measures. In negotiations at plant level, the CFDT was able in several instances to improve on the provisions agreed at national level [Chaskiel and Villeval, 1988, pp. 95-96].

provision for the early retirements that had already been agreed as well as for internal transfers (with appropriate retraining wherever necessary), which were supplemented, however, by a "solidarity rule". Even in plants not affected by job losses, some employees were offered early retirement in order to make room for workers transferred from other parts of the sector. In addition, a government programme provided financial incentives for foreign workers to return home.

However, the social plan did contain some new elements. The so-called *"congés de reconversion"* or *"congés de formation conversion"* - "reconversion leave" or "training and conversion leave (TCL)" - are intended to come into play when other measures prove inadequate. These "reorientation periods" last a maximum of two years. They are open to employees under 45 years, who have lost their jobs; those aged 45 to 50 may apply only if they have "individual plans" (self-employment or a new job) and renounce their right to take early retirement at some future date. During their period of leave, employees are paid 70 per cent of their gross wage, which is equal to about 84 per cent of their previous net wage. The cost is divided between the company, which pays 30 per cent, and the state, which pays the remaining 70 per cent. Employees may go on training courses, the costs of which are borne in equal part by the company and the government. During or at the end of this reorientation period, the company must offer them a choice of employment between two permanent jobs, matched as closely as possible to their qualifications. One of these jobs must be in their home region. The employment contract is suspended during the period of leave and is not terminated until the employee has been successfully placed in another job or declines the offer of employment. If the new job pays 10 per cent less than the previous one, additional compensation of 20,000 FF is paid. Workers can leave training courses as soon as an offer of employment is made. The entitlement to subsistence allowance can be cashed in at any time: 65 per cent of the remaining allowance[58] (calculated on the basis of a maximum leave period of 24 months) is paid at this point. Training and conversion leave is the subject of regular consultations with trade unions and works councils.

2.   The application of the 1984 social agreement in Lorraine

A.   Entries into and exits from training and conversion leave

The social agreement was introduced in mid-1986, and between then and the end of 1986 the number of jobs in the Lorraine steel industry fell by almost 40 per cent, from 41,828 to 25,677. In the largest steel company, Unimetal, which was particularly affected by job losses during this period, the workforce fell from 18,295 in June 1984 to 6,505 in December 1987, a reduction of 65 per cent. The number of people opting for training and conversion leave (4,143, plus

---

[58] Since there is a chance that the company will offer individuals two jobs after only a few months, there is a financial incentive to accept redundancy pay. Only if the period of leave lasts for the full 24 months will individuals receive more money than is paid in the event of redundancy.

a further 321 who went on internal further training courses) was even greater than the number taking early retirement. A further 1,483 individuals were transferred to a special "anti-crisis department". These were mainly the 45- to 50-year-olds whose jobs had been lost but who were already past the age limit for training leave. At 4,730, the number of individuals originally planning to take training and conversion leave was even higher; however, 427 people were transferred internally or found a new job without claiming leave (Figure 9; Table 13).[59]

The average duration of training and conversion leave was 7.5 months. More than 80 per cent ended their period of leave after less than 12 months and 90 per cent did so within 15 months. Thus only a minority took advantage of the maximum period of 24 months [*Bilan Lorrain*, 1987, p. 121]. The majority of those ending their leave cashed in their entitlement to a subsistence allowance and became self-employed or found new wage work; 9.2 per cent were transferred to jobs that fell vacant within the steel industry and 11.5 per cent were placed in new wage work outside the sector. At the time of writing, about 20 per cent were still on training leave, although only 6.8 per cent were on further training courses; 4.5 per cent were taking part in acclimatisation courses in other companies[60] intended to facilitate their subsequent placement and the rest were waiting for offers of training or employment.

The implementation of training leave has been characterised by the rapid throughput of individuals, the high take-up rate for redundancy pay and a marked preference for re-employment over training. Indeed retraining, which was supposed to be the main plank of the new arrangements, has been marginalised.

The company was initially slow to develop training programmes of its own and encouraged its employees to accept redundancy pay. This relieved it of the obligation to make the two job offers to the affected workers and to organise training courses. In the absence of a link between employment and training, hitherto decisive in fashioning individual motivation to retrain, employees were not clamouring for places on training courses. Considerable pressure had to be exerted by the trade unions, particularly the CFDT, before plans for further training were drawn up and implemented [Chaskiel and Villeval, 1988, p. 120].

The training courses lasted on average only 311 hours or 8 weeks [*Bilan Lorrain*, 1987, p. 85]. By the end of 1986, not even one-third of the individuals who had taken conversion leave had been on any kind of training course; they

---

[59] The numbers of people taking training leave shown in Table 13 are higher than the figure given in Figure 9. There are overlaps between the various headings. For example, an individual could be transferred from training leave to a job within the steel industry. The figures in Table 13 are based on original entries into training leave, while Figure 9 gives information on whereabouts on the reference date at the end of 1987.

[60] During this acclimatisation period they remain employed by the steel company. This means that the other companies can try out the new workers without risk or cost to themselves: if they take them on, they will have saved themselves the costs of recruitment and acclimatisation.

Figure 9:   Measures of workforce reduction at Unimetal between 1984-87

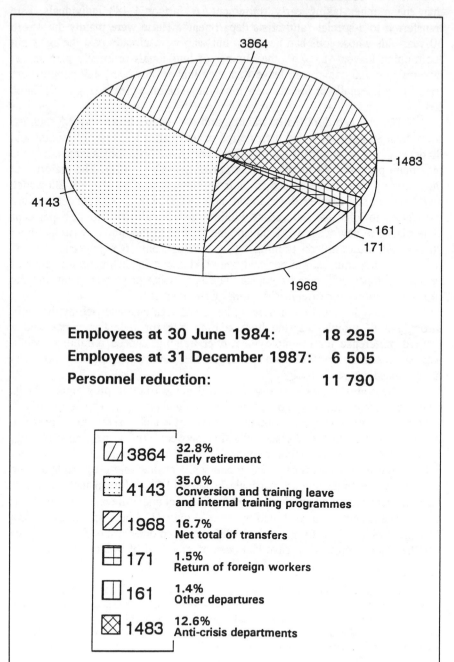

Employees at 30 June 1984:   18 295
Employees at 31 December 1987:   6 505
Personnel reduction: 11 790

3864   32.8%
        Early retirement

4143   35.0%
        Conversion and training leave
        and internal training programmes

1968   16.7%
        Net total of transfers

171   1.5%
        Return of foreign workers

161   1.4%
        Other departures

1483   12.6%
        Anti-crisis departments

Table 13: Training and conversion leave (TCL): entries and exits, June 1984 to December 1987

Applications for TCL	4,730	%
Rejections	0	
Immediate placement in employment	427	
Total entries to TCL	4,303	100.0
Exits immediate cashing-in:		
- for self-employment	483	11.2)
- for new wage work	821	19.1)
		)
Cashing-in during reconversion:		) 47.4
- for self-employment	143	3.3)
- for new wage work	595	13.8)
Placement in new wage work	496	11.5
Transfer within steel industry	398	9.2
Other exits[1]	193	4.5
Total exits	3 129	72.7
Number remaining	1,174	27.3
Current TCL programmes including: Further training:	853	19.8
- in the company	9	0.2)
- external	274	6.4) 6.6
Acclimatisation period in other companies	195	4.5
Waiting to begin a course or for initial counselling	61	1.4
Waiting for other measures	21	0.5
Recall to work	45	1.0
Others[2]	248	5.8
Further training in firm	321	7.5

Notes: [1] Return to home country; dismissal for failure to accept offer of job.
[2] Mainly those waiting for offer of employment.

Source: Unimetal.

had on average tried two courses. Actual vocational training accounts at most for half of the further training on offer. The training offered to unskilled and semi-skilled workers was mainly practical refresher courses not leading to a recognised qualification. Higher vocational training degrees could be obtained more readily by skilled workers, technicians and foremen, all of whom were already accustomed to receiving training.

The second component of the training programme was aimed less at refreshing or extending technical knowledge, but rather at preparing steelworkers psychologically for employment in another sector. The following objectives were outlined:

- "determination at plant level of individuals' vocational and social capabilities;

- familiarisation with new working environment;

- formulation and analysis of new employment reality;

- changing habits associated with former employment in order to find a new job;

- building up individuals' confidence in their own abilities".
  [*Bilan Lorrain*, 1987, Annexes, p. 183 ff.]

In addition, and on a smaller scale, literacy and general educational courses were organised for workers who had left school without any qualifications, in order to equip them for subsequent training courses.

At the same time, the company was also developing its own internal training programme in order to be able to manage technological change with a reduced workforce. The number of people (321) currently taking part in internal further training courses organised within the framework of the newly created reconversion structures is greater than the number of those on the dismissal list (283). In contrast to the arrangements for training and conversion leave, here the link between further training and employment has been maintained. The aim of virtually all the internal training courses is to expand vocational qualifications, but they also include general educational modules for employees with low attainment levels in education and training.

B.   The reconversion structures

Such extensive job losses, which were not implemented solely through redundancies but also by placing numerous obligations on companies, could not be managed by personnel departments already burdened with their everyday tasks. Joint committees were set up at the company level, in which discussions on the implementation of the social plan were held with the trade unions that were signatories to the agreement.[61] As far as implementation itself was concerned, it was necessary to set up new structures. Depending on the scale of the job losses, these ranged from releasing individual reconversion administrators from their normal duties to setting up independent departments (Unimetal, Ascometal).

In 1985, Unimetal set up the so-called "Unimetal-Conversion", which had representatives at four sites. Its purpose was twofold: to make available the personnel and financial resources required for reconversion and at the same time to bring some clarity to the calculation of costs by avoiding any ambiguity in the allocation of operating and restructuring costs. Consequently, the staff allocated to Unimetal-Conversion were relieved of any responsibility for the day-to-day running of the company and obliged to fulfil their tasks within a given budget. At each of its four sites, Unimetal-Conversion was made up of three departments: organisation of training leave, Unimetal-Service and protected workshops.

For every 25 to 30 individuals nominated for training leave, there was one adviser, often foremen who would subsequently be taking retirement themselves, but also officials of the CFDT, which alone among the participating unions has its own organisational structures at plant level. Discussions were held with each individual about his/her future employment opportunities; then, after consultations with local training agencies and the public employment service,[62] offers of employment or training were made and advice was given on the opportunities for becoming self-employed. Initially, the advisers had to work in a tense, hostile atmosphere, a situation which was noted even in the official report [*Bilan Lorrain*, 1987, p. 50]. However, the structures that had been set up made it possible to avoid an immediate break with the company. Links with the familiar environment were maintained and support was provided to ease the transition into training, another job or self-employment, which workers threatened with redundancy in other sectors did not receive.

Unimetal-Service took on all those aged between 45 and 50 whose jobs had disappeared but were not on training leave (1,483 individuals between 1985 and 1987). Most Unimetal-Service employees are waiting to take early retirement, although others are to be transferred back into the company or allocated to other activities. They are to be involved in three areas of work:

- work of "general interest" in the company, mainly demolition work at plants that have shut down;

- work that used to be contracted out (cleaning, gardening, painting and maintenance work);

---

[61] The CGT, the strongest union in the steel industry, was not represented on these committees since they had not signed the social agreement (on the position of the CGT, cf. *Bulletin de Liaison CGT d'Usinor - Sacilor*, No. 2, No. 4, No. 14, 1987).

[62] Tripartite training commissions were established at regional level. The placement service set up "employment exchanges" in plants. Steel workers were given preferential treatment.

- temporary work at Unimetal or other steel companies at cost price.

At Longwy, where the largest Unimetal-Service departments are located, the company estimates that this strategy has led to a 10 per cent reduction in the subcontracting out of work in the region [*Bilan Lorrain*, 1987, p. 54].

In order to promote self-employment as an option for former steelworkers and to create new jobs in the region, *Industrialisation Usinor Sacilor* (*Industrialisation 1988*) was set up, with departments in all steel-producing regions. Employees in the steel industry wishing to become self-employed can obtain advice from some of the 30 experts employed by *Industrialisation Usinor Sacilor* and are eligible for ten-year loans of up to 50,000 F at a rate of interest of 1 per cent. Advice is also given to local companies seeking to expand, and loans at a favourable interest rate of 6 per cent are available for such expansion projects. Additional subsidies are paid if former Usinor and Sacilor employees are appointed to newly-created jobs in these companies. *Industrialisation Usinor Sacilor* concentrated its efforts on small and medium-sized enterprises in the region, since it is here that the greatest opportunities for expansion are reckoned to exist. There is no assistance for companies seeking to relocate from another region where jobs are also to be created within the framework of a reconversion programme.[63]

These economic development companies set up by Usinor Sacilor received considerable subsidies from the French state. In 1987 these amounted to 200 million FF, with a further 192 million FF being given in 1988. On two occasions Usinor Sacilor has been active in the development of small and medium-sized enterprises away from its own sites. By increasing the capital of the various regional economic development companies in the group, it will be possible for local chambers of industry and commerce and other companies to take a stake in them. Obviously thought is being given to ways of keeping the now well-developed expertise of these companies in the region and utilising it in the interests of regional employment policy.

C.   Employee selection and destination on leaving

With a few exceptions, those employees over 50 years were all given early retirement. For the other measures, however, there was a selection process, conducted for the most part by management. No data were available on the skill structure of those who remained in employment and that of employees who took training leave or were transferred to Unimetal-Service. However, it is

---

[63] This objective is formulated in a considerably more explicit way with respect to the economic development of the French Saint Gobain group. The head of the regional economic development agency writes: "There are few potential investors who are not 'premium or subsidy hunters'; moreover, there is very strong competition between towns and cities seeking to attract new companies. And can we really say that 'vacating Peter's apartment in order to give Paul a roof over his head' provides a genuine solution? For these reasons, we have chosen instead to support small and medium-sized enterprises that are already in the region and in a position to create new jobs" [Bertherat, 1988, p. 70].

barely conceivable, given the technological change that is currently taking place and the increasing labour shortages, that the companies would have dismissed their younger, reliable and more highly skilled workers. In most cases, the trade unions exerted no influence over the selection process (or were unable to do so), and their involvement in the subsequent implementation of the various measures was restricted to an advisory role (to those on training leave) performed by some CFDT officials and the following up of individual complaints. The CGT, the strongest union in the steel industry, pursued a policy of non-co-operation. It demanded that jobs in the steel industry should be saved by means of new employment programmes, and wanted no part in the job losses. Early retirement was so popular among employees that even the CGT accepted it as a means of shedding labour. However, the union demanded that for each worker taking early retirement a young worker should be appointed in his place. The union's opposition was focused primarily on training and conversion leave, which it described as a "prelude to unemployment". Those CGT members who had been selected for training leave were abandoned to their own devices. CGT members requiring advice on further training measures were sent by their works council members to the CFDT; as a result, the union gave up any opportunity of influencing developments. However, the CFDT had so little influence on the day-to-day running of the company that it was unable to exert any control at all.

In the case of transfers, selection is carried out by the receiving plants or departments. Applications by foreign workers were clearly rejected outright and stringent requirements were laid down with respect to qualifications and age. Thus, after the closure of the Pompey works, 27.9 per cent of the French workers (excluding those who retired) were transferred, compared with only 7.4 per cent of the foreign (i.e. North African) workers; the corresponding figure for unskilled workers was only 9 per cent, compared with 29 per cent for skilled workers and 39 per cent for the higher-grade white-collar workers (Table 14).[64]

Investigation of workers leaving Pompey shows, moreover, that:

- It was mainly skilled manual and white-collar workers who chose self-employment. However, in doing so, most of them made no use of their professional skills, but have gone into the retail (45 per cent) and hotel and catering trades (16 per cent) [*Bilan Lorrain*, 1987, Annexes, p. 216].

- Training leave creates a reservoir of manual workers, particularly semi-skilled workers, who would be most likely to be downgraded on changing sector. However, unskilled workers are slightly under-represented: they have shown a marked preference for immediately cashing in their entitlement to redundancy pay. This may be attributed to the fact that the market for

---

[64] The closure of the Pompey works is being investigated by a research team from the University of Nancy. The personal files of about 1,400 employees were evaluated (excluding those who retired). In addition, a survey of 370 individuals was carried out in 1987. The details of the closure are described in Chaskiel and Villeval [1988]. Preliminary results were kindly made available to us by the research team.

unskilled employees is still relatively large in France, as a result of the underdevelopment of the initial training system. On the one hand, therefore, many areas are still dominated by working-class environments, in which vocational training has not yet been accepted as an essential component of job security. On the other, the size of the unstructured labour markets means that workers are more likely to find another job than they are in the Federal Republic of Germany.

Table 14: Reconversion of former Pompey employees (%)

	Transfers	Self-employment	Cashing-in	TCL	Return home	Total
Unskilled workers	9	9	58	20	4	(N = 209) 100
Semi-skilled workers	29	13	31	27	1	(N = 721) 101
Skilled workers	29	17	32	22	-	(N = 147) 100
Technicians and foremen	22	25	38	14	-	(N = 63) 99
Higher-grade technicians and foremen	28	17	44	11	-	(N = 104) 100
Lower-grade white-collar workers	11	21	57	11	-	(N = 120) 100
Higher-grade white-collar workers	39	19	39	3	-	(N = 31) 100
Total	24	14	39	21	1	(N = 1395) 99

Source: Villeval [1988].

In 1987, 370 of the affected workers at Pompey (excluding those who retired) were interviewed once again about their current employment. Initial evaluation shows that after leaving the company many workers have either lost their job once again or never found alternative employment after cashing in their redundancy pay. The following trends can be discerned: 18.2 per cent of former Pompey employees are currently unemployed, compared to an unemployment rate of 10.2 per cent for Lorraine as a whole. *Self-employment and cashing-in of redundancy pay were the most likely routes to unemployment.* Those who chose one of these two options account for more than 20 per cent of the current unemployment rate and for 40 per cent of those who have been unemployed at some time since the closure of the works, compared with an overall rate of 30 per cent (Table 15).

Table 15: Unemployment after closure of the Pompey steelworks (%)

Reconversion measure	Unemployed in 1987	Unemployed at some time after shut-down
Transfer	1.1	9.7
Cashing-in	26.7	41.8
TCL	16.7	26.4
Self-employment	23.7	39.5
Total	18.2	30.4

Source: Villeval [1988].

Those currently unemployed rapidly used up their redundancy pay. Those who chose self-employment and are now unemployed lost their redundancy payment by going bankrupt very quickly, while those who found another job only to lose it again received unemployment benefit for a period of only 15 months after obtaining their first redundancy payment. In addition, the receiving companies often paid newly-hired steelworkers lower than average wages to begin with, justifying this action by arguing that their redundancy pay provided a temporary cushion. As a result of this practice, part of the redundancy payments did not find its way directly into the steelworkers' hands.

The job losses in the Lorraine steel industry were accompanied by an expansion of the tertiary sector, which was reflected in an increase in poorly paid and, above all, precarious jobs. Many of the former steelworkers were forced into the more unstable areas of the labour market. Only a few of them benefited from the more stable jobs created in the new companies set up with the aid of government subsidies. The metalworking companies established on the site of the old Pompey works recruited only a few former steelworkers, all skilled workers. Only 19 per cent of the 1,495 new jobs created there were filled by former steelworkers, and if the new appointments made by the two subsidiaries of the steel group Sacilor - parent company of the shut-down firm - are deducted, even this figure falls to just 7 per cent. The French researchers summarise the situation thus: "With the introduction of training leave, the process of reintegrating the redundant workers began to be individualised. The establishment of a large number of small firms led to a process of 'economic Balkanisation' motivated less by a desire to reintegrate the redundant workers than by a search for government subsidies. There was a lack of co-ordination between the reconversion policy directed towards redundant workers on the one hand, and the policy of economic regeneration applied to the site of the old works on the other, with the two policies being implemented at different paces" [Chaskiel and Villeval, 1988, p. 129].

To a large extent, therefore, the aim of reconversion policy as actually implemented was *systematically to prepare workers for the transition to a more precarious, individualised working environment*. Many steelworkers, fearing this, took their redundancy pay and tried to avoid this demotion by taking the initiative to seek employment elsewhere. In so doing, however, they put themselves under great pressure of time and often met with failure in the unfavourable conditions that existed in the external labour market.

Retraining and systematic job search and placement, assisted by the company, offered a relatively greater chance, if not an absolute guarantee, of obtaining a new job than the individual routes represented by the early cashing-in of redundancy pay or self-employment.

D.   The new social agreement of 1987

The 1984 social agreement expired in 1987. In the middle of 1987 a new social agreement was signed, which was to be accompanied by the loss of a further 30,000 jobs between 1988 and 1990. The conclusion of this new agreement seemed to hang in the balance for some time. The trade unions were weakened by their lack of unity and their unsuccessful campaign against the job losses. In the light of this situation, the companies wanted to bring the regulations governing job losses down to the level of the general protection offered against dismissal. In order to "keep the social peace", however, the employers' association and the government agreed on a new, considerably less generous agreement, under the terms of which the option of early retirement is to be extended for the "last time" because of the high costs involved [*Sidérurgie: Nouvelle CGPS*, 1987].

Additional social security contributions mean that subsistence allowances for those taking early retirement are reduced by 10 per cent. The maximum length of training and conversion leave is reduced to 12 months; only for those over 45 years and people completing a longer course of vocational training can it be extended to 24 months. Participants will now receive only one job offer each. In 1984, the sole objective of TCL was further training. Since 1987, equal emphasis has been given to placement and evaluation of each individual's scope for action. Practical experience in another company is expressly classified as further training, since a placement could result from it. And entitlement to redundancy pay is still calculated on the basis of a hypothetical 24-month period of TCL, which significantly increases the financial incentive to cash in that entitlement immediately.

While the further training components of TCL are being downgraded, in-firm training is being developed with the aid of government funds. Agreement has recently been reached on so-called "internal training contracts for the steel industry". Depending on the resources available - the level of which is agreed each year with the government - employees whose job disappears are released for up to 12 months, during which they receive a minimum of 9 months' further training. They are then re-employed within the steel industry. Preferential treatment is to be given to those aged between 45 and 49, who are too young to be considered for early retirement. As is the case with TCL, their subsistence allowances will be topped up to 84 per cent of their previous net wage, with government bearing 30 per cent of the cost. Companies are obliged to set up their own organisational structures to implement these measures, unless a low take-up rate for TCL makes this impractical. Other tasks that will be carried out within these structures include studies of the chances of success for individual projects (self-employment) and appropriate counselling.

Thus, the contradiction between short-term placement and the medium and long-term perspectives of TCL, which had already become apparent in practice, is being resolved in favour of placing people in jobs. The report on the 1984 social agreement states that the low level of interest among steelworkers in further training had been underestimated. In practice, direct placement in employment predominated. However, one positive comment is that it proved possible to use the new organisational structures to prepare steelworkers for employment in a different firm and sector [*Bilan Lorrain*, 1987, pp. 148-149]. The person in charge of training leave at Unimetal described the original concentration on further training as "naive and optimistic". According to him, the majority of people left their TCL programme within a year. This had been taken into account. Special regulations could be invoked to enable those really willing to undertake further training to go on two-year courses.

Judgement of the new social agreement must certainly be equivocal. On the one hand, the old regulations are being extended, even if they are now less favourable; on the other hand, however, agreements in the steel industry are being reduced to the level of the general legislation providing protection against dismissal. This is clearly undermining the pioneering role that the steel industry has long played in the formulation of social policy.

III. The legal framework for reconversion and its implementation

1. The laws of 1985, 1986 and 1987

By the middle of 1985, reconversion as a means of managing job losses with government support had spread to sectors such as steel, shipbuilding and motor manufacturing, all dominated by large firms. In 1985, on the basis of the experience gained in these sectors, the measures were incorporated into general labour law (the *Code du Travail*); this meant that all firms announcing operational redundancies for cyclical or structural reasons could now claim financial assistance from the government for the implementation of reconversion programmes [*Congés de Conversion*, 1985].

Firms wishing to introduce a reconversion programme can apply for assistance; the application must list the number of redundancies, the skill structure of those affected, the objectives of the reconversion programme, the period of time within which employees have to make their decisions (a minimum of 15 days), the length of leave, the level of the subsistence allowance and the state assistance required; the application must be discussed with the works council.

Employment contracts are suspended during the reconversion programme, which must last for at least four months. There is no restriction on the maximum duration. However, the longest period for which state support is provided is ten months. Subsistence allowances must not be less than 65 per cent of previous gross earnings or 85 per cent of the legal minimum wage.

A worker can be made redundant in the course of a reconversion programme if he does not accept an offer of training or employment or if he is placed in a job. At the end of the reconversion period the employment contract is revoked. Employees are then entitled to redundancy pay equivalent to two months' wages; after this, full unemployment benefit can be claimed.

Various levels of government assistance are available for reconversion programmes. This assistance depends on the situation in the regional labour market as well as the involvement of the company in the reintegration of its employees. At most, the state pays half of the legal minimum subsistence allowance and half of the retraining costs.

On this basis, 1,185 reconversion agreements were concluded between 1985 and 1987, and 14,329 redundant workers embarked on reconversion programmes. This was equivalent to barely one-fifth of the workers made redundant by the companies in question. The rest preferred to take their redundancy pay and to look for a job on their own initiative. Statistical surveys also reveal the following trends [Marioni, 1987; 1988]:

- Of the 922 agreements concluded between 1985 and 1986, 117 were national agreements for larger companies with several establishments, which accounted for 50 per cent of the redundancies in signatory companies.

- Small firms with fewer than 50 employees account for about 86 per cent of all firms in France, but for only 25 per cent of signatories.

- Reconversion programmes are used mainly in the event of mass rather than individual redundancies. On average, 3.5 operational redundancies were announced per company, whereas the corresponding figure for companies signing agreements was 47.

- 62 per cent of the companies signing agreements were in the manufacturing sector. The service sector was significantly under-represented.

- 61.4 per cent of the individuals on reconversion programmes were manual workers and only 17.5 per cent were white-collar workers. The proportion of technicians and master craftsmen is surprisingly high at 15.1 per cent.

- The average length of reconversion programmes in 1984-1986 was six months, although the mean variation was very high. In around 11 per cent of firms the length of the programme exceeded ten months, while in 38 per cent it was four months, the legal minimum. In 1987, the average duration rose to seven months.

- In virtually all firms the subsistence allowance paid did not exceed the legal minimum.

- For the period 1984-1986, the state paid on average 33 per cent (35 per cent in 1987) of the cost of subsistence allowances and 28 per cent (32 per cent in 1987) of further training costs. However, there were wide variations in government support. It can be concluded from this that the level of subsidies was decided after examination of the particular circumstances pertaining in each individual case.

- By the end of 1987, 5,418 of the 14,329 individuals taking part in reconversion programmes (37.8 per cent) had been placed in employment,[65] although there were considerable variations from one regional labour market to another. The placement rate also depends on the active involvement of the companies, which have been only partially successful in developing their own reconversion structures.

It is evident from this analysis that the legal framework made reconversion programmes an acceptable means of managing job losses in the event of mass redundancies, although only for *workers in larger manufacturing firms*. And even such companies have made relatively little use of it compared with other instruments such as redundancy pay.

However, 55 per cent all operational redundancies in France occur in firms with fewer than 50 employees, and about half of all redundancies involve individuals or groups of up to 10 people. In these cases, there is not even provision for a social plan. In order to eliminate these gaps in dismissal protection, employers and unions, negotiating at central level, signed an intersectoral agreement in 1986 that extended the reconversion policy to small firms and individual redundancies. At the end of 1986 the French government supported the agreement with legislation [*Contrats de conversion*, 1987]. Reconversion programmes are now obligatory in the event of operational redundancies in the following instances:

- involving fewer than ten employees within a period of 30 days irrespective of size of firm;

- involving ten or more employees in firms with fewer than 50 employees and in firms in which the workforce has no representation.

They are optional for operational redundancies involving ten or more employees in firms employing at least 50 people and in which there is a works council. Thus reconversion is compulsory for all small-scale redundancies, in small firms and in firms without employee representation, but not in the event of mass dismissals in larger firms. The logic of these new regulations lies in the correction of the inequalities between employees in large firms, who are better protected in the event of mass redundancies because of the greater influence of trade unions and works councils, and those with less protection for whom optional arrangements would not be effective in the absence of a player capable of taking action.

---

[65] Since at the end of December 1987 there were still about 2,620 people on reconversion programmes, the placement rate quoted is not yet meaningful.

However, the obligations on firms are considerably reduced by the 1986 law. The state no longer has to authorise operational redundancies. This had long been demanded by the employers, who considered the government approval procedure to be an unacceptable restriction on their flexibility. The local employment service is now the agency responsible for reconversion programmes. The company pays to the local employment offices the two months' pay per employee that it would otherwise have had to pay out in redundancy money; small firms with fewer than ten employees pay a one-off sum of 4,000 FF into the reconversion fund, which, moreover, is credited against the further training levy.[66]

Employees made redundant are entitled to claim only if they are under 56 years of age and have worked for the same firm for two years. During the reconversion programme they receive 70 per cent of their gross income for a maximum of five months. However, if workers are simply dismissed they are not entitled to the two months' wages as redundancy pay, and unemployment benefit is paid for two months less if no claim is made for reconversion. The legal status of an individual on a reconversion programme is the same as that of participants in a government supported further training scheme.

In the middle of 1987 these regulations were further extended. Reconversion programmes are now compulsory for all operational redundancies arising out of bankruptcy or settlement proceedings [*Conventions de conversion*, 1987].

The 1985 Law on Conversion Leave is still in force. However, claims under the terms of the 1985 legislation on conversion leave and that of 1986 on conversion agreements cannot be made simultaneously. In qualitative terms, the agreements have become significantly more important than leave. In 1987, 12,012 agreements were signed (18,772 in 1988) and 11,846 employees (26,237 in 1988) were granted assistance. In 1988, 29.1 per cent of all employees made redundant by signatory firms, and 5 per cent of those made redundant throughout the country, took part in a reconversion scheme. Almost 50 per cent of all participants in schemes arranged under the provisions of the 1986 agreement come from firms with fewer than 50 employees; 45 per cent were from the service sector; 56 per cent are white-collar workers.

In France, therefore, there are two different legal frameworks governing reconversion programmes. The 1985 law is applied in the case of mass redundancies in large manufacturing firms, while the 1986 law is used primarily in small firms, in individual redundancies and also in the service sector or for white-collar workers. This expansion of reconversion policy into the small firm sector was possible only after considerable cutbacks. Firms were not placed under any obligation to organise reconversion programmes themselves. Reconversion is rather the state's responsibility - ties with the former employer are cut. The philosophy that originally underlay the reconversion programme has

---

[66] Every French company has to pay a further training levy of 1.1 per cent of its wages bill; this sum can be reclaimed if further training programmes are organised.

been reduced to a sort of improved placement service made available in the first few months following redundancy, the effects of which are alleviated by a new status that does not yet carry the stigma of unemployment. This status increases the chances of finding a new job, since it helps to differentiate between "innocent" (operational) and "guilty" redundancies, i.e. those arising out of individual failings or behaviour.[67]

For companies, the 1986 regulations entail less cost than redundancy, unlike the 1985 law. As in the event of an ordinary dismissal, the company has to pay two months' wages as severance pay to the state but, on the other hand, the employment contract is terminated more swiftly than is the case with redundancy. For the state, the programme is cost-neutral or even cheaper in the short term because the severance pay is refunded; in the long term, however, it becomes more expensive if a new job is not found. However, the state can recoup this additional expenditure by reducing the period of entitlement to unemployment benefit [Vernaz, 1987]. For redundant employees, reconversion programmes are financially less favourable than a normal dismissal if the average monthly subsistence allowance is used as a basis for comparison; however, individuals may well benefit from the special efforts made to find them alternative employment and from their new status.

2. Workforce restructuring and reconversion

The detailed structures of the implementation of legislation on reconversion (including a few cases of reconversion managed independently by companies) were examined in a total of 33 establishments owned by 25 companies [Ardenti and Vrain, 1988]. Even in these establishments, job losses were largely managed by traditional means. "Classic measures" such as redundancies and early retirement were used for 63.4 per cent of the jobs lost and 9.1 per cent were accounted for by internal transfers; 19.7 per cent of those affected found employment through various reconversion measures (help in setting up companies or in settling into a new company, further training, etc.) and 6.2 per cent were dismissed after completing a period of training leave.

Of greater interest than these average values, however, is the extraordinarily wide variation in the take-up rate for reconversion programmes, which ranged from 0 per cent of the potential beneficiaries to virtually 100 per cent. What are the causes of these huge differences between firms?

The process of shedding labour in the firms investigated had often begun many years earlier; most companies had given older employees early retirement, stopped recruiting skilled and semi-skilled workers and started to hire skilled workers only. The freeze on recruitment had, over a period of years, led to an unfavourable age structure among the least well-qualified members of the

---

[67] All investigations of plant closures and mass redundancies show that prejudice against re-employing those affected is less than in the case of single redundancies, since personal "blame" is more likely to be attached to individuals made redundant (see pp. 16-17).

workforce. Such an *adverse age pyramid* was not a sound basis for the succesful implementation of a reconversion programme.

The aim of the companies' personnel policy during the reconversion period was also to *restructure the skill profiles of their workforces*. The main objective was to dismiss less skilled employees. "Professional competence" was a much more important criterion in the selection of those to be dismissed than it had been in the past. The use of this criterion was not usually admitted openly in order to avoid conflict. The authors see in this a long-term trend towards a loosening of companies' ties with their core workforce and the encouragement of permanent exchanges with the external labour market. The reconversion programme, which has also been introduced by some firms on their own initiative, has served primarily as a means of intensifying external mobility while at the same time avoiding conflict [Ardenti and Vrain, 1988, p. 81].

However, most firms seem to have offered training leave only after the intervention of the public employment service, which for a long time has played an important role in France in the negotiating of social plans. On the one hand it has to authorise mass redundancies, while on the other it can make such authorisation dependent on certain measures, including early retirement and TCL, which it can also help to finance. All too often, reconversion programmes proposed by the employment service have been implemented without any great enthusiasm on the part of companies.

The amount of effort firms devoted to reconversion programmes depended particularly on the *skill levels of their workforces*. Reconversion programmes were aimed primarily at skilled employees who were more easily accommodated in the external labour market. Where there was a high proportion of unskilled workers, redundancy pay and early retirement schemes predominated. Foreign and female workers were particularly disadvantaged when it came to reconversion [Ardenti and Vrain, 1988, p. 160]. Indeed, they were virtually excluded from the programmes.

The differing situations in the local labour markets meant that the reconversion programmes produced very different results. In the Paris labour market, the specificity of which lies in high inter-firm mobility, placement in other firms, for example, with or without further training, was easier than in other labour markets. The worst results were seen in local labour markets dominated by one firm or industry and with above average unemployment rates.

Finally, the *industrial relations situation* both before and during reconversion was a decisive factor in the success of the programme. In firms where mass redundancies were bitterly contested, mutual suspicion often accumulated, creating a situation dominated by the "synergy of mistrust" [Ardenti and Vrain, 1988, p. 179]; trade unions and employees no longer took the reconversion programme seriously, seeing it rather as a particularly treacherous means of shedding labour. Reconversion was successful when firms showed that they were not going to take the easy option of simply revoking employment contracts and were not afraid of getting to grips with the problems posed by a difficult reconversion programme. The trade union reaction at the plant level was different from that at the national level. In several cases, local CGT branches co-operated in the implementation of TCL, in defiance of the negative attitude of their headquarters, although they often also opposed such schemes "for structural reasons", since it was the CGT which represented the unskilled workers, foreign and female workers who remained excluded from reconversion programmes. Assistance to those wishing to become self-employed and for the creation of new jobs in the region was given only by the *newly-created economic development companies* set up by a few large French companies. In this manner, these firms were able to find alternative employment for almost 20 per cent of their redundant workers.[68]

Finally, the successful implementation of reconversion programmes was dependent on the use of company resources. In the first place, the company had to be willing and able to deploy qualified personnel to oversee the programmes; in branch establishments in particular, where there was a high proportion of unskilled workers, such personnel were not available. It was necessary to have at least one supervisor for every 20 employees on reconversion programmes. External employment agencies usually achieved only "modest" results, since they were operating on a purely commercial basis and were interested only in quick success; consequently, they systematically ignored workers who were difficult to place (female workers, unskilled workers and foreign workers). It is true that, in conclusion, Ardenti and Vrain note the importance of *targeted vocational training* for a planned new occupation, but they also consider an excessively long period of vocational training to be an obstacle to a rapid and successful placement, particularly in the case of unskilled workers.

IV. The specific characteristics of French reconversion policy

Unlike in the Federal Republic of Germany, the initiative for the "social management of structural change" in France came from the government. *For the socialist government in France, reconversion was a necessary measure at a time of rapid structural change*, the pace of which had been forced by *a restrictive economic policy.*

With government assistance, large French companies have now set up regional economic development companies, which even operate outside the companies' immediate localities and in fields unconnected with the original

---

[68] The numbers of newly-created jobs published by the companies are not always reliable. For example, the companies included jobs that were to be created over a period of several years. In one case - probably the most quoted study on the reconversion programme at Creusot-Loire - a re-employment rate of 90 per cent was given [Deck, 1986]. However, this figure was based on the assumption that all employees claiming redundancy pay had found alternative employment. However, subsequent research revealed that 20 months after the closure 44.2 per cent of the Creusot-Loire employees were unemployed [Outin et al., 1988, p. 31].

reason for their establishment, namely the need of a particular company to shed labour. The intention clearly is to use them as the permanent infrastructure for the regional development of small and medium-sized firms. It is true that complaints are still being heard about the lack of professionalism of these organisations; however, this could be improved by ending their temporary status and introducing greater continuity.

The limitations of regional diversification policy can be seen most clearly in local labour market conditions. Local labour markets that are isolated and/or dominated by a single firm or industry and that have a low proportion of small and medium-sized firms operating independently of the shut-down firm constitute extremely difficult terrain for the entrepreneurial economic development companies. In such labour markets, any attempt to reindustrialise is sometimes abandoned completely, with a change of job being the only option offered to redundant workers [Bertherat, 1988, p. 72]. It often takes several years to create new jobs. The minimum period required for a successful start to regional diversification is often said to be two to three years. Thus the *time scale of regional diversification and that for the reconversion of redundant employees are not compatible*. However, the economic development companies, under pressure to justify their existence, often publish false figures that reflect long-term prospects rather than short-term successes.

The centrepiece of reconversion policy is training and conversion leave. Even this is often offered only under pressure from the local employment service. With assistance from the *Fonds National de l'Emploi*, the French employment service has been able not only to be very flexible in its dealings with firms but also to offer varying degrees of financial support, depending on the measures to be introduced. A lack of readiness on the part of the employment service to provide support does not appear to have been a problem in France. A greater obstacle was the traditionalist approach to personnel policy adopted by many firms, which all too frequently provoked bitter conflict through their policy of not providing adequate information about redundancies. The lack of unity among the trade unions - with most unions often simply acquiescing to firms' proposals and the CGT remaining unrepentantly hostile, frequently made TCL programmes very difficult to implement.

Attempts to put such programmes into practice came up against considerable *objective restrictions*, which lay particularly in the *occupational specialisation of workers* and in the *geographical division of labour practised by large firms*. Placement in new firms, whether with or without training leave, and help in setting up new companies were most successful in the case of well-qualified workers in large urban areas and most difficult in that of unskilled workers from firms in marginal regions. Unskilled workers, particularly those who were female, and foreign workers were virtually excluded from reconversion programmes. This reflects the trend towards a restructuring of the skill profiles of workforces, both in the firing as well as in the hiring firms, which was associated with a simultaneous intensification of discrimination against women and foreign workers.

However, given similar labour market situations and similar occupational profiles, reconversion programmes assisted a higher proportion of redundant workers to find alternative employment than was the case with traditional severance agreements.

In most cases, however, those made redundant - even those who benefited from a reconversion programme - had to accept wage cuts of between 15 and 25 per cent, since they transferred to more poorly paid sectors (services), types of firms (small and medium-sized firms) and employment forms (self-employment).

The original intention was to facilitate placement primarily through the provision of further vocational training. The main obstacle to placement was reckoned to be the redundant workers' lack of training. However, the implementation of reconversion in the steel industry and in other pioneering sectors led to fundamental changes in the philosophy underlying reconversion policy in France. Training as the route towards successful placement has clearly retreated into the background, and in the case of unskilled workers is even seen as an unhelpful waste of time. The main objective now is direct placement and preparation of employees for new working environments through a wide range of "training in flexibility" intended to cast doubt upon the classic expectations of core employees with respect to stability and wages. This was reflected in the revised version of the agreements in the steel industry and in the legal regulations, which both put the emphasis on short-term placement.

There were also solid financial reasons for this change of philosophy. The "costs per case" are reduced by short-term placement. Only after it had been slimmed down in this way could the reconversion programme be applied to small firms. The 1986 law also released firms from their obligation to set up organisational structures for putting reconversion into practice. Employees entering a period of training leave are even less well-off financially than if they had simply been made redundant. Nevertheless, *they do acquire a certain status, half-way between employment and unemployment, which can make placement easier.*

A political dynamic has arisen in France out of the *continuous intertwining of a progressive element of social policy with a strategy of flexibilising the standard employment relationship.* This political dynamic has to be understood against the background of the weakness and disunity of the French trade union movement, which has lost more members than virtually any other European trade union movement.[69] It proved itself unable to take up the government's initiative on reconversion policy at the firm level and to establish it firmly in its members' expectations as a precondition for further development of the concept. Indeed, reconversion policy actually exacerbated the disunity in the trade union movement. The terms of the debate on the prospects for reconversion have been determined largely by the government, firms and academics. The trade unions, in contrast, have tended either to accept it or reject it lock, stock and barrel, rather than attempting actively to influence policy.

---

[69] In 1970, 21.3 per cent of all workers were union members; by 1985 the figure had fallen to 14.5 per cent [Visser, 1990].

Chapter 6

Employment plans in practice

The starting point of this investigation was to ascertain whether external or internal job changes could be managed in a more socially acceptable way by means of employment plans than with the methods used hitherto (see pp. 11-13). It is hardly possible to offer a general answer, since the individual employment plans varied considerably in design and were implemented to differing extents, depending on the particular objective labour market situation of the affected workers and the behaviour of all the actors involved (management, works councils, trade unions, Federal Labour Office and workforces). Before we embark upon a provisional assessment of employment plans (see Chapter 7), these differences should be highlighted. Only in this way will it be possible to clarify the conditions under which employment plans can be a practicable and - depending on the observer's aims - desirable instrument of labour market policy for the future.

I. Training without diversification

According to the debate within the trade union movement, employment plans are actually intended to link training to diversification, as they do in Sweden. On completion of their retraining programme, those affected are supposed to transfer to a newly-created job, whether internal or external. However, this deliberate linking of retraining and diversification required considerable *government investment in regional restructuring programmes*, which were called for in the Federal Republic of Germany but never implemented [Löwe and Wand, 1987]. Companies trying to go it alone found diversification considerably more difficult. At Grundig and Krupp, joint committees were set up and given the task of producing proposals for *internal product diversification*. However, these plans for diversification never came anywhere near reaching fruition. Grundig and Krupp gave scant support to the work of these committees. Grundig vetoed the use of outside experts and failed to employ its own expertise (from R & D departments and head office) in support of the committee's work. It is quite obvious that both companies gave in to one of the demands made by the trade union in order to take some of the tension out of the negotiations and in the expectation that they would not subsequently have to stick to the agreements. As a result, trade unions and works councils were wasting their energies with their demands for product diversification. The company management teams were presumably hoping to neutralise the considerable explosive potential of such approaches (co-determination in product and investment decisions).

However, the practical difficulties of product diversification at the *company level* should not be overlooked. All the companies investigated were making efforts to extend their product ranges. In the light of contested markets, long lead times for product development, competitors' innovative capacities, the specialisation of firms linked together within a group and the many proposals for products that had already been rejected on the grounds that "they did not rate", the diversification of products that have already been developed at considerable cost is a perilous undertaking that cannot be implemented synchronistically with retraining programmes in any but the most exceptional cases.

This is all the more true of those companies that had got into a crisis because of past failures to modernise (e.g. Berthold and Präwema) or as a result of sectoral crises beyond their control (shipyards, steel firms). It is true that they began to modernise production, but at the same time it was clear that they would survive only if their workforces were considerably reduced.

The difficulty of planning for successful diversification or the expectation that the company would have to scale down its operations meant that most companies would not agree to the creation of new jobs,[70] which from their point of view could lead only to unrealistic illusions about the company's situation and to delays in shedding labour that would be damaging to the company as a whole. At the Sürken shipyard, the favourable economic situation and an extension of the product range did in fact lead *ex post* to the creation of new jobs within the company and to an unexpectedly successful linking of retraining and diversification. In most of the other companies, however, the economic situation started to look up just as the retraining programmes were coming to an end. This made it possible to implement *an internal structural change that would not have succeeded under different economic conditions.* Moreover, the improved economic situation increased the opportunities for inter-firm mobility. Particularly in regions with a favourable local labour market situation (e.g. Villingen-Schwenningen), many employees left jobs they considered to be at risk, thus creating more vacancies for those completing training courses than would have arisen from natural wastage alone. The employment plans actually left open all the options for reintegration of this kind, whether it was because employment contracts had not been terminated before retraining commenced (as at Blohm & Voss, for example) or because another test

---

[70] Only at Krupp Rheinhausen was a company agreement on the creation of replacement jobs signed; however, this could be attributed not to diversification within the existing company, but rather to the transfer of previously planned investment to different sites within the group. Nevertheless, this investment was based on past diversification within the group. In France, where the steel groups have remained pure steel companies, the planning of investment on a plant basis is simply not possible.

procedure was introduced after completion of the training programme, during which attempts are made to ascertain whether those affected cannot after all be reintegrated into the company.

Only at Thomson in Villingen-Schwenningen was an attempt at *external diversification* made, on the lines of the French examples. The "Industry and Technology Park Management Company" (ITM) was created, to act as a sort of private economic development company which was to encourage new firms to set up on the site of production units that had been closed down. The ITM managed to attract a number of company subsidiaries, thus stabilising the position of the Villingen-Schwenningen site within the group as a whole. And in future the ITM may take over some aspects of the local authority's industrial settlement policy. Against the background of comparable French experiences, it can be assumed that such diversification programmes need a starting-up period of two to three years. They may help *to create jobs in a region* that had previously suffered a bleeding of its resources as a result of the job losses, without the *the redundant workers* necessarily benefiting, since the creation of new jobs requires a considerably longer period of time than retraining courses. This means that, as a result of such external diversification, some sort of measures to cushion the blow of redundancy are far from being superfluous. "In practice, regional restructuring and the reorientation of former employees are *two entirely separate things*", remarked one interviewee.

II.   Training and waiting-loop models

During company negotiations and the subsequent implementation of agreements, there was a change of objective from diversification to retraining or even to a waiting loop. *In virtually every case, employment plans were pure training or waiting-loop agreements.* They were financed on the one hand out of firms' own resources and on the other by the Federal Labour Office; in several cases there were also additional subsidies from the *Land*. The interests of the firms influenced the model just as much as the institutional structures of the Federal Labour Office. Problems arose as a result of differences in concept between employment plans negotiated at firm level and the Employment Promotion Law. The aim of employment plans is the training of whole groups of employees threatened by redundancy; and although § 2 of the Employment Promotion Law does make reference to an abstract duty in the area of structural policy, the entire act is conceived around individuals who have to fulfil certain requirements in respect of insurance contributions and aptitude for training. And since, according to the Federal Labour Office's interpretation of the regulations, the retraining of employees is basically the responsibility of firms, employees can only be paid a subsistence allowance if their retraining serves a particular objective of labour market policy. Such an objective is deemed to be served if unskilled and semi-skilled workers are to be trained for a recognised vocational qualification, and if employees are threatened with unemployment, which training will help them to avoid.

These regulations produced two types of training plans. Unskilled and semi-skilled workers and those with a high risk of becoming and/or staying unemployed receive training. In the first model, their employment contract remains in force indefinitely (see Table 16). If they cannot then be offered employment, redundancies take place or a new group of employees are sent on retraining courses; a rotation strategy of this kind means that the time available for restructuring of the company is extended (Sürken shipyard). Those companies that implement the dismissal procedures they expect to be necessary before the retraining begins offer only a fixed-term employment contract during the re-training period (model 2). In both the first two models, retraining is the only alternative to redundancy. This means that a considerable *selection threshold* is built into the model. All employees who, for the widest possible range of reasons, cannot take part in a training programme, are forced to leave the firm. It is true that in most of the firms investigated this selection threshold was lowered as a result of negotiations over the group of eligible individuals, but it was not entirely eliminated. Both models are based on the assumption of *close co-operation between employment offices and companies*. Employment offices have to be prepared to train all eligible employees, even if it puts a considerable strain on their budgets, and to exploit the legal regulations to the full, parti-cularly when it comes to the definition of "threat of unemployment" (see Chapter 3). This co-operation worked in a number of cases. In most cases external political pressure was also necessary.[71] Most officials at the Federal Office regard the employment plans, which were initially agreed at firm level and only sub-sequently negotiated with the employment offices, as an unacceptable attack on their autonomy. On several occasions, there has been talk of "regaining our autonomy" after the conclusion of this first generation of employment plans. The implementation of the economy measures already decided upon at the Federal Labour Office[72] makes such autonomy necessary, because otherwise expendi-ture on training programmes cannot be controlled.

Because of the difficulties involved in co-operating with the employment office, several firms changed over to the *waiting-loop model* (see p. 43 and pp. 106-109). This shift relieved them of numerous obligations, from the need to clarify the legal position with the employment office to the organisation of training programmes. Four types of waiting-loop models emerged (see Table 16). There were waiting-loop models without any obligation to retrain (models

---

[71] As part of the shipyard programme, the Federal Government asked the Federal Labour Office to apply the Employment Promotion Law particularly in the shipbuilding industry. This political pressure helped to strengthen the willingness of employment offices to give preferential treatment to shipyard employees.

[72] The ninth amendment to the Labour Promotion Law, which came into force on 1.1.89, reduced the resources available for further training programmes from 6.37 billion DM to 5.76 billion DM.

3 and 4). Workers with widely differing training requirements and of different ages enter the waiting loop, where they may or may not begin a course of training, depending on their individual requirements. From the employers' point of view, these models are suited to the rapid implementation of mass redundancies and the weeding out of inefficient workers.

Table 16:   **Basic models of training plans**

Training of employees Employment contract suspended	**1** Indefinite employment contract *Example*: Blohm & Voss	**2** Fixed-term employment contract for duration of training *Example*: HDW-Ross
Waiting-loop model without commitment to training	**3** Agreement to re-employ *Example*: Krupp	**4** No agreement to re-employ *Example*: Saarstahl (but moral obligation to re-employ)
Waiting-loop model with commitment to training	**5** Agreement to re-employ *Example*: Klöckner-Becorit steel foundation	**6** No agreement to re-employ *Example*: Voest-Alpine steel
Employment company	**7** Training and employment company *Example*: Thomson (further training, short-time working, external and internal placement)	
Internal labour pool short-	**8** Personnel deployment departments in the steel industry on time basis *Example*: Hoesch (without training)	

When the waiting loops involve a commitment to training (models 5 and 6), the selection thresholds for re-entry into the company are significantly higher. Those affected must seek training for themselves (e.g. Klöckner-Becorit). Re-employment is offered only to those individuals who have successfully completed a training course. Here, too, attempts were made to filter out of the waiting loop any employees who would subsequently fail to cross the selection threshold. If such a model is used in the management of mass redundancies, the company is most definitely obliged to organise the corresponding training and counselling schemes. One of the major differences between the Saarland and Voest-Alpine steel foundations is the far greater resources made available by the Austrians for training and counselling. Depending on the company's objectives and the interpretation of the Employment Promotion Law by the local employment office, waiting-loop models could be designed with or without a binding promise to re-employ those allocated to the waiting loop. The emergence of models 3 and 4 in the Federal Republic of Germany (cf. Table 16) can be attributed wholly to the different interpretations of the law made by the employment offices in North Rhine-Westphalia and the Saarland. In the Saarland, the paying of unemployment benefit when a guarantee of re-employment had been given was held to be illegal.

A seventh model was developed at Thomson. By maintaining the old employment contracts, the company's training and employment company stabilised workers' links with their employer, while at the same time its institutional separation from the parent company made it easier both to establish training courses for those at risk of unemployment and to make applications for short-time benefit. With its own management, such a company is in a position both to organise the targeted placement of employees and to employ them by winning orders or loaning workers. This creates the opportunity to offer those affected a combination of training and job placements. However, the potential of such companies cannot be exploited if they have to accept the weakest employees who can be neither trained nor placed in alternative employment.

We did not investigate the internal labour pools set up in the steel industry. These were the so-called "personnel deployment departments" (model 8), most of whose members were older workers who could be transferred to other departments to cover in the event of temporary personnel shortages. For the most part, however, they had nothing to do and drew a maximum of 24 months' short-time allowance from the employment office until they were able to take early retirement; this benefit was topped up by the company to between 85 and 90 per cent of previous net income. These internal labour pools can be combined with training programmes. However, such schemes were developed only from mid-1990 onwards in the former German Democratic Republic. Unlike the West German programmes, they contained substantial amounts of retraining.

The models described here cannot be evaluated in the abstract; they emerged out of particular circumstances prevailing in companies and in the fields of politics and labour market policy. However, the following general points can be made:

(1) Because of its excessively restrictive interpretation of the "threat of unemployment", the Federal Labour Office allowed companies to change over to waiting-loop models of Type 3 and 4. Because of the payment of unemployment benefit to contributors, these models are hardly any more favourable in terms of costs than retraining models, and in terms of structural policy they are significantly less advantageous: they encourage firms to temporarily get rid of less efficient workers who are on the verge of early retirement rather than setting up training programmes that may also contribute to regional restructuring.

(2) All the models are compatible both with internal and external structural change, depending on whether they guarantee re-employment within the company or do not revoke the employment contract from the outset. Models 1, 3 and 5 are explicitly directed towards internal structural change in the workforce, while in models 2, 4 and 6 the contractual relationships are dissolved or weakened to an extent that almost channels employees towards external mobility,[73] although without entirely excluding re-employment within the firm.

---

[73] However, the Saarland steel foundation aims primarily at internal change. It was only because of intervention by the employment office that re-employment was not guaranteed.

(3) The fundamental condition for the functioning of all models proved to be the selection processes by which employees were selected for the programmes on offer and through which they might also be able to return to the company. These selection procedures are at least as important to the progress of the training programmes and the waiting period as the institutional frameworks that the models seem to provide. Models with tough selection criteria can cater only for a certain proportion of those made redundant.

III.   Company restructuring and participant selection

In all the firms there was an enormous contradiction between ambitious targets for the retraining and placement of "superfluous" workers and the firm's own concern to use the job losses to improve the structure of its workforce. This contradiction can only partially be resolved. It is scarcely conceivable, in a period of rapid technological and organisational change, that firms would seek to dispose of their best workers or loosen their ties with the company by offering them the opportunity to acquire marketable skills, simply because they can easily obtain alternative employment.

The chances of successfully surviving future competition also depend on having a highly skilled and efficient workforce. However, the legal requirement to carry out a selection process based on social criteria in the event of redundancies forces firms into making compromises with works councils; they are unable simply to select the best workers, since the selection process gives particular protection to older workers, those with long seniority and employees with dependent families. Company managements agreed to new models for managing redundancies only to the extent that they did not reduce the scope the previous legal situation offered them in the area of personnel selection, particularly if the retraining models introduced an additional, external negotiating partner, in the shape of the employment office, that interfered in personnel selection by deciding on suitability for training.

Because of concern for their companies' future success, works councils did not always insist on fully exploiting the legal opportunities available to them with respect to the selection process, preferring instead to seek a compromise between their concern to protect weaker workers on the one hand, and to keep the best workers in the company on the other. In the words of one works council member: "Nobody in the company would understand if we supported those whose efficiency has decreased at the expense of their workmates without understandable reasons such as illness or family problems".[74] In most firms, the

---

[74] It is known from earlier studies that the attitude of works councils depends very much on the reason for dismissal. Works councils often consent to dismissals for reasons of behaviour (such as a criminal offence or inexcused absence from work). It can be assumed that they are supported in this by the workforce and are even put under pressure to agree to the dismissal. Works councils are most likely to oppose dismissals on the grounds of illness or age-related

parties to the discussions were concerned not to allow the details of personnel selection to become public knowledge,[75] since such compromises between a selection process based on social criteria and the company's long-term interests always contain individual decisions that can be contested in court, particularly when the actual criteria on which decisions are made are negotiated in public. To that extent, the criteria for personnel selection in the event of redundancies remain somewhat opaque to empirical social research. It would be a mistake to assume that the publicly declared selection principles and procedures actually reflect reality.

Moreover, since it was only in individual cases that we obtained data on age structure, skill levels and state of health of the workforce as a whole and of those opting for the various alternatives (retraining, redundancy), our picture of the processes of personnel selection remains incomplete. And in the Federal Republic of Germany, unlike in France, there is also a lack of studies of workforce reductions that might throw more light on these selection processes. However, our case studies do provide a number of clues that indicate the widely differing ways in which the contradiction between selection procedures based on social criteria, "negative selection" and the determination of suitability for training by the employment office was dealt with. Four different types of procedures can be discerned; in some companies, more than one type was used, either concurrently for different groups of employees or in sequence.

(1) *Redundancy or retraining*: Some companies used training programmes as a way of getting round the social selection required in the event of redundancies. At Blohm & Voss, for example, a list of those to be made redundant was drawn up. Prior to any intervention by the works council or the employment office, those listed were given a choice between "training and redundancy", and some left the company - as management had expected and hoped they would. Under the same pressure, some employees chose training courses, so that motivation and thus the chances of the training programmes succeeding were correspondingly low. This pressure was alleviated to some extent by the intervention of the works councils and the employment office's assessment of suitability for training, and it also became clear that voluntary participation had to be encouraged. Management subsequently expressed the criticism that "it had been left with workers who could no longer be used". Grundig planned a similar approach after the conclusion of the first employment plan; the company had drawn up a "transfer list" of older and less skilled workers whom they intended to present with the choice between "training or redundancy". This was opposed

---

reductions in efficiency. It is considered that no blame can be attached to individuals in these circumstances, which are caused largely by the stresses and strains of work [Höland, 1983, p. 73].

[75] Personnel selection in France is very aptly described as a policy of the "unspoken comment" [Ardenti and Vrain, 1988, p. 61].

by the works council. Management subsequently lost interest in training programmes, and the 1985 employment plan was never implemented.

(2) *Improvement of workforce structure through early retirement and compromises in the selection of participants for training courses*: In most of the companies investigated, only a small proportion of the job losses were implemented through training programmes. Companies significantly improved the age structure of their workforces through early retirement, having already restructured them in favour of younger and more highly-skilled workers by halting the recruitment of unskilled and semi-skilled workers and taking on those who had successfully completed their apprenticeships. There must also have been other individual dismissals for personal or behaviour reasons, which increase when companies are in crisis, without companies making an explicit connection between these dismissals and the planned job reductions (see footnote 17, p. 24). It was precisely when the training programmes had ceased to be mass programmes that company management were prepared to compromise. In most of these companies, extensive discussions with works councils and employment offices removed much of the stigma of being a substitute for redundancy from further training and created the conditions for voluntary participation. At Klöckner-Becorit in Castrop-Rauxel and at the Sürken shipyard in Papenburg, ability to take part in training, for example, was a criterion for selection, with the upper age limit being set at about 40 years. In other firms, all training programmes were based on voluntary decisions (Grundig 1988/89).

(3) *Room for compromise increased by government financial support*: In cases where the company did not have to bear the costs of a social plan because of the availability of government funding for training programmes, it could attempt to use this financial assistance to improve the skill structure of its workforce and to prevent key workers from leaving by offering longer-term employment prospects. The selection of employees for dismissal, which might prove necessary at some point, could be postponed and possibly even avoided altogether. An example of this is the Sürken shipyard, where a training programme made it possible to dispense with an expensive round of redundancies and to build up a workforce that is now better qualified than before.

(4) *Reduction of opportunities for selection through unplanned labour turnover*: Because of the favourable situation in the external labour market and the general feeling of uncertainty created by job losses, employees, particularly skilled workers, left the firm. As a result, the firm was no longer in a position to choose its "élite workers" because of its bad image in the labour market and became more interested in keeping its employees and retraining them.

The selection process can be much more drastic in the waiting-loop models than in the training models, since firms no longer have to take account of suitability for training and the employment office does not act as a third partner in the process (see section II below). However, works councils will support such a model only if re-employment in the company is guaranteed and if social benefits are maintained should employees take early retirement or find employment in another firm. These conditions existed in the case of Saarstahl. In the then favourable economic situation, the company re-employed the mostly young workers who were not able to take early retirement during their time with the foundation; in re-hiring these former employees, the company applied lower standards than would have been the case if it had been hiring from the external labour market. Such waiting-loop models also existed within other companies. So-called "personal deployment departments" were set up in several steel firms; these departments accommodate workers made redundant by various partial closures and rationalisation measures who are on short-time or acting as a temporary reserve labour force until they can be transferred to other parts of the firm or take early retirement. And in Grundig's No. 11 Works there was a "parking lot" for a number of employees for whom retraining was out of the question and who were then distributed among various other plants. Some of these allegedly "weaker workers" settled very well into new departments. Clearly, they had either become outsiders in the rigidified social structures of their old workforces and were unable to develop until their social circumstances had changed, or the assessment of their abilities reflected the common prejudice of supervisory staff in favour of those who display subservience rather than independence. *Some of the alleged "improvements in the structure of the workforce" failed not only because of the unexpected departure of key workers, but also because the social structures that inhibit co-operation and productivity were not removed.*

IV. The limited input of resources by firms

In none of the investigated firms was an employment plan more costly than a traditional social plan. For some of the companies the employment plans were cost-neutral, while for others they were in fact less costly.

In the shipyards and at Saarstahl, subsistence allowances and unemployment benefit were topped up by the *Länder*. Saarstahl was spared the expense of a very costly social plan, and the Hamburg shipyards of Blohm & Voss and HDW Ross were also saved from paying out large sums of redundancy money, although in this latter case the savings were somewhat offset by the continued payment of holiday and Christmas money to employees on training courses.

Those firms that used their own resources to top up subsistence allowances or unemployment benefit took the amounts paid out into consideration when calculating the severance pay due when an employee left the firm. If the extra allowances paid exceeded the estimated severance pay due, the payments either ceased or were dropped (cf. Table 7), so that the "unit costs per job reduction" were only slightly higher than those incurred under a social plan. Only at Thomson was the deduction of the extra subsistence allowance from redundancy pay alleviated by the introduction of a hardship clause. In most cases, redundancy pay was not claimed because workers were re-employed soon after completion of their training course, so that the companies' costs were actually lower than if they had simply offered everybody redundancy pay. To that extent, a distinction has to be made between the *potential costs* of an employment plan (maximum use of subsistence allowance followed by payment of balance of redundancy pay on departure) and the *actual costs*. The full potential costs arise only in an extraordinarily blocked labour market. Only Thomson, on the basis of its French experiences, planned for greater labour market mobility, which would make it easier both to transfer workers from the training and employment company back into the company and to place employees in other companies after their training period. As a result, the company offered more generous subsistence allowances than other companies. This more generous financial assistance undoubtedly gave individual employees more security and time to plan their future employment, even though it was not used to the full because of the labour market mobility already mentioned.

Most of the companies do not seem to have fully realised, however, that the employment plans were cheaper, or at least no more expensive, than social plans: they tended rather to view them as a financial risk. Consequently, the companies made every effort to avoid committing any additional resources to employee counselling or the planning of training programmes. With the exceptions of Saarstahl, the Sürken shipyard, Ruhrkohle AG and Sietas, they did not take part in the development and implementation of training programmes, preferring to leave this task to works councils, trade unions and employment offices. The main reasons for this were the pressure to reduce the workforce as quickly as possible and the fear that comprehensive training programmes would waste time and be more costly. Furthermore, companies feared that their active participation would give employees the impression that they wanted them to return to the company. The involvement of the employment office necessarily meant that the search for new employment was directed towards the external labour market, and companies did not want this search to be reversed.

For the same reasons, the training courses took place for the most part outside the companies. This was intended to loosen employees' ties with the company and to accustom them to the idea of working elsewhere. An in-house training programme would only have endangered this process of individualisation. Moreover, the labour director at Blohm & Voss did not want any "underemployed workers on site who might stir up trouble". The works councils tried to make up for this lack of support from the companies by maintaining regular contacts with participants on external training courses. They took up their complaints, made preparations for their return to the firm, and so on.

Greater interest in the organisation of training programmes was shown by those companies that wanted to use the programmes to take up the slack in their underutilised training facilities (Saarstahl, Sürken shipyard, Ruhrkohle AG); they could only compete with other training agencies if the quality of their training provision was particularly high. Since steel and mining companies in particular are planning to maintain and market their training capacities in the long term, they played an active and decisive role in the implementation of the training measures agreed upon [Heimann, 1989], which had the effect of strengthening employees' ties with their companies. The commitment of some companies waned when it became clear that the Federal Labour Office would not support training programmes to the same extent as previously. This was clearly the case with the part-time training courses at Ruhrkohle-Bergbau.

Since re-employment in the company was a feature of virtually all the employment plans drawn up in the Federal Republic of Germany, any active participation by companies in the implementation of the plans threatened to strengthen employees' ties with their firms. If companies wished to support these ties, they co-operated with works councils and employment offices in the implementation of the employment plan (Sietas, Sürken, Saarstahl, Ruhrkohle AG). If their main aim was external change,[76] implementation was left solely or mostly to the works council (Klöckner-Becorit, Grundig, Blohm & Voss, HDW Ross) and sometimes failed because of a lack of support from management in dealing with the employment office (Berthold, Präwema). These companies lacked the courage and the ability to conceptualise in order to contribute to the determination of the external mobility process. Conservative and unimaginative short-term thinking predominated.

With the establishment of the training and employment company, the Thomson Foundation and the ITM management company, Thomson was the only company to create institutional structures to deal systematically with the placement of employees, even those seeking employment in other companies. This reflects a completely different company philosophy, in which the company, within the limitations of its budget, is responsible for both the fate of its employees in the labour market and for the development of the region in which its sites are located. West German companies do not for the most part accept such responsibility (see footnote 4, p. 5). Thus, their commitment to employment plans faces a twofold ideological barrier: they do not wish to co-operate in internal change, since they fear that staff reductions will be delayed, nor are they willing to commit themselves to a socially acceptable form of external change, since in their view this is exclusively a task for the government and other public bodies. Their approach to the implementation of the employment plans resembled that of the ostrich: sign agreements involving little financial risk and no legally enforceable obligations, and then bury your head in the sand.

---

[76] Resolving the problem by moving people out of the company.

V.   Social plans and employment plans

All the training plans were concluded on the same legal basis as social plans. All the agreements also contain the traditional provisions relating to redundancy payments, early retirement and transfers. These provisions informed the strategies of management as well as the attitudes of works councils and the decisions taken by individual employees. It is true that employment plans were conceived as a collective solution to the problems of groups threatened by unemployment. As we have seen, however, these groups were reduced by the employment offices to individuals with differing claims on the insurance system and aptitudes for training. The employment plans further extended individuals' scope for action, which was assessed and exploited in different ways by those involved.

In virtually all the firms, more people opted for redundancy pay and early retirement than for training courses. It was common practice for a whole group of employees (manual workers or white-collar workers up to middle management grades) to be given early retirement provided they had all reached the necessary age. A certain proportion of the job losses were effected in this way. The level of take-up for training courses was then determined by the decision of those remaining to accept redundancy pay or a place on a training course. Many people "voted with their feet" (i.e. they left the firm) against the new and untried training programmes. The following factors played a part in determining individual decisions:[77]

(1) *The atmosphere surrounding counselling and implementation*: There is no doubt that fear about job security was a decisive factor in the decision of many individuals to opt for training. However, this fear alone was not sufficient motivation. Decisions to undertake training have far-reaching consequences for the lives of individuals, particularly if the courses are to last a considerable length of time. Those embarking on such courses have to accept financial penalties and additional burdens in order to improve their position in the labour market in the medium term and possibly gain access to more satisfying jobs. Those employees who have no personal experience of training and who have little confidence in their own ability to successfully complete a course of retraining are unlikely to take such decisions without *good advice and persuasion from the works councils, the employment office and company management*. When these three parties jointly advocated training and also had sufficient time for counselling, and when employees were given sufficient time to make their decisions, a relatively high proportion of employees could be convinced of the benefit of training

---

[77] These are for the most part the factors described on pp. 30-37 as structuring the consequences of mass redundancies. However, our opportunities for analysis are limited, since we have not carried out follow-up studies on the careers of individual employees, whether they took training courses or not. The following statements should be taken as rough estimates based on discussions with experts.

courses. However, as soon as training programmes became a subject for dispute, employees received inadequate counselling and were also placed under pressure by the hectic pace of job losses, they were unable to develop any confidence in this alternative and so decided in favour of redundancy.

(2) *Financial incentives*: Since participation in a training course usually brought little, if any, financial benefit, many employees naturally wondered whether it would not be better to accept their redundancy pay immediately. Those who found a new job immediately were financially better off in the short term. In the long term, however, some of these people were to lose their jobs again, which made them realise that their employment situation had been destabilised. In the shipyards, on the other hand, subsistence allowances were topped up with government funds. Only those employees who opted for training courses were able to claim these extra payments without at the same time reducing their entitlement to redundancy pay. This favourable situation certainly contributed to the large numbers of shipyard employees who opted for training. In individual cases, the extra subsistence allowance offered by the company was so low (e.g. Klöckner-Becorit, where a maximum of 150 DM (approx. £55) per month was offered) that single wage-earners with families could not see how they could afford to go on a training course. In the waiting-loop models (Krupp, Saarstahl), those on training courses were not any better off financially than if they had been unemployed; since any training course requires additional expenditure,[78] they were even worse off. Consequently, many Saarstahl employees preferred just to twiddle their thumbs, and some even requested a transfer from training to the waiting loop.

(3) *The local industrial labour market*: Virtually all the employees (mainly manual workers) who found jobs in other firms, either voluntarily or because they declined an offer of training, moved within the manufacturing sector. In order to limit their pay cuts, most of them seem to have remained within that *segment of manufacturing firms that pay above standard rates*. So given the difference in wage rates between the various segments of the labour market, the criterion for their change of job was the external labour market situation in the more highly paid manufacturing segment of the labour market. A favourable local labour market situation in this segment made external mobility easier and gave younger and skilled workers in particular the opportunity to change jobs without having to take a large pay cut. A favourable labour market situation of this kind existed in Villingen-Schwenningen, where both the general rate of unemployment and that of individual occupational groups were below the Federal average. But *even in geographically concentrated labour markets with above-average unemploy-*

---

[78] Such expenditure can be incurred, for example, because there is less time during a training course for general household tasks and second jobs, so that trainees have to resort to buying goods and services in the market place (e.g. repairs and child care).

ment rates the supply of manufacturing jobs rose as a result of the economic upturn, at least in those regions not entirely dominated by declining industries. Thus in the Ruhr and in Hamburg, where the labour markets are not quite so dominated by a single industry, younger employees and skilled workers found jobs in other firms. The labour market in the Saarland, on the other hand, appeared to be blocked by the dominance of the crisis-hit steel and coalmining industries; moreover, the above-average wage rates at Saarstahl meant that virtually nobody considered transferring to a smaller firm with lower wage rates. In geographically isolated, dispersed labour markets with high regional unemployment rates, the external labour market offered little in the way of job mobility. In the two East Frisian shipyards virtually all the affected employees preferred training to a change of job.

(4) *Individual training needs*: One of the main arguments in favour of employment plans was the hypothesis that they would encourage participation in training courses by those workers who could not be reached in the anonymity of unemployment or who could not be motivated in the absence of a concrete prospect of employment. Since we do not have access to data on participant structure or to the results of surveys on the subjective views of participants, any statements we make must be treated with great caution.

The relatively high proportion of employees without any recognised vocational qualifications taking part in the training programmes offered by some companies (the East Frisian and Hamburg shipyards and Saarstahl) is an indication that employment plans can help to encourage unskilled and semi-skilled workers to stabilise their employment prospects by entering a vocational labour market. For virtually all of them, as well as for most of the skilled workers on further training courses, the decisive motive seems to have been the opportunity to stabilise their position within the company, now restructured in favour of a more highly-skilled workforce, while at the same time improving their chances of competing in the external labour market.

Most of those taking part in training courses were under 40 years of age. Older participants were mainly skilled workers seeking an additional qualification. Age, state of health and, in many cases, the ability to take stress (often determined by family circumstances) were the decisive entry thresholds, particularly for unskilled and semi-skilled workers whose last experience of education was usually their schooldays. "Further training is like going to the dentist's" said one works council member of that particular entry threshold. Only if the content of further training is linked to existing educational experience is it possible to motivate older workers (those aged between 40 and 45), unskilled and semi-skilled workers, foreign workers and women. At Grundig, preparatory courses created a certain degree of enthusiasm for training among unskilled and semi-skilled women which could be built upon in the implementation of the employment plan. In several other companies the entry threshold was lowered by special pre-training programmes. At the Jansen shipyard at Papenberg a pre-training course gave trainees an opportunity to become reaquainted with learning techniques. In Hamburg, the *Land* government provided additional funds to its economic action programme for the development of curricula for retraining foreign workers. In preparatory courses held at the Foundation for Vocational Training and Support for the Unemployed (*Stiftung Berufliche Bildung, Arbeitslosenwerk*), which lasted up to 11 months, language courses, general education components and preparation for vocational training were combined in such a way that even foreign workers with a very low level of educational qualifications were able to take part in training courses. However, the whole course ran for up to 35 months (11 months' preparation, 24 months retraining) and was open to only a small number of people because of the high costs involved.

These various subjective and objective influences could reinforce each other or work against each other. At the Sürken shipyard, for example, the poor situation in the local labour market, the co-operative climate in which the training was provided, the good counselling that was offered, the extra subsistence allowances paid by the *Land* and special pre-training courses had the effect of increasing participation. At Klöckner-Becorit, on the other hand, the improved labour market situation and the lack of financial incentives encouraged a surprisingly large number of workers to seek alternative employment, despite the good counselling that was offered. Because of the multiplicity of factors at work, *a low take-up rate for the new instruments contained in employment plans should not necessarily be taken to indicate failure.* It is not the aim of an employment plan to put a stop to all external mobility, which may be a precondition for a necessary structural change; rather their purpose is to soften the exigencies of the external labour market for those made redundant and to increase the options open to them. An extremely high take-up rate for training programmes also indicates a *blocking of structural change* caused by the underdevelopment of the regional economy, as in East Frisia, for example. All too frequently, however, inadequate implementation meant that *the potential of employment plans was not exploited.* In several cases (e.g. Klöckner-Becorit, Thomson), some of those affected have come to realise this: they opted to accept redundancy pay rather than retraining and are now unemployed.

VI. Employment plans for firms or regions?

Employment plans originally grew out of a concept that went beyond individual firms in an attempt to reduce overall unemployment and to restructure the firms and regions in question. As has already been made clear, this diversification hardly ever happened. Only Krupp Rheinhausen agreed to replace the jobs lost through the closure of its steelworks by investing in other Krupp subsidiaries. By setting up a regional industrial settlement company, Thomson made available the sites and resources required to attract new firms and by the end of this investigation had at least created a number of new jobs in the region by influencing company decisions on plant location. The restructuring plan drawn up by EWD in Villingen-Schwenningen helped *to strengthen and in certain respects improve regional economic development policy.*

In the other companies, employment plans did not help to create new jobs, but merely *redistributed employment opportunities* by setting up training programmes and not making redundant those workers who were unable to compete in the external labour market. This redistribution process is undoubtedly advantageous to the regions, since the labour market is not encumbered by the dismissal of poorly qualified workers who would have little chance of finding another job.[79] Sengenberger uses the term "social pollution" to describe such private strategies for transferring the cost of redundancies to the state [Sengenberger, 1989]. Thus, employment plans helped to prevent social pollution and to internalise the costs of structural change.

Regional skill profiles were also improved by the *contents of further training programmes.* Employment offices generally insisted that any skills acquired should be transferable to the external labour market. Consequently, training programmes had to lead not only to a generally recognised qualification but also to the acquisition of skills that could be used in other firms in the region. Retraining programmes concentrated on trades that are always in demand (fitter, electrician, lathe operator, etc.), while advanced training courses gave skilled workers the opportunity to fill the gaps in their knowledge of new technologies (CNC, pneumatics, hydraulics, data processing for clerical staff, etc.). Only in very few cases did employment offices sanction further training courses that were mainly firm- or sector-specific (welding courses in three shipyards, retraining in crafts specific to the iron and steel industry), because in these instances they assumed that the companies would survive; they also realised that theoretically less demanding courses that built upon existing knowledge would improve the skills of workers for whom other training courses would probably have been out of the question. It was precisely because it was by no means clear when the objectives of the training programmes were first drawn up whether future jobs would be located within or outside the firm, thus making it impossible, *a priori*, to link diversification and training, that *training programmes had to be flexible and open to future developments.* In training policy terms, the insistence on *generally recognised vocational qualifications* is the correct response to this uncertainty about the future. From the regional point of view, such a training strategy is preferable to purely firm-specific adjustment programmes, because on completion of their training programmes those involved are more mobile and not chained to the firm. Because of the type of training offered, training plans differ significantly from the usual firm-specific further training plans implemented without assistance from public funds.

---

[79] Because of the consequent long-term unemployment, social production of this kind gives rise to high costs for the unemployment insurance system. Furthermore, the inadequate supply of skilled labour gives rise to high adjustment costs for firms.

With their high training quotas, the above-mentioned steel and mining firms are making a particular contribution to the formation of a regional stock of skilled workers (see pp. 92-101). In a number of firms not included in our investigation (Krupp Rheinhausen, Thyssen Niederrhein, Thyssen Hattingen), management agreed, in connection with employment plans, to maintain their company's training capacities for the time being. To this end, new institutional structures were created for the training centres, in which municipal authorities, employment offices and other institutions are now represented, in addition to the firms. These training centres are to take over some of the responsibility for initial and further vocational training in the region [Heimann, 1989]. They will probably trigger off a debate on *further training requirements in the region* and possibly provide the impetus for more systematic planning of further training.[80]

In implementing employment plans, companies did not generally set up their own organisational structures that would have been available to the region for the management of possible future mass redundacies after the company had concluded its own restructuring. Only Thomson, with the establishment of its training and employment company, created a particular institution which can perhaps be taken over by the local authorities and other firms as a *regional reception company* for use in the management of personnel reductions. The Hamburg employment company Öko-Tech and the "Charitable Employment and Training Company" (*Gemeinnützige Gesellschaft für Beschäftigung und Qualifizierung*) set up by Saarstahl could also in the long term continue to exist as sources of job creation schemes and develop new job creation measures for the long-term unemployed (in areas such as environmental protection, conservation of monuments, etc.).

However, most employment plans were conceived only as *special measures implemented for a limited period of time in order to manage a clearly defined programme of personnel reductions*. They made it possible to reduce the "social pollution" caused by such job losses. However, their pioneering character will ensure that they leave their mark on the shaping of regional employment policy and may inspire other firms to imitate them. Only in very few cases will employment policy structures developed in connection with employment plans continue to exist.

VII. Employment plans and reconversion policy compared

German employment plans and French reconversion policy both developed for the same reasons: in both countries, personnel reductions in large firms in the sectors affected by structural crisis (coalmining, iron and steel, shipbuilding, consumer electronics, etc.) could no longer be managed with the

---

[80] An empirical investigation in two regions shows that at present there are virtually no indications of systematic planning of further training at regional level [cf. Bosch et al., 1987].

early retirement schemes and redundancy programmes that had predominated until the early 1980s. The older age groups had already been thinned out considerably by previous early retirement schemes and a further reduction of the age limit could not be contemplated for reasons of cost. The high unemployment rate reduced workers' willingness to quit their jobs voluntarily and accept redundancy pay. There was thus a prospect of classic redundancy programmes, which would be resisted in those firms where the trade unions were well organised (e.g. at Longwy in France and later at Krupp Rheinhausen in the Federal Republic).

However, the reaction to these problems and to the process of industrial restructuring is formed by the particular economic, political and institutional structures of the two countries, which differ considerably. The most important differences are outlined below:

(1) Reconversion has now become an established element of government economic and social policy in France. After the collapse of its expanionist policy of stimulating demand, the socialist government forced the pace of structural change in the economy and put forward its reconversion policy as a means of legitimising and softening the impact of this change of direction in economic policy. And after the nationalisation of the large companies, the French government possessed enough leverage to force companies to first accept and then implement the new measures. Thus reconversion was introduced *at the insistence of the government*; it was implemented initially through sectoral agreements in those sectors affected by crisis and then through *intersectoral agreements and legislation* in the economy as a whole.

In the Federal Republic, comparable government strategies existed only at *Land level*, and even there they were targeted at individual sectors or firms. The Federal Government's shipyard assistance programme was used by Hamburg and in part by Lower Saxony to finance retraining schemes. The Saarland set up the steel foundation in order to accelerate the pace of structural change in the Saar steel industry without, in the process, producing any further mass unemployment. The remaining employment plans were implemented solely at *firm level* by committed works council members and trade unionists. Only at Thomson did the initiative come from management, and in this case one that had already had experience of French reconversion policy. These decentralised initiatives did not form a basis for the extension of individual company agreements to cover whole sectors or regions.

In both countries, despite the differences that exist between them, the initial impetus for these approaches to labour market policy came not from the rather conservative managements of the companies themselves but rather from the state, the *Länder*, the unions or works councils.

(2) However, *financial incentives* were required before political influence could be exerted over firms. The combining of government resources made available as part of labour market policy with funds released by companies

for the implementation of social plans opened up attractive opportunities for companies to shape the restructuring process. In France, government support was easy to institutionalise. However, unemployment insurance, the employment service and an active labour market policy are kept strictly separate in institutional terms. The active labour market policy is financed directly from the government's budget; consequently, funds are not made available in accordance with the insurance principle but can be targeted as required by labour market or structural policy considerations. The financial assistance made available from the *Fonds National de l'Emploi* was negotiated directly with firms or, in the case of sectoral agreements, with representatives of both trade unions and employers in the sector. The fund can react flexibly to differing problems at both firm and sector level and can also, for example, financially reward a particular commitment made by firms. The external financial assistance available for reconversion in France was sufficient to avoid the creation of bottlenecks. Indeed, the government sought to make reconversion financially attractive and to secure its position as an element in company personnel policy.

The allocation of funds by the Federal Labour Office in the Federal Republic of Germany was based on the insurance principle; in other words, each individual case was taken on its merits. As a result there was not a great deal of scope for negotiations between firms and the Federal Labour Office. Furthermore, the federal authorities pursue a restrictive policy towards assisting employees, since they consider further training to be the responsibility of firms and not of employment policy. Thus it was difficult for the firms to get agreement on financial assistance from the Federal Labour Office; moreover, it was impossible to estimate the level of assistance since each individual case was examined on its own merits. This bureaucratic and financial bottleneck limited both the take-up rate for the training programmes on offer and the extension of employment plans to other firms.

(3) The different *labour market situation* in the two countries helped to determine the objectives of industrial restructuring within firms. Reconversion was aimed almost exclusively at *external mobility*, while employment plans were intended to assist both *internal* and *external* mobility; to a certain extent, the decision on this was left open until the end of the training period. This difference is linked to the fact that job losses in French manufacturing industry were much more drastic, particularly in the crisis-hit sectors.[81] The number of employees in manufacturing industry in France fell each year between 1977 and 1986 by 2.1 per cent (4.2 per cent in crisis-hit sectors) compared with 0.7 per cent in the Federal Republic of Germany (2.8 per cent in crisis-hit sectors) [OECD, 1989, p. 172]. In France it was reckoned there would be little chance of reintegrating those

---

[81] The sectors in crisis include those sectors in which employment has fallen by more than average since 1973 [OECD, 1989, p. 170].

affected into their firms. For this reason, most workers entering a reconversion programme severed permanently their ties with their former employer. And since the unemployment rate was significantly higher in France than in the Federal Republic of Germany[82] and the general employment trend, including the service sector, less favourable,[83] the circumstances in which reconversion, as a more global policy, was implemented were less auspicious than those in which employment plans were put into practice; almost all of these were concluded in firms in which they had a real chance of success.

In so far as employment plans in the Federal Republic of Germany furthered external mobility at all, this mobility took place for the most part *within industries*. Manufacturing is by far the largest sector in terms of numbers employed, accounting for 31.9 per cent of all jobs (1987). This is a higher proportion of the workforce than in any other OECD country. The corresponding figure for France was 22.1 per cent, with a sharply downward trend. External mobility was more strongly associated with a *pluralisation of subsequent careers* than in the German firms investigated. Not all employees were able to remain within manufacturing industry; some were forced into the artisanal or service sectors, a move which brought with it a change of status from permanent employment to self-employment or unstable employment. Because of the wage differentials between sectors, particularly for workers without qualifications who stand no chance of employment in well-paid service activities such as banking or insurance, the reductions in the working and living conditions of those made redundant in France were much more serious. After the closure of the steelworks in Pompey in France, for example, 14 per cent of those made redundant became self-employed, most of them reluctantly [Villeval, 1989]; after the closure of AG Weser in Bremen, only 1.2 per cent of the former employees went into self-employment [Gerdes et al., 1990]. This gave rise, understandably, to the completely divergent explicatory model. The German investigation merely skirts around the subject of structural change and focuses particularly on the effects of internal and occupational labour markets, while structural change is at the heart of the theoretical deliberations in the French study.

Considerably more resources were allocated to reconversion policy, in order at least partially to compensate for these disadvantages. Assistance was offered to those wishing to become self-employed, wage cuts caused by a change of firm were reduced over a lengthy period by compensatory payments and companies set up economic development companies in the places hit by crisis in order to create new jobs in the region. Despite the

---

[82] The standardised OECD unemployment rate was 10.3 per cent in France compared with 6.2 per cent in the Federal Republic of Germany.

[83] Between 1979 and 1986, the number of employees fell in France by 0.2 per cent per year; the corresponding figure for the Federal Republic was 0.1 per cent [OECD, 1989, p. 15].

greater commitment shown by firms in France, it was not sufficient to avoid a generally higher rate of unemployment following restructuring. In the Federal Republic of Germany, on the other hand, the recent favourable employment trend has tended to confirm companies in their faith in the market and their reservations towards an active structural policy, and has called a halt to debate on new responsibilities for firms in the shaping of regional structural change.

(4) In both countries, *vocational training was seen initially as the key to obtaining a new job*. Although it is very difficult to make quantitative comparisons, further training seems in practice to have played a less important role in reconversion policy than it did in the Federal Republic of Germany. In the majority of cases, the purpose of reconversion was to use a process of individualisation and dissolution of old collective ties in order psychologically to accustom displaced workers to new, less stable employment relationships and to worse or unfamiliar working and living conditions. Moreover, in comparison with the Federal Republic of Germany, occupational labour markets are less important in France than internal labour markets (see pp. 18-30). In 1982, for example, 29.8 per cent of employees in the Federal Republic of Germany had no vocational qualification, compared with 56 per cent in France in the same year.[84] In France, labour market opportunities are allocated mainly through internal labour markets. Seniority within the firm plays a significantly greater role in wage determination in France than in the Federal Republic of Germany [Sengenberger, 1987, p. 1985]; for these reasons, average seniority is longer and inter-firm mobility less highly developed than in the Federal Republic of Germany [ibid., p. 204]. In the case of an enforced change of firm, as is stated in labour market theory, employees in internal labour markets take greater wage cuts and lose more status than those in occupational labour markets (cf. Figure 1). When seniority is so decisive in determining access to sought-after, highly-paid jobs, as is the case in France, it makes good sense to give priority to rapid placement in employment over retraining, unless attempts are made, through an active retraining policy, to shift these labour market structures somewhat in favour of occupational labour markets.

In the Federal Republic of Germany, on the other hand, employment opportunities are allocated mainly through vocational training. The increasing competition in the labour market brought about by high unemployment has tended to further strengthen employees' vocational orientation. This rise in the importance of occupational labour markets is strongly reinforced by the high geographical density of the labour market in the Federal Republic of Germany, which, on the one hand, encourages employees with vocational qualifications to be highly mobile and, on the other, gives firms the opportunity to adopt employment structures that

---

[84] The figures are taken from French and German census data.

reflect vocational qualifications. In the Federal Republic of Germany, a larger population than that of France is distributed over a territory of less than half the area. Only the Paris labour market, which is not typical of the country as a whole, can be compared in density to that of the Federal Republic of Germany (the Ile de France has 822 inhabitants per km^2, cf. Table 17).[85] Empirical studies also confirm that reconversion is more likely to be successful in Paris than in other regions of France [Ardenti and Vrain, 1988, p. 168]. In a geographically dense labour market, each individual can reckon on a certain degree of fluctuation which may give him an opportunity of finding a vacancy, particularly if he has improved his chances by completing a course of retraining.

(5) *Trade unions* in the two countries have played very different roles in company restructuring. Employment plans were developed in the 1970s in response to trade union demands. The conclusion of the first plans was widely regarded as a major success for the unions. As a result, works councils and trade unions have tried to bring their idea to fruition by participating actively in the implementation of the agreements. In those sectors where IG Metall represents workers' interests, a demand for employment or training plans is now a fixed item in the list of union claims submitted whenever large-scale redundancies are announced. Until unification, however, German trade unions had not had to face the challenge of helping to implement employment plans aimed primarily at external mobility in such unfavourable labour market conditions as those in France. There is considerable potential here for conflict within the trade unions.

In France, on the other hand, reconversion policy was developed by the socialist government as an explicit alternative to a policy based on the expansion of demand and a reduction in working hours. The CGT did not accept this policy change and saw reconversion merely as a transitional stage leading to unemployment. There were also structural reasons for the CGT's negative attitude. The crisis-hit sectors form the union's organisational base, and it stood to lose a great deal of influence as a consequence of the job losses; moreover, its membership in these sectors is made up of workers who would scarcely benefit from a successfully implemented reconversion policy (unskilled and foreign workers). The CFDT participated actively in reconversion policy at central level. Its members, mainly skilled workers and management personnel, benefited from reconversion. At company level, however, the CFDT acting alone was too weak even to keep track of the measures taken, let alone have a hand in shaping policy. The split between the unions and their inability to participate in the management of reconversion meant that firms were able to seize the initiative when it came to implementation, and that the government was able to do the same with

---

[85] The only available basis for comparison is relatively large geographical entities (such as Federal *Länder*). Differential analysis would show that France actually has other geographically dense labour markets, such as those around Lyons, Marseilles and Bordeaux.

Table 17: Regional unemployment and labour market density in the Federal Republic of Germany and France

Federal Republic of Germany

Region	Population in 1,000[1]	Population per km²	Unemployment rate[2]
Schleswig-Holstein	2 614	166	7.1
Hamburg	1 592	2 109	10.4
Lower Saxony	7 216	152	7.8
Bremen	666	1 649	11.4
North Rhine-Westphalia	16 704	490	8.0
Hessen	5 535	262	4.7
Rheinland Pfalz	3 624	183	5.6
Baden-Württemberg	9 241	258	3.5
Bavaria	10 958	155	4.4
Saarland	1 051	409	10.0
West Berlin	1 849	3 852	7.9
Total	**61 049**	**246**	**6.2**

France

Region	Population in 1,000[1]	Population per km²	Unemployment rate[2]
Nord-Pas-de-Calais	3 934	317	14.2
Normandy-Picardy	4 817	98	11.7
Ile-de-France	10 206	850	8.7
West	7 328	86	11.0
Central	5 226	55	10.5
East	5 000	104	9.5
Auvergne-Limousin	2 072	48	10.0
Southwest	5 053	58	10.7
Rhône-Alpes	5 124	177	8.6
Mediterranean	6 018	102	13.1
Corsica	247	28	12.2
Total	**55 062**	**101**	**10.5**

Notes: [1] 1985 figures.

[2] Average for 1987. Standardised rates of unemployment were used, which compare the number of unemployed to all those in employment rather than to persons in dependent employment.

Source: OECD, *Employment Outlook 1989*, Paris, pp. 115 ff.

respect to policy formulation. The German trade unions, on the other hand, were able to use their unified and relatively strong organisational structures at company level to play a fairly decisive role in the implementation of employment plans and to develop and put into practice their own initiatives.

(6) Reconversion policy in France was subject to a considerable *dynamic of political development*. It was initially a substitute for an expansionist economic policy; consequently, it was rooted in the large-firm sectors, was renewed there under worsening conditions and finally extended, under even worse conditions, to the economy as a whole. Its enshrinement in law was accompanied by the introduction of new, lower standards, making it necessary to adapt, step by step, the pioneering arrangements introduced in the steel and shipbuilding industries. Reconversion is one element in the policy of flexibilising employment relationships, which, in contrast to a policy of pure deregulation, not only cuts the provisions of social plans and rights to protection against dismissal, but at the same time creates new safeguards for employees made redundant and converts passive labour market instruments, such as unemployment benefit and redundancy pay, at least partially into active instruments, such as funding for training programmes and placement services.

A corresponding dynamic of development is not yet discernible in the Federal Republic of Germany. The Federal Government has made some small adjustments to the provisions of social plans, without offering anything to replace them with, as has been the case in France. On the other hand, employment plans did enable the trade unions, particularly in large firms, to extend the provisions of social plans and the social protection available to employees affected by redundancy programmes. Some *Länder* with a Social Democrat government are considering implementing a more systematic training policy as a means of managing structural change. At the moment, the Federal Government's policy on the deregulation of social plans, the *Länder's* more active structural policy and the trade unions' strategies for the development of employment plans are disconnected and conflicting. When the next large-scale redundancy programme is announced, these strategies will enter a collision course. Depending on political circumstances, matters could develop in accordance with one of several possible scenarios (see pp. 168-170).

Chapter 7

A provisional assessment

I.   Labour market policy: the untapped potential

Has the enormous amount of energy expended on employment and training plans been worthwhile, and should this strategy be pursued further when other sectors are hit by crisis? Answers to this question will certainly vary considerably, depending on initial expectations of what was to be gained from the plans and attitudes to labour market policy. However, since many of the employment plans have not yet been fully implemented, and many of them were purely experimental in nature and, moreover, their long-term consequences cannot yet be predicted because of the short period of time that has elapsed since the signing of the first plans, therefore it is not possible to deliver anything more than a provisional judgement. It is felt that an apparently more definitive verdict would serve only to hinder future development. It is the purpose of this study to avoid such hindrance and to stimulate further debate on the role of employment plans.

For those who hoped that employment plans would contribute to the rapid creation of new jobs in the region, as was the case during the restructuring of the Swedish shipbuilding industry, the interim results will be disappointing. The failure of the companies in question to diversify can be attributed on the one hand to the practical difficulties of such diversification at firm level and on the other to the failure of structural policy to provide any additional assistance. Blame for this latter failing should be attributed not to the employment plans themselves but rather to the political framework within which they were drawn up. *In practice, employment plans became primarily in-firm training plans.* Consequently, they can only be assessed as such, although this should not necessarily lead to the complete abandonment of more ambitious structural policy objectives.

In my view, the consequences of employment plans are largely positive, although even this assessment is not entirely free of reservations. The ambivalence arises out of the not easily reconcilable contradiction between the employers' aim of getting rid of less skilled, less efficient workers and the labour market policy objective of enhancing the employment opportunities of workers threatened by unemployment by offering them high-quality training courses. This contradiction has been partially resolved by the granting of additional state support for further training programmes and the modification of firms' selection procedures by works councils, but nevertheless continues to affect each firm.

One of the positive achievements of employment plans has been the avoidance of mass redundancies. The immediate pressure to dismiss workers was reduced by the training programmes. The time thus gained made it possible for many of the retrained workers to return to their firms, where their newly-acquired skills helped to stabilise their position. Furthermore, their additional vocational training has significantly enhanced their chances of external mobility in the future. Just as in France, the chances in the Federal Republic of Germany of becoming unemployed after claiming redundancy pay were considerably higher than after a change of employer on completion of a training course. The individual route to the labour market, which may initially appear lucrative because of the large amounts of redundancy pay on offer, is thus significantly riskier than the one linked with the guarantees offered by employment plans or reconversion programmes. This experience confirms the actions of all those trade unionists who committed themselves to the implementation of employment plans and calls into question those strategies that, out of mistrust of management or disappointment at the inadequate level of support from government structural policy, advised employees against participation in training courses, as the CGT did in France.

Firms were obliged to show greater commitment to internal structural change and to refrain from substituting employees in a way that merely places strain on the labour market. This made it possible to protect groups of employees (unskilled and semi-skilled workers, older people and women) who may well have become long-term unemployed if left to the vagaries of the external labour market. They were protected directly, by participating in further training courses and thus gaining access to occupational labour markets, and indirectly, by other workers being trained in their place. In individual cases, employment plans led to a development of planning for further training and the creation of new employment policy institutions for the region (such as the employment companies).

Employment plans are an instrument for the development of internal labour markets. However, since an employee's long-term future in a firm is uncertain, the additional protection is based on strengthening an individual's ability to compete in occupational labour markets, resulting in a strengthening of occupational labour markets.

One of the negative consequences of employment plans was that in a few cases unsuitable or inadequately prepared workers were faced with a choice between training or redundancy and forced out of the firm. In these cases, the legal requirement for a selection process based on social considerations was circumvented. In several firms, the training programmes offered were inadequately tailored to the particular training requirements of unskilled and semi-skilled workers; there was a lack of preparatory and motivating courses, with the result that the entry thresholds remained high. Furthermore, it is obvious that in many cases the hectic pace of personnel reductions left little time for employees to receive proper counselling; the resultant atmosphere of mistrust encouraged them to act rashly and accept redundancy pay. Those who subsequently became unemployed or found themselves in unstable jobs regretted that they had not accepted the opportunities offered by employment plans. In a few cases, the time constraint and hectic pace were deliberate ploys, introduced to accelerate the departure of certain workers from the firm. Firms did not wish to give employees the impression that they were interested in continuing to employ them. Finally, the Federal Labour Office proved to be something of an obstacle: on the one hand, its frequently mean-spirited interpretation of the law hindered the implementation of training programmes, while on the other it was restricted in the support it could give employees by the Employment Promotion Law, which is based on the insurance principle and thus oriented towards individual workers.

However, it should not be forgotten that our predominantly positive assessment is being made against the background of recent favourable economic trends in the Federal Republic of Germany, which facilitated the reintegration of employees and made it possible in most cases to avoid external mobility or, if it did become necessary, to ensure that it took place in favourable labour market conditions. Moreover, virtually no employment plans were concluded in firms in which the chances of success were limited, such as, for example, in firms with a high proportion of women or foreign workers among those threatened by unemployment.[86] Attempts at implementing reconversion programmes were made in such firms in France, and these had a negative effect on the outcome of the policy as a whole.

In short, the *potential of employment plans remains untapped*. Co-operation between works councils, trade unions, management and labour market policy-makers would undoubtedly have allowed more employees threatened by unemployment to retrain and remain with their employers. However, it is uncertain whether all parties are interested in such co-operation and whether it is possible to create the conditions that are required for such co-operation to be feasible in future. In any event, the political influence of the trade unions and of committed politicians has hitherto led only to the conclusion of single-firm agreements and not to a more widespread adoption of the concept of employment plans.

---

[86] In firms employing a high proportion of female and foreign workers, the chances of success are low, for a variety of reasons. Even after completing vocational training courses, both groups of employees come up against discrimination in the labour market, which cannot be eliminated through training strategies alone. Moreover, women are generally less flexible than men, in terms of both mobility and working hours, and are thus dependent on a structural policy that places greater emphasis on linking diversification and retraining (see pp. 18-30).

II.   Four scenarios for future development

Unlike reconversion policy in France, employment plans are by no means firmly established as an instrument of labour market policy and continue to attract controversy.

The *trade unions'* assessment of the experience of employment plans is largely positive, despite the disappointment at the failure of structural policy to provide adequate support. In addition to the direct consequences for labour market policy, the political consequences will also be examined here. Employment plans have given workforces and trade unions a goal for political activity in crisis situations of a structural nature. The political process they have set in motion is considered to be one of the most important factors in making clear the need for further initiatives in both labour market and structural policy. Without the disputes at Rheinhausen and Hattingen, for example, there would have been no round of talks on the coal and steel industries. Furthermore, the right of works councils to express their opinion on further training programmes was strengthened; this has dealt with one of the trade unions' future problems, since the growing importance of further training had not until this point been accompanied by any significant role for the unions in shaping the training programmes.

In virtually all large-scale redundancy programmes in the sectors covered by IG Metall, employment plans are now on the union's list of demands, and this demand is already on the way to becoming firmly established in the trade union agenda. However, the debate on employment plans has hitherto been restricted exclusively to the sectors covered by IG Metall and has not yet reached other trade unions. Even within IG Metall, attempts at drawing up or implementing employment plans have occasionally broken down because of the traditionalism of some trade unionists and works councils, who see redundancy payments as providing solid financial advantages for employees and mistrust long-term personnel strategies whose outcome is initially unclear. In many firms, the policy of trade unions and works councils is still too directed towards short-time financial gains for them ever to initiate long-term personnel strategies.

The majority of *employers* see employment plans as a restriction of their freedom to manage, an unacceptable extension of rights of codetermination and a means of postponing necessary personnel reductions and of building up new, long-term and costly regional responsiblities for firms. Their willingness to top up redundancy payments, in order to buy off those employees interested in the "new" ideas, seem to be greater than their courage in implementing new personnel policies. This conservatism also reflects their ideological inability to manage the implementation of employment plans, either on the organisational or conceptual levels. Only a handful of personnel managers in the Federal Republic of Germany seems to possess the skills that this task would require. The harshly critical attitude of the metal industry employers towards the training and employment company set up by Thomson (see pp. 83-92) leads one to fear that this negative attitude will even become enshrined in the programmes of employers' associations, and that this will happen more quickly if IG Metall includes employment plans in its own programme. A more flexible, but obviously minority school of thought within firms is more receptive to the notion of employment plans; it realises that it will be more difficult in the 1990s to manage personnel reductions by means of early retirement schemes and that it will be possible, in co-operation with trade unions and works councils and with financial support provided by labour market policy, to open up opportunities for introducing less confrontational and more socially acceptable personnel strategies, which need not be more costly than traditional social plans.

The assessment of the effect of the state will lie somewhere between those of the trade unions and employers, depending on their political complexion. However, it has become clear that government has room for manoeuvre. Indeed, *it alone is in a position, through political pressure and financial incentives, to resolve stalemates and help employment plans become firmly established*. If it opts to take this course, it will be able to count on the support of trade unions, works councils and workforces; under certain circumstances, even firms are ready to co-operate. Thus it is entirely possible that a future government will take up some of the ideas contained in employment plans, such as the training components or the employment companies for older and unskilled workers, and encourage their implementation in certain sectors or regions in order to render structural change more acceptable and to lessen the disadvantage of inadequately qualified groups of workers.

Against this background, the following scenarios can be sketched out for the years to come:

(1) *The conservative market model*: The conservative tendency in the employers' camp incorporates opposition to employment plans into its programme and thus blocks any initiatives taken by more progressive member companies. The Federal Government cuts the provisions of social plans and the resources to support training programmes (a measure currently under consideration). Companies use their new freedom to manage redundancy programmes to introduce a harsher, less costly selection process; the consequences of this "social pollution" will not be absorbed by labour market policy, with the result that the strengthening of market forces leads to an increase in long-term unemployment and intensifies the disputes surrounding personnel reductions.

(2) *The status quo model*: The conservatives do not succeed politically in extensively deregulating protection against dismissal, just as the trade unions fail to push through new training or structural programmes. Employment plans continue to be negotiated individually and at the firm level and implemented more or less successfully, depending on conditions within the company and the region. The present unequal treatment of employees threatened by unemployment in large firms with employment plans and in small firms without such plans persists.

(3) *The redistribution model*: As in France, attempts are made to increase firms' responsibility for structural change, and particularly to develop training

programmes in the event of involuntary changes of job. However, in order not to place any additional financial burdens on companies, this is to take place without extra expenditure. Firms' new responsiblities can be made more acceptable by redistributing the resources available for social plans in order to provide support for hard-to-place workers and through targeted government assistance.

(4) *The progressive model*: The current regulations governing social plans and dismissals are basically maintained, although the conversion of lump-sum financial entitlements (e.g. redundancy pay) into active protective measures (training programmes, etc.) is made easier. Through the use of additional labour market and structural policy resources and instruments, employment plans are applied more generally and extended to small and medium-sized firms (see section IV below).

III. The philosophy of employment plans: the need for elaboration

In a critical assessment of employment plans, Olaf Sund (president of the Employment Office in North Rhine-Westphalia) has correctly pointed out that the debate on employment plans conducted within firms frequently "has more static elements (new jobs for the *same* workers, at the *same* site, on the *same* terms) than is consistent with the dynamic, one might almost say the arbitrariness of economic development... Mobility, even if it is involuntary, is an element in economic structural change which must be speeded up, particularly in the regions hit by crisis. Consequently, the general aim cannot be to protect employees threatened by redundancy from re-orientation with respect to their employer, their job, their place of work, etc." [Sund, 1989, p. 54]. Sund's polemical conclusion is: "Not training instead of redundancy, but rather training and then redundancy". The legitimate core of this overstated conclusion lies in the reference to the possible need for external mobility, which is undoubtedly also a consequence of company restructuring and must be taken into account in labour market and employment policy.

Thus, the philosophy of employment plans must be considered from the point of view of *a more dynamic approach to labour markets* than has been the case hitherto. This becomes all the more necessary the greater the attempt to extend the basic philosophy of employment plans to small and medium-sized firms, which because of their size offer few opportunities for purely internal mobility. The philosophy is also in need of further elaboration in the following respects:

(1) Employment plans were called for as an alternative to social plans, in the hope that pure social policy measures could be converted into elements of structural policy. Experience to date shows that this is probably an illusion. Not all employees threatened by redundancy can be retrained or transferred

to other jobs. *Social policy cannot be turned entirely into structural policy,* unless certain less mobile groups are excluded and inalienable minimum safeguards are taken away from others. Thus social plans and classic social policy measures are still a justified and necessary means of managing personnel reductions. *Social plans and employment plans complement each other,* and only by being used in concert can they cover the wide range of problem situations that arise within labour market policy and avoid creating new difficulties.

(2) The content and chronology of *diversification and retraining* can be synchronised only if assistance can be given through government structural policy, as in Sweden, for the creation of new jobs either at the time of the dismissals or on completion of the training programmes. Such demonstrations of the power of structural policy have not been forthcoming in the Federal Republic of Germany in recent years. At most, *a smooth transition* to a new job is offered, through targeted public or private investment, to a proportion of those made redundant. The rest are left, on their own or with the limited protection provided by social policy, to find a new job *in the labour market,* where they may or may not benefit from the new jobs created by government economic development programmes. This reveals more clearly the *autonomous nature of the various spheres of action in the field of labour market policy.* Since the employment prospects of those affected remain uncertain, which is not the case with planned company restructurings, retraining should not be closely linked to specific production processes or products, because this would merely narrow the range of options open to each individual. With the establishment of broad basic occupations, vocational training policy has in part provided a properly institutionalised answer to this problem.

(3) Not everyone will take part in training programmes, and for those who have completed courses there will be periods of waiting that will have to be bridged if they are not to lose the protection afforded by employment plans. To deal with this, *the stock of labour policy concepts will have to be extended,* otherwise passive waiting-loop models will inevitably come into use. On the one hand, sensible employment opportunities should be created. For example, further consideration could be given to the notion of using employment and training companies to form regional labour pools which would represent a socially acceptable form of temporary work and help to reduce overtime in the region. On the other, the policy of providing support for those seeking employment, which predominates in France, remains largely undebated; this could also be one of the functions of such training and employment companies.

(4) If the *potential* of employment plans is to be better exploited than hitherto, there must be financial incentives to participate in training programmes and better social protection, particularly for employees threatened by unemployment, which could be provided by redistributing the resources

available for social and employment plans. The growing inequality of oppportunity in the labour market between the trained and the untrained means that *equal levels of redundancy pay contrast with increasingly unequal destinies in the labour market.* It is precisely unskilled and semi-skilled workers who most need financial incentives to participate in further training, in order to reduce the growing deterioration of their position in the labour market. The subsistence allowances paid during further training must be raised relative to unemployment benefit, and this is largely a task for labour market policy. But a contribution towards this objective can also be made at the firm level. The financial rewards for participation in a training programme should be greater than those for "waiting"; some of the funds available for social plans could be reserved for the provision of special assistance for unskilled and semi-skilled workers and those who are difficult to place in employment.[87]

IV. The need for initiatives in both labour market and structural policy

Active support for employment plans will also make it easier for labour market policy to fulfil the objectives laid down in para. 2 of the Employment Promotion Law (see Chapter 3). It will help to prevent long-term unemployment and increase the chance of success in the labour market for those employees without any or with outdated vocational qualifications; it will also improve the structure of regional labour markets. Labour market policy can also promote further training within firms, so that firms are encouraged, over and above the immediate requirement of the redundancy programme, to invest more in their employees. Finally, employment plans could help to make more effective use of the resources available for labour market policy, since government funds and private social fund resources would be combined and additional non-material resources mobilised. One of the most important of these resources is the commitment of works councils and possibly also of personnel departments to motivating and counselling employees, developing training programmes suitable for those employees and monitoring the implementation of those programmes.

---

[87] A special social plan fund could be set up to provide financial assistance for pre-training courses for unskilled and semi-skilled workers. The training and employment company set up at Thomson provides a model for the redistribution of redundancy pay that is worth discussing. In the case of those workers who can be offered an acceptable new job by the company, the extra subsistence allowances they received during their training period are offset against any redundancy pay they may receive. Workers made redundant without being offered a job receive their full redundancy pay, even after two years of extra subsistence allowances. However, this aspect of redistribution is undoubtedly an explosive issue for trade unions and works councils. Redundancy pay is popular precisely because of inequalities in the labour market. Many employees prefer redundancy schemes, because they expect to find a new job quickly.

With their limited staffing, employment offices are not in a position to devote so much attention to individual cases.

It is our central conclusion that labour market policy should seize these opportunities and play the role of an active and well-informed midwife in the processes of restructuring taking place at the firm, regional and sectoral levels, instead of reluctantly supporting external initiatives.

At the same time, however, this investigation has undermined our optimism that the Federal Labour Office itself will be able to fulfil this active role in the foreseeable future. Because of its commitment to a narrow interpretation of the insurance principle, conceptualising in terms of structural policy is completely alien to it. The predominant viewpoint within the administration is based on the assumption that the Office does not have any responsibility for structural policy; in consequence, its potential for intervention in labour market policy is deliberately restricted. *Initiatives for the further development of labour market policy must come therefore from outside the Federal Labour Office and be formulated in the political arena.* The task of future political and academic debate should be to develop and define appropriate models for further discussion along the following lines:

(1) The *Employment Promotion Law could be opened up*, making possible a broader interpretation of the threat of unemployment. As with short-time work allowances, which in the crisis-hit steel industry can be retained for up to three years, jobs could be declared at risk for a given period of time in a particular sector, region (e.g. one with above-average unemployment) or type of firm (firms making workers redundant for operational reasons) and support for a restructuring phase extended accordingly.

(2) Those responsible for labour market policy could draw up a *special programme of training courses* (possibly limited to a specified period of time) in regions or sectors hit by crisis, which would be financed by the Federal government and freed from the constraining legal framework of the Employment Promotion Law. In this way, as with the special labour market programme of 1979, training programmes with an entitlement to higher subsistence allowances than those provided for by the Employment Promotion Act could be financed.[88]

(3) A *flexible, easy-to-manage restructuring fund* could be established. Firms in which social plans are agreed because of imminent job losses would be able to apply for government subsidies provided they use their social plan resources, or a part of them at least, for active labour market measures, having first obtained the agreement of works council to do so. A fund of this kind could be used to finance vocational training courses, particularly

---

[88] On the experiences with the special labour market programme [cf. Bosch et al., 1984]. The error in the design of this programme was that high wage cost subsidies (80 per cent of the wage) were used to support exclusively in-firm training programmes, the quality of which was not adequately verified.

general educational courses for unskilled and semi-skilled workers, employment companies for older workers, some of the employment companies' permanent workforce, and so on; and in addition to specific measures, the fund could also finance more experimental projects. Increased government subsidies could be made available if the company, the municipal authorities or the governments of the *Länder* agree to participate or to increase their commitment, in order to produce diversity of funding and synergy effects.

(4) All the measures listed so far tend to favour employees in large firms. There seem to be two possible routes *for extending these innovations to small and medium-sized firms*, which can be combined with each other:

(a)   Each employee made redundant for operational reasons who has no vocational qualification or one not suited to the new occupational images would receive a legal entitlement to retraining. Older and hard-to-place workers (e.g. those to whom no reasonable job offer could be made within a given period of time) would be entitled to a place on a job creation scheme;

(b)   When making employees redundant, companies must - as in France - help those dismissed either to obtain a new job or, in collaboration with the employment office, offer them retraining or a place in a local employment company (perhaps as part of a job creation scheme). Local authorities could set up reception companies for redundant workers which could help small and medium-sized firms to develop their placement and training services (e.g. regionalised Thomson model). In sectors with high mobility and a fluctuating workforce, firms themselves could also set up such labour pools (e.g. in the building industry) and use them when necessary instead of loan workers and overtime. These measures could be financed partly out of social plan resources and partly from government funds. As with employment plans, participants could contribute a proportion of their redundancy pay.

All these models for further discussion could be organised quite differently from both the legal and financial point of view and could be linked to each other. Thus, for example, the opening up of the Employment Promotion Law could be combined with a special labour market programme, which would top up the resources available under the Employment Promotion Law. Models 3 and 4 would undoubtedly provide the most flexible solutions. They would make it possible to use public funds for measures other than training, which excludes a certain proportion of employees. At the same time, financial incentives could be offered to firms, local authorities and *Länder* in return for their increased involvement, which would be one way of preventing firms withdrawing from their social plan obligations through increased use of government funds.

Figure 10: Employment companies

Employment levels of steel workers affected by reductions in
production capacity and whose contract of employment remains in force

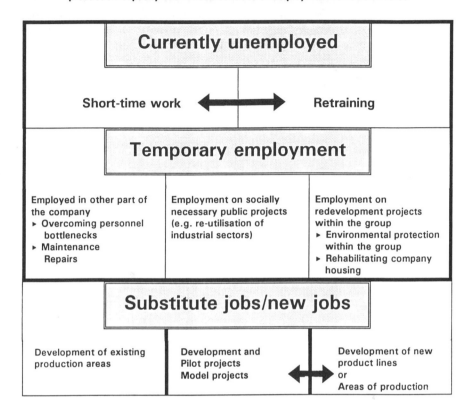

Source: IG Metall, 1989.

However, such initiatives derived exclusively from the sphere of labour market policy merely redistribute employment opportunities in favour of redundant employees who are disadvantaged in the labour market. The number of jobs in the region is, as a result, increased only temporarily (e.g. through the establishment of employment companies implementing job creation schemes). In order to avoid shifting the burden of job losses on to the next generation or other hard-to-place workers, additional structural policy measures designed to create new jobs in the region are needed to deal with mass redundancies and closures in firms of importantance to the region. The Hamburg Economic Action Programme (see pp. 61-71), which included an attempt to link labour market policy and regional structural policy, could be further developed. Thus schemes for reclaiming areas of disused land could combine job creation and training programmes with other appropriate public tasks. These possiblities could be extended further through the establishment of regional employment companies that had their own management and were thus in a position to make active contributions in the areas of labour market and structural policy. The limits of such links lie in the fact that labour market and regional structural policy cannot be completely synchronised. *Labour market policy provides immediate assistance for the protection of workers in the event of mass redundancies, whereas regional structural policy can usually only stimulate the creation of new jobs in the medium term*, thus providing assistance to a largely different group of individuals. However, some of these gaps can be bridged. The employment companies proposed by IG Metall (cf. Figure 10) are the most concrete idea for such a bridge put forward so far, the design of which needs further refinement [cf. IG Metall, 1989].

Bibliography

Aaron, B. 1964. *Plant closings: American and comparative perspectives*, Los Angeles, University of California Reprint No. 328.

Aballea, F. et al. 1988. *Le reclassement des ouvriers de la téléphonie dans le Trégor, Recherche méthodologique sur l'évaluation*, Commissariat Général du Plan.

Adamy, W.; Bosch, G. 1989. "Arbeitsmarkt", in Kittner, M. (ed.): *Gewerkschaftsjahrbuch 1988*, Cologne, Bund-Verlag.

---. 1989: "Arbeitsmarkt", in Kittner, M. (ed.): *Gewerkschaftsjahrbuch 1989*, Cologne, Bund-Verlag.

Agence Nationale pour l'Emploi. 1988. *Etude sur les plans sociaux des entreprises en restructuration et les congés de conversion: Etude d'une population de licenciés économiques*, Paris, Direction des Etudes et des Statistiques.

Aiken, M. et al. 1968. *Economic failure, alienation and extremism*, Ann Arbor, University of Michigan Press.

Anderson, M. et al. 1979. *Regional employment and economic effects of a Chrysler shutdown - Preliminary data and analysis*, Cambridge, Mass., U.S. Department of Transportation.

Arbeitsmarktanalyse. 1988. *Arbeitsmarktanalyse 1988 anhand ausgewählter Bestands- und Bewegungsdaten*, Nuremberg, Bundesanstalt für Arbeit.

Ardenti, R.; Vrain, P. 1988. *Les restructurations dans les grandes entreprises: Politiques de recomposition de main-d'oeuvre et plans sociaux d'accompagnement des suppressions d'emplois*, Paris, Centre d'Etudes de l'Emploi.

Atkinson, J. 1986. "Employment flexibility and internal and external labour markets", in *Neue Arbeits- und Tätigkeitsformen*, Dublin, Europäische Stiftung zur Verbesserung der Lebens- und Arbeitsbedingungen.

Autorengemeinschaft. 1977. *Sozialplanpolitik in der Eisen- und Stahlindustrie Köln*.

Bäcker, G.; Steffen, J. 1988. *Altessicherung der Zukunft*, Hamburg, VSA-Verlag.

Bandemer, J.D. v.; Ilgen, A.P. 1963. *Probleme des Steinkohlenbergbaus*, Basel, Xyklos; Tübingen, Mohr.

Bellet, M.; Boureille, B. 1986. *Pôle de conversion: Outil de restructuration du marché du travail? L'exemple de Loire-Sud*, 6e Journée de l'Association d'Economie Sociale, Lille, 25/26.9.1986.

Belleville, P. 1988. "...et les friches sociales?", in *Economie et humanisme*, No. 304, November-December, Paris.

Berglind, H. 1988. "Happy losers? A study of laid-off metalworkers and the Swedish Welfare System", in *ALC*, Stockholm.

Bergner, S. 1987. *Fortbilden statt entlassen*, Interim Report, Freie und Hansestadt Hamburg, Behörde für Schule und Berufsbildung, Amt für Berufs- und Weiterbildung.

---. 1988. Working paper for the meeting of the advisory council of the Hans-Böckler Stiftung on the project "Qualifizieren statt Entlassen", Hamburg (manuscript).

Bernaud, I. et al. 1988. "Peugeot-Sochaux: une mutation rapide", in *Economie et Humanisme*, No. 304, November-December, Paris.

Bertherat, J. 1988. "Saint-Gobain, la reconversion industrielle et le développement local: Entretien avec J. Bertherat", in *Economie et Humanisme*, No. 304, November-December, Paris.

Berufsbildungsbericht. 1988, Bonn, Bundesminister für Bildung und Wissenschaft, Bonn.

Beschäftigungsrückgang. 1985. Personalpolitische Beurteilung von Maßnahmen und Mittel zur Anpassung an Beschäftigungsschwankungen, Teil I: Beschäftigungsrückgang, Studien zur Mitbestimmungstheorie und Mitbestimmungspraxis, Arbeitsgemeinschaft "Engere Mitarbeiter der Arbeitsdirektoren Eisen- und Stahl" in der Hans-Böckler-Stiftung Nr. 13, Düsseldorf.

Bilan Lorrain de trois années de conversion, 1987, Nancy, Cabinet du Préfet délégué.

Bluestone, B.; Harrison, B. 1982. *The deindustrialisation of America*, New York, Basic Books.

Böhle, F.; Lutz, B. 1974. "Rationalisierungsschutzabkommen - Wirksamkeit und Probleme", in *Bd. 18 der Schriftenreihe der Kommission für wirtschaftlichen und sozialen Wandel*, Göttingen.

Bosch, G. 1978a. *Arbeitsplatzverlust. Die sozialen Folgen einer Betriebstillegung*, Frankfurt/New York, Campus-Verlag.

---. 1978b. "Soziale Probleme bei einer Betriebs- stillegung", in *WSI-Mitteilungen 4.*

---. 1985a. "West Germany", in Cross, M. (ed.): *Managing workforce reductions. An international survey*, London & Sydney, Croom Helm.

---. 1985b."Betriebliche Initiativen zur Sicherung der Beschäftigung - Chancen für neue Produkte?", in WSI and DGB, *Regionale Beschäftigungspolitik und gewerkschaftliche Interessenvertretung.* Düsseldorf, WSI and DGB experts' meeting.

---. 1987. "Qualifizierungsoffensive und regionale Weiterbildungsplanung", in *WSI-Mitteilungen 10.*

---. 1989. "Qualifizieren statt Entlassen: Ergebnisse eines empirischen Forschungsprojektes", in *Soziale Sicherheit*, No. 2.

Bosch, G.; Seifert, H. 1984. "Das geplante Beschäftigungsförderungsgesetz - ein arbeitsmarkt-politisches Notstandsgesetz", in *WSI-Mitteilungen 10.*

Bosch, G. et al., 1974. *Bedingungen und soziale Folgen von Betrienstillegungen*, Dortmund, Interim Report.

---. 1984. *Arbeitsmarktpolitik und gewerkschaftliche Interessenvertretung*, Cologne, Bund-Verlag.

---. 1987. *Beschäftigungspolitik in der Region*, Cologne, Bund-Verlag.

Brun, F.; Brygoo, A. 1987. *Etude sur les congés de conversion à la NORMED*, Centre d'études de l'emploi, Paris, ANPE.

Büchtemann, Ch. 1985. Infratest Sozialforschung (1983). *Die Bewältigung von Arbeitslosigkeit im zeitlichen Verlauf. Repräsentative Längsschnittuntersuchung bei Arbeitslosen und Beschäftigten 1978-1982*, Research Report Vol. 85, Bonn, Bundesminister für Arbeit und Sozialordnung.

Bulletin de Liaison CGT d'Usinor-Sacilor, 1987, No. 2, No. 4, No. 14.

Burdillat, M. 1987. *La reconversion des salariés - Eléments exploratoires*, Paris, Groupement d'intérêt public "Mutations Industrielles".

Casey, B. 1984. "Teilzeitarbeit nach der Lehre - ein neues Arbeitsmarktphänomen?", in *MittAB*, No. 3.

Chaskiel, P.; Villeval, M.C. 1988. *Pompey. Crise/Fermeture/Reconversion*, Nancy, Presses Universitaires de Nancy.

Chauchard, J.L. 1985. *Restructuration et plan social*, Paris, Les éditions d'organisation.

Chérèque, J. 1988. "L'Etat-partenaire: Entretien avec J. Chérèque", in *Economie et Humanisme*, No. 304, November-December, Paris.

Christensen, J.F. 1988. "Transforming industrial destruction into industrial renewal - the case of Elsinore", in Roskilde University Centre, Grenoble Social Sciences University: *Industrial flexibility and work. French and Danish perspectives*, Paris.

Congés de Conversion. 1985. "Conventions d'allocations spéciales du Fonds national de l'emploi (FNE)", in *Liaisons Sociales*, No. 5696, 11.9.1985.

Contrats de Conversion. 1987. "Régime d'assurance-conversion et adaptation de l'assurance-chômage", in *Liaisons Sociales*, No. 5900, 28.1.1987.

Conventions de Conversion. 1987. "Entreprises en redressement ou liquidations judiciaires", in *Liaisons Sociales*, No. 5989, 13.8.1987.

Convention Générale de Protection Sociale dans la Sidérurgie. 1984. in *Liaisons Sociales*, No. 5522, 9.8.1984.

County Employment Board. 1987. *The Uddevalla shipyard. Labour market policy programmes*, Gothenburg (manuscript).

Cramer, U. 1987. "Klein- und Mittelbetriebe: Hoffnungsträger der Beschäftigungspolitik", in *MittAB*, No. 1.

DA A FuU. 1987. *Durchführungsanweisungen zur Anordnung über die individuelle Förderung der beruflichen Fortbildung und Umschulung*, Nuremberg, Bundesanstalt für Arbeit.

Dahremöller, A. 1987. "Existenzgründungsstatistik", in *Schriften zur Mittelstandsforschung*, No. 18 NF, Stuttgart.

Deck, J.P. 1986. *La reconversion c'est possible*, Toulouse, Ed. Erés.

Dedering, H. et al. 1970. *Die Mobilität von Arbeitnehmern bei Betriebsstillegungen*, 3 vols., Frankfurt, Zentrum für arbeits- und sozialwissenschaftliches Untersuchungen.

Deeke, A. 1983. "'Arbeitskräftepool' - ein Modell beschäftigungssichernder Bewältigung des technischen Wandels?", in *KVR/ITZ, Strukturanalyse Ruhrgebiet. Bilanz-Kritik-Perspektiven*, Proceedings of a joint KVR/ITZ event held on 23/24.3.1983 in Gelsenkirchen.

Dobischat, R.; Neumann, G. 1987. "Betriebliche Weiterbildung und staatliche Qualifizierungs-offensive - Qualifizierungsstrategien zwischen privatwirtschaftlicher Modernisierung und staatlichem Krisenmanagement", in *WSI-Mitteilungen 10*.

Dolleschka, B. et al. 1988. *Die Stahlstiftung. Eine Idee wird Wirklichkeit*, Linz, Voest-Alpine, Stahlstiftung zur Förderung der beruflichen Wiedereingliedrung.

Dombois, R. et al. 1982. "Vom Heuern und Feuern zur stabilen Mindestbelegschaft. Drei Jahrzente betriebliche Beschäftigungspolitik eines Schiffbauunternehmens", in *Mehrwert, Beiträge zur Kritik der politischen Ökonomie*, Vol. 23, Berlin.

Dragendorf, R. et al. 1988. *Beschäftigungsförderung durch Flexibilisierung. Dynamik befristeter Beschäftigungsverhältnisse in der Bundesrepublik Deutschlands*, Frankfurt/New York, Campus-Verlag.

Drewes, C. et al. 1982. *Vorstudie Arbeitskräfte-Pool*. Endbericht zur sozialwissenschaftlichen Begleitsforschung, Göttingen.

Eberwein, W.; Tholen, J. 1987. *Borgwards Fall. Arbeit im Wirtschaftswunde Borgward Goliath Lloyd*, Bremen, Steintor-Verlag.

Edin, P.A. 1988. *Individual consequences of plant closures*, Thesis, University of Uppsala, Stockholm, Lamquist & Wiksell.

Ehrmann, A. et al. 1988. *Folgenwirkungen von Betriebsstillegungen am Beispiel des AEG-Werkes "Brunnenstraße" in Berlin-West*, Working papers published by the Arbeitskreis Sozialwissenschaftliche Arbeitsmarktforschung (SAMF 1988-1), Paderborn.

Falke, J. 1983. "Kündigungspraxis und Kündigungsschutz", in Ellermann-Witt et al. (eds.): *Kündigungspraxis und Kündigungsschutz und Probleme der Arbeitsgerichtsbarkeit*, Opladen, Westdeutscher-Verlag.

Falke, J. et al. 1981. *Kündigungspraxis und Kündigungsschutz in der Bundesrepublik Deutschland*, An empirical investigation carried out by the Max-Planck-Institut für ausländisches und internationales Privatrecht, Hamburg, Vols. 1 and 2, published by the Bundesminister für Arbeit und Sozialordnung, Bonn.

Flaim, P.O.; Seghal, E. 1985. "Displaced Workers of 1979-83: How well have they fared?", in *Monthly Labour Review*, No. 108, pp. 3-16.

Förderung der beruflichen Weiterbildung. 1988. *Ergebnisse der Teilnehmerstatistik über berufliche Fortbildung, Umschulung und Einarbeitung im Jahr 1987 und im 1. Halbjahr 1988*, Nuremberg, Bundesanstalt für Arbeit.

Garnier, B. 1986/87. *Atouts et limites d'une politique de reclassement: Les congés de conversion - le cas de trois entreprises de la région nazarienne*, Dissertation, University of Nantes.

Gerdes, J. et al. 1987. *Folgewirkung einer Betriebsstillegung: Mobilitätsprozesse auf dem lokales Arbeitsmarkt*, Bremen, Universität, Zentrale Wissenschaftliche Einrichtung "Arbeit und Betrieb".

---. 1990. *Betriebsstillegung und Arbeitsmarkt. Die Folgewirkungen der Schließung der AG "Weser"*, Bremen, Edition Temmen.

Gesamtsozialplan. 1968. "Gesamtsozialplan über die öffentlichen und betrieblichen Leistungen und Vorsorgemaßnahmen für die von Stillegungen betroffenen Arbeitnehmer des Steinkohlenbergbaus von 15", in *Bundesanzeiger*, No. 94.

GEWOS/GfAH/WSI. 1988. *Strukturwandel und Beschäftigungsperspektiven der Metallindustrie an der Ruhr*, Hamburg, GEWOS Institut für Stadt-, Regional- und Wohnforschung.

Glücklich, F. 1988. "Kapitulation vor der Dauerarbeitslosigkeit - Welchen Weg nimmt die Bundesrepublik?", Stiftung berufliche Bildung, Arbeitslosenbildungswerk, Hamburg.

Gonäs, L. 1989. *Labour market adjustments to structural change in Sweden*, Stockholm, Arbeitslivscentrum.

Gottsleben, V. 1987. "Randgruppen in der zertifizierten Arbeitsgesellschaft? Zur abnehmenden Bedeutung der nicht formal Qualifizierten am Arbeitsmarkt", in *MittAB*, Vol. 1.

Hamburg Aktionsprogramm Wirtschaft. 1986. *Bürgerschaft der Freien und Hansestadt Hamburg*, circular 12/137, 30.12.1986.

Hansen, G.B. 1988. "Layoffs, plant closings and worker displacement in America: A serious problem in need of a national solution", in *ALC*, Stockholm.

Harris, C.C.; Candee, S. 1984. "The magnitude of job loss from plant closings and the generation of replacement jobs: Some recent evidence", in *The Annals of the American Academy of Politic and Social Science*, Vol. 475, Philadelphia.

Harris, C.C. et al. 1984. "Redundancy in steel: labour-market behaviour, local social networks and domestic organisation", in Roberts, B. et al. (eds.): *New approaches to economic life*, Manchester University Press, pp. 154-166.

Hase, D. et al. 1988. *Die Praxis von Interessenausgleichen und Sozialplänen in der Bundesrepublik - eine empirische Analyse*, Berlin, Forschungs- und Beratungsstelle für betriebliche Arbeitnehmerfragen.

Heimann, K. 1989. "Perspektiven des Ausbaus der Ausbildungsstätten der Stahlindustrie zu regionalen Bildungszentren", in *WSI-Mitteilungen 4*.

Hemmer, E. 1988. *Sozialplanpraxis in der Bundesrepublik. Eine empirische Untersuchung*, Cologne, Deutsches Instituts Verlag.

Herron, F. 1975. *Labour market in crisis*, London, Macmillan.

Heseler, H. 1987. *Europäische Schiffsbaukrise und lokale Arbeitsmärkte. Eine Untersuchung über die Folgen von Betriebsschließungen in Schweden, der Bundesrepublik Deutschland und Dänemark*, Universität Bremen, Forschungstransferstelle des Kooperationsbereich Universität/Arbeiterkammer.

---. 1989. "Gegen den Trend. Arbeitsmarkt- und Strukturpolitik in Schweden", in *WSI-Mitteilungen 4*.

Heseler, H.; Roth, B. 1988. "Die Auswirkungen der AG 'Weser'-Schließung auf dem Bremer Arbeitsmarkt", in *Individuelle und sozialstrukturelle Folgen der Massenarbeitslosigkeit*, Arbeitskreis sozialwissenschaftliche Arbeitsmarktforschung, Arbeitspapier 1/1988, Paderborn.

Hillen, K.B. 1971. *Arbeitnehmer nach einem Arbeitsplatzverlust*, Opladen, Westdeutscher Verlag.

Höland, A. 1983. "Das Verhalten von Betriebsräten in der Kündigungssituation", in Ellermann-Witt et al. (eds.): *Kündigungspraxis und Kündigungsschutz und Probleme der Arbeitsgerichtsbarkeit*, Opladen, Westdeutscher Verlag.

IAB. 1986. Kurzbericht, 29.9.1986, Nuremberg.

IG Bergbau und Energie. 1988. *Sondertarifvertrag über Teilzeitarbeit von Berufsanfängern im Anschluß an die Ausbildung bei der Ruhrkohle AG.*

IG Metall. 1984. *Unterhaltungselektronik, Arbeitsplätze wie Schnee im Sommer*, Frankfurt/M.

---. 1986. *Zum weiteren Vorgehen bei Grundig in bezug auf die Umsetzung des Beschäftigungsplanes*, IG Metall discussion paper, Nuremberg.

---. 1987. *Beschäftigung sichern und neue Arbeitsplätze schaffen. Eine Rahmenkonzeption für eine Beschäftigungs- gesellschaft Stahl*, Frankfurt/M.

---. 1989. *Strukturpolitische Alternativen zur gesellschaftlichen Arbeitslosigkeit. Programmatischer Rahmen und praktische Ansätze, Ein strukturpolitisches Memorandum der Industriegewerkschaft Metall.*

Industrialisation Usinor Sacilor. 1988. Paris.

Iversen, L. 1987. "Some health effects of the closure of a Danish shipyard. A three year follow-up study" in Pedersen, P.S. (ed.): *Unemployment theory, policy and structure*, Berlin/New York, de Gruyter-Verlag.

JHK des Saarlandes. 1982. *Saarhütten in der Neuordnung*, Special publication by "Saarwirtschaft 1982", Saarbrücken, Industrie- und Handelskammer.

Jones; Mackay. 1987. *Redundancy and redeployment*, University of North Wales (manuscript).

Judith, R. et al. 1980. *Die Krise der Stahlindustrie - Krise einer Region. Das Beispiel Saar*, Cologne, Bung-Verlag.

Jürgenhake, U. et al. 1988. *Fallstudie "Saarstahl/Völklingen"*, Dortmund, Sozialforschungsstelle.

Jürgens, U. et al. 1989. *Moderne Zeiten in der Automobilfabrik. Strategien der Produktionsmodernisierung im Länder- und Konzernvergleich*, Berlin, Springer-Verlag.

Kahn, H. 1962. *Repercussions of redundancy*, London, Allen & Unwin.

Kern, H.; Schumann, M. 1985. *Das Ende der Arbeitsteilung*, Munich, Beck-Verlag.

Klebe, T.; Roth, S. 1989: "Beschäftigungsplan statt Sozialplan: Zwischenlagerung eines Problems oder Perspektive? Betriebsverfassungsrechtliche Aspektet und Durchsetzungsbedingungen", in *DB*, Vol. 30, p. 1518 ff.

Klees, B. 1983. "Ausgewählte probleme des Kündigungsschutzes in Gegenwart und Zukunft", in Ellermann-Witt et al. (eds.): *Kündigungspraxis und Kündigungsschutz und Probleme der Arbeitsgerichtsbarkeit*, Opladen, Westdeutscher-Verlag.

Kohl, H. 1978. "Personalplanung und Gewerkschaften - Bericht über eine empirische Untersuchung bei Betriebsräten und Gewerkschaften", in *WSI-Mitteilungen 4*.

---. 1982. "Die Antikrisenabteilung in der Luxemburger Stahlindustrie", in *Die Mitbestimmung*, No. 11.

Koistinen, P.; Asko, S. 1988. "Plant closings and the functioning of local labour markets. Theoretical and empirical findings in the socio-economic context of Finland", in *ALC*, Stockholm.

Laballe, M. 1985. Inspecteur Général. Enquête sur la société de conversion de Thomson (le GERIS), Paris, Ministère de Redéploiement Industriel et de Commerce Extérieur.

Larsson C.; Sigfridson, R. 1989. *Structural changes in Swedish industry - the Udevalla Case*, Deindustrialisation, Local Labour Markets and Policy Measures for Industrial Renewal. Experiences from West Germany, United Kingdom and Sweden, International Conference, Bildungsstätte der Angestelltenkammer Bad Zwischenahn, March 1989.

Löwe, W.; Wand, K. 1987. *Arbeit für eine Krisenregion*, Cologne, Bund-Verlag.

Lutz, B.; Sengenberger, W. 1974. *Arbeitsmarktstrukturen und öffentliche Arbeitsmarktpolitik - eine kritische Analyse von Zielen und Instrumenten*, Vol 26, Schriftenreihe der Kommission für wirtschaftlichen und sozialen Wandel, Göttingen, Schwartz-Verlag.

Mackay, D.I. 1972. *Redundancy and re-engagement: A study of car workers*, The Manchester School of Economic and Social Studies, Study No. 3, September.

Mackay, D.I. et al. 1980. *Redundancy and replacement*, Research Paper No. 16, Department of Employment, London.

Malmberg, A. 1989. *Old industries and uneven regional development. The case of Sweden*, Deindustrialisation, Local Labour Markets and Policy Measures for Industrial Renewal. Experiences from West Germany, United Kingdom and Sweden, International Conference, Bildungsstätte der Angestelltenkammer Bad Zwischenahn, March.

Marioni, P. 1987. *Les congés de conversion. Dossier statistique du travail et de l'emploi*, Supplément au Bulletin mensuel de statistique du travail, No. 3435, October.

---. 1988. "Les dispositifs de conversion", in *Bilan de l'emploi 1987*, Supplément aux Dossiers statistiques du travail et de l'emploi (INSEE), No. 43/44.

Martin, R.; Fryer, R.M. 1973. *Redundancy and paternalist capitalism*, London, Allen & Unwin.

Massey, D.; Meegan, R. 1982. *The anatomy of job losses*, London, Methuen.

Méhaut, Ph. 1984. *Public and private policies for the development of human resources in France*, Paris, OECD.

Mehrens, K. (ed.). 1985. *Alternative Produktion. Arbeitnehmerinitiativen für sinnvolle Arbeit*, Cologne, Bund-Verlag.

Mendius, H.G. et al. 1983. *Qualifizierung im Betrieb als Instrument der öffentlichen Arbeitsmarktpolitik*, Research Report No. 89, Der Bundesminister für Arbeit und Sozialordnung, Bonn.

---. 1987. *Arbeitskräfteprobleme und Humanisierungspotentiale in Kleinbetrieben*, Frankfurt/New York, Campus-Verlag.

Mukherjee, S. 1973. *Through no fault of their own*, London, MacDonald & Co.

Nowak, Th.; Snyder, K. 1983. "Women's struggle to survive a plant shutdown", in *The Journal of Intergroup Relation*, Vol. XI, No. 4.

Ochs, P. 1976. *Analyse betrieblicher Sozialpläne*, Saarbrücken, Institut für Sozialforschung und Sozialwirtschaft.

OECD. 1987a. *Labour Force Statistics*, 1965-1987, Paris.

---. 1987b. *Employment Outlook*, 1987, Paris.

---. 1988. *Employment Outlook*, 1988, Paris.

---. 1989. *Employment Outlook*, Paris.

Ohio Public Interest Campaign. 1988. "Industrial exodus hits minority workers the hardest", in *Economic Dislocation and Equal Opportunity*, Report prepared by the Illinois Committee to the United States Commission on Civil Rights.

Outin, J.L.; Silvera, A. 1988. "La reconversion en marché: l'exemple du Creusot", in *Economie et humanisme*, No. 304, November-December, Paris.

Outin, J.L. et al. 1988. *Que sont devenus les non-repris de Creusot-Loire?*, Supplément au Bulletin Régional d'Information Travail et Emploi, No. 101, May.

Paine, D. (no date). *Closure at Linwood: A follow-up survey of redundant workers*, Manpower Services Commission, Edinburgh.

Pellul, W. et al. 1983. "Arbeitskräftepool - ein Ansatz zur Lösung der Werftenkrise", in Heseler, H.; Kröger, H.J. (eds.): *Stell dir vor, die Werften gehören uns*, Hamburg, VSA-Verlag.

Perrucci, C. et al. 1987. "Plant closing: A comparison of effects on women and men workers", in Lee, R.M. (ed.): *Redundancy, layoffs and plant closures*, London, Croom Helm.

---. 1988. *Plant closings, international context and social costs*, Berlin/New York, de Gruyter-Verlag.

Projektgruppe Videocolor am Institut für Soziologie der Universität Münster, 1987. *Der Sozialplan ersetzt mir ja nicht den Arbeitsplatz, Betriebsschließung und Besetzungsstreik bei Videocolor Ulm*, Cologne, Bund-Verlag.

Pyke, F. 1982. *The redundant worker, work, skill and security in an engineering city*, Durham, University of Durham, Working Paper No. 18.

Pyke, F. et al. 1990. *Industrial districts and inter-firm co-operation in Italy*, Geneva, International Institute for Labour Studies.

Rhyope, A. 1970. *Pit closures. A study in redeployment*, Department of Employment and Productivity, Her Majesty's Stationery Office, London.

Roth, S.; Kohl, H. (eds.). 1988. *Perspektive: Gruppenarbeit*, Cologne, Bund-Verlag.

Ruhrkohle AG. 1988. *Handbuch für Teilzeitarbeit von Berufsanfängern*, Essen.

Sagét, F. 1986. *Reconversion économique et création d'emplois, la pratique des opérations de reconversion des groupes industriels*, Paris, Syros.

Savatier, J. 1985. "La nature des congés de conversion et leurs effets sur l'électorat dans l'entreprise", in *Droit Social*, No. 4.

Schäfer, H. 1986. *Betriebliche Ausländerdiskriminierung und gewerkschaftliche Antidiskriminierungspolitik*, Berlin.

Schultz-Wild, R. 1978. *Betriebliche Beschäftigungspolitik in der Krise*, Frankfurt/New York, Campus-Verlag.

Sengenberger, W. 1987. *Zur Struktur und Funktionsweise von Arbeitsmärkten. Der Bundesrepublik Deutschland im internationalen Vergleich*, Frankfurt/New York, Campus Verlag.

---. 1988. "Mehr Beschäftigung in Klein- und Mittel-betrieben: Ein Flexibilitätsgewinn?", in *WSI-Mitteilungen 8*.

---. 1989. *Labour standards and industrial restructuring: Issues and perspectives*, Paper prepared for the Second Meeting of the International Working Group of Researchers and Trade Unionists, Düsseldorf, 30 and 31 May.

---. 1990. "Flexibility in the labor market - Internal versus external adjustment in international comparison", in Appelbaum, E.; Schettkat, R. (eds.): *Labor market adjustments to structural change and technological progress*, New York, Praeger.

"Sidérurgie: Nouvelle CGPS", in *Liaisons Sociales*, No. 5987, 12.8.1987.

Skogö, I. 1988. "Experiences of some major company closures in Sweden", in *ALC*, Stockholm.

Soltwedel, R. 1984. *Mehr Markt am Arbeitsmarkt. Ein Plädoyer für weniger Arbeitsmarktpolitik*, Munich/Vienna, Philosophia-Verlag.

Storrie, D. 1988. *Structural change and labour market policy in Uddevalla*, Paper for ALC conference on Structural Change and Labour Market Policy.

Strath, B. 1987. *The politics of deindustrialisation - The contraction of the West European shipbuilding industry*, London, Croom Helm.

Sund, O. 1989. "Arbeitsmarktpolitik und Qualifizierung für Beschäftigte aus Krisenbranchen - Handlungsmöglichkeiten und Handlungsprobleme der Bundesanstalt für Arbeit", in *Sozial Sicherheit*, No. 2.

Tessaring, M. 1988. "Arbeitslosigkeit, Beschäftigung und Qualifikation: Ein Rück- und Ausblick", in *MittAB*, No. 2.

Vennin, B. 1988. "Conversion industrielle: une affaire d'Etat?", in *Economie et humanisme*, No. 304, November-December, Paris.

Vernaz, C. 1987. "Rupture pour motif économique", in *Liaisons Sociales*, 9 July.

Vertrauensleute und AK Alternative Fertigung Blohm & Voss. 1985. *Zukunftsperspektiven - aus der Sicht von Beschäftigten - Überlegungen des Arbeitskreises alternative Fertigung u.a. zu Schiffs- und Meerestechnik, Panzerproduktion und Fregattenexport, Arbeitsplatzentwicklung*, Hamburg.

Villeval, M.C. 1988. *Employees' reconversion paths and new employment relationships*, Paper presented at Xth International Working Party on Labour Market Segmentation, Porto.

---. 1989. "Die Politik der Rekonversion der Arbeitskräfte in Frankreich. Ein Instrument zur Restrukturierung der Beschäftigungsverhältnisse", in *WSI-Mitteilungen*, No. 4.

Villeval, M.C. et al. 1989a. *La reconversion de la main-d'oeuvre, Reflexions autour d'un analyseur des recompositions du travail et de l'emploi*, Université Nancy II, Nancy.

---. 1989b. *La reconversion de la main-d'oeuvre, Bilan des problématiques (1950-1988)*, Université Nancy II, Nancy.

Visser, J. 1990. "In search of inclusive unionism", in *Bulletin of Comparative Labour Relations*, Deventer/Boston, Kluwer Law and Taxation Publishers.

Vogt, A. 1974. *Sozialpläne in der betrieblichen Praxis*, Cologne, Otto Schmidt-Verlag.

Walker, A. et al. 1984. "From secure employment to labour market insecurity: The impact of redundancy on older workers in the steel industry", in Roberts, B. et al. (eds.): *New approaches to economic life*, Manchester University Press, pp. 319-337.

Warbruck, K. 1988. *Krise der Stahlindustrie? Ansätze zu einer betrieblichen und überbetrieblichen Bewältigung am Beispiel Krupp Rheinhausen*, Duisburg, Dissertation, Universität Gesamthochschule.

Wedderburn, D. 1964. *White-collar redundancy*, Department of Applied Economics, Occasional Paper, Cambridge University.

---. 1965. *Redundancy and railwaymen*, Department of Applied Economics, Occasional Paper, Cambridge University Press.

Weitzel, E. 1986. "Bescheidende Beschäftigungswirkungen durch Neugründungen", in *IFO-Schnelldienst*, No. 7.

Wood, S.; Dey, J. 1983. *Redundancy, case studies in cooperation and conflict*, Aldershot, Hampshire, Gover.

Young, E. 1974. "The Armour experience: A case study in plant shutdown", in Somers, G. et al. (eds.): *Adjusting to technological change*, Westport, Greenwood Press.

Zukunftsperspektiven. 1985. *Überlegungen des Arbeitskreises Alternative Fertigung u.a. zu Schiffs- und Meerestechnik, Panzerproduktion und Fregattenexport, Arbeitsplatzvernichtung*, Hamburg, Vertrauensleute Blohm & Voss.